A World ot Becoming

A John Hope Franklin Center Book

A World of Becoming

William E. Connolly

DUKE UNIVERSITY PRESS

Durham & London

2011

© 2011 Duke University Press
All rights reserved
Printed in the United States
of America on acid-free paper ∞
Designed by Amy Ruth Buchanan
Typeset in Carter + Cone Galliard by
Keystone Typesetting, Inc.
Library of Congress Cataloging-in-
Publication Data appear on the last
printed page of this book.

To my graduate students,

past and present.

————————————

Contents

Prelude, 1

Chapter 1.   Complexity, Agency, and Time, 17

Chapter 2.   The Vicissitudes of Experience, 43

Chapter 3.   Belief, Spirituality, and Time, 68

Interlude, 93

Chapter 4.   The Human Predicament, 97

Chapter 5.   Capital Flows, Sovereign Decisions,
              and World Resonance Machines, 124

Chapter 6.   The Theorist and the Seer, 148

Postlude, 176

Acknowledgments, 178

Notes, 181

Bibliography, 199

Index, 205

Prelude

In the closing scene of the Coen Brothers' film, *Barton Fink*, a young woman in a bathing suit strolls down a beach. Barton Fink, a frustrated young screenwriter, who has spent too much time talking to a man who turned out to be a psychotic killer, walks toward her carrying a box just large enough to contain a severed head. Barton may not know what is in the box. The woman sits down on the sand, exchanging a few words with Barton, who replies politely. She then turns toward the ocean, leaning on her left arm with her right hand cupped above her eyes. The scene freezes, but the waves continue to break onto the shore. The visual image soon dissolves and the sound of the waves lingers a moment longer before the credits roll.

The final scene recalls a crude painting of the woman in that same arrested pose, which had hung on the wall of the writer's dingy room. That picture had been too ordinary for Barton or us to note. He had been unable to write a script about ordinary people, because he could not relate to them, a failing exhibited by his unwillingness to listen to the crazy guy in the next room who was ready to fill him full of tales about the derangements of ordinary life. "I could tell you lots of stories," the strange, affable neighbor would say before Fink would interrupt him to recount his desire to break his writer's block by engaging ordinary life. That postcard painting had peered at us from time to time, and at the writer too, as he stared through it in the struggle to compose a sentence. It just hung there, in a film at once satirical about Hollywood and elemental in its presentation of life.

As the credits roll, we the viewers are now drawn back to that painting as a figure of arrested movement. On its surface the waves are frozen in mid-motion; even the froth at the top of each is arrested. There is no sound. The woman's face and eyes are fixed in an immobile gaze. The muscles holding her left arm in the pose are locked in place, as are those in her legs, stomach, shoulders, and buttocks. The gentle breeze kicking up a few grains of sand has stopped, holding the grains in midair. The woman's breath, pulse, per-

Figure 1. *Barton Fink*, closing scene.

spiration, hormones, thinking, hopes, and fears are placed on ice too. Even the pull of gravity is suspended. The arrest of gravity, thought, body, waves, wind, sound, and skyline frame each other.

But we are not simply pulled back to that picture on the wall. We move back and forth between the picture and the closing scene, as we ponder the human condition. As we do so, we find ourselves plunged into a moment of time without movement, engaging different zones of temporality coursing through and over us. For that scene arrests multiple sites and speeds of mobility that impinge upon one another when in motion. We may commune for a moment with a drop of time itself before we ease up from our seats to ramble out of the theater. Soon we start our cars and race home, stopping habitually at each red light on the way . . .

We belong to time, but we do not think often about the strange element through (or "in") which we live, breathe, act, suffer, love, commune, and agitate. Indeed, it would be unwise if we focused on this register of experience too often. We would lose our ability to act with efficacy, confidence, and fervor in the world. For action requires simplified perception to inform it. We barely glance at the cup of coffee before picking it up, refusing to tarry over its size, texture, shape, colors, odor, and distance. And there is no time to note the color and make of that car rushing at you before you dive out of its way. But still it does make both thought and action more subtle to dwell in time periodically. Perhaps reflection about the larger cosmos and our place in it requires, as Henri Bergson and Marcel Proust both insist, periodic attention to time as "duration."

The power of the first scene was amplified involuntarily for me a few days after first pondering it. On a cold morning (15 January 2009), I was waking slowly from a dream only dimly available for review. As I sometimes do, I allowed my eyes to remain closed to defer the demands of the day. I was soon transported back to a party I attended in eighth grade at a popular ninth-grade girl's house. She had us playing spin the bottle: seven or eight of us forming a polite circle, taking turns spinning a milk bottle, with only one couple already "going steady." If, when it was your spin, the bottle pointed to someone of the same sex, an uncomfortable jolt of laughter would note the event. Very little, almost nothing. You would then spin again, to ac- knowledge an implicit structural limit to this game of chance at that time. This was a collective nod during a second of hesitation to an issue that would explode onto the politics of becoming a decade or so later. What I will later call a moment of mere incipience. If the next spin stopped at a girl you and she were "obliged" to kiss. The kiss could be modest or a bit more intense, brief or prolonged slightly, depending on the attraction of each to the other. Everyone read the tea leaves during each kiss, so to speak, to determine whether a secret attraction was disclosed, or whether a hesitation by one or both disclosed something else. Laughter, shyness, attraction, uncertainty, anticipation, jealousy, and twinges of discontent filtered through an eerie politeness, all mixing into that little game of chance.

The atmosphere was electric, suffused with awareness that something fateful could emerge. Would the bottle point to the girl or boy of your dreams? Who was that, anyway? Recollections of previous flirtations and slights permeated the room (for everyone in that school discussed every- thing in the halls, lunch room, and locker room behind the back of each person). There was a sense of hovering between the licit and the illicit, the innocent and the informed, the present and the future, the playful and the fateful. We were poised in hesitation. An attempt at humor was received eagerly by everybody, either to laugh with it or to condemn it in exaggerated tones. We were alert, too, not to go too far with a kiss, so as to sustain the delicious energy and uncertainty in the room.

I have "remembered" this little event occasionally in the past when I encountered a fellow player during a visit to my hometown, or when I was told about the death of one of them, or when I responded to an adult proposal to play charades with the suggestion that we play spin the bottle, to a mixture of laughter and ridicule. We don't play that game anymore, and if we did we would no longer play it in that way. We are stuck with charades . . .

But to recall such an event is not equivalent to having a layered, multi-sensory memory of it wash over you on its own as you slide from sleep to wakefulness. The difference is that between casually viewing a snapshot of a past event (like the picture on Barton's wall) and absorbing the atmosphere in which it occurred. To recall an event like a snapshot differs from the experience of being suspended in a moment in which the sensory richness of the event resonates back and forth with the world you now inhabit: it is the divergence between a stereotyped recollection versus layered memory in which disparate sensory elements fold into each other in a new way. Suppose an older girl had let you kiss her two seconds longer than expected, spurring surges of anticipation about a date that, doubtless because she had other interests, went nowhere. Do such little surges of warmth and anticipation — even when unfulfilled then and not recollected later as events — flow some-how into future feelings and actions, infusing and inflecting a sense of humor, a style of regret, a mode of empathetic identification, a sense of anxiety, even a political sensibility? Do fugitive possibilities not acted upon in the past ac-cumulate below recollection to make a difference to thought and action in the future? Nietzsche and Proust both thought so, with the former calling these energetic elements "the powers of the false" and the latter enacting such powers in his text. Do such pressures, in conjunction with the accumulation of numerous such events, help to propel the past into the future even when it is not being recollected, especially when it is not?

What if such a game had involved the demand to commune experimen-tally with one of five gods contending in the world or one of three modes of godlessness, depending upon where the spinning stopped? That would be a game, I suppose, played on and by us at various junctures in life: a game in which chance and fate (or grace) meet in the disjunction of the moment before receding into a past that merely helps to condition the future.

I am aware that the rich memory of an event and the event from which it draws are not identical. All the better. It is the reverberations back and forth between past and present, with each folding into the other and both surging toward the future, that make all the difference to life. We participate in at least two registers of temporal experience, action-oriented perception and the slower experience of the past folding into the present and both flowing toward the future. The first is necessary to life; the second is indispensable to its richness. It is the possible interactions between the two modes that need to be underlined.

A traumatic event could be reviewed with some of the characteristics of my early morning memory in January, carrying different tones. Such events also make a profound difference. But when we are moved by positive, simmering memories that flow over us in a new setting, an enhanced sense of belonging to time may emerge. We may even become more alert to our modest participation in a much larger world of temporal force-fields marked by an element of real creativity. Disparate experiences fold into each other in everyday life, mobilizing energy into action-oriented perception, sometimes setting the stage for truly novel thoughts. Such processes help to mobilize actions and ethical sensibilities, and — when collected and amplified through micropolitics — to infuse the ethos of politics embedded in institutional settings in one way or another.

A force-field, roughly speaking, is any energized pattern in slow or rapid motion periodically displaying a capacity to morph, such as a climate system, biological evolution, a political economy, or human thinking. As we shall explore in chapter 1, different force-fields display differential capacities of agency. We inhabit a world of becoming composed of heterogeneous force-fields; and we also participate in two registers of temporal experience, each of which can help us to get bearings in such a world. It is when the story of multiple force-fields of different types, in and beyond the human estate, is linked to the exploration of two registers of temporal experience in the human estate that things get interesting. Nonetheless, the themes of this book may carry little weight for anyone who finds nothing of interest in the Barton Fink scene or in a moment from their own past that resonates somehow with the scene I have painted from mine. You may give singular priority to the demands of punctual time while I seek to maintain a tense balance between the incorrigible demands and pleasures of operational perception set in punctual time (the kids' attention to that spinning bottle as it drew to a halt) and the need to dwell periodically in protean moments that exceed the operational demands of action.

You may initially connect the temper I commend to "optimism" or "romanticism" rather than to the pessimism, coolness, realism, or abiding sense of the negative that you respect. I don't see it that way, though. My sense is that those who jump to such a conclusion have too limited an arsenal of ontological alternatives available. To appreciate two registers of experience in a world of becoming can also help us come to terms with tragic possibility. Such an appreciation encourages us to embrace the world as we act and intervene resolutely in it, even though it is replete with neither divine providence nor ready susceptibility to human mastery. Indeed, I don't read the absence of providence or mastery as a "lack," finding the use of that term by some to express a hangover of previous views inadequately overcome in the view officially adopted. I also know that shared experiences of grief or loss can help to consolidate connections with others, and that collective anger, resentment, and indignation are often indispensable spurs to critical action. So there is no sense here that "thinking it is so makes it so" or that "optimism is always healthy." These orientations are attached to a different take on existence than that advanced here, though there are people who confuse the two. I do suspect that when inordinate drives for individual self-sufficiency, unity, community, consensus, or divine redemption are severely disappointed, things can become dangerous. These disappointed drives — I am sure there are others as well — readily cross over into entrenched dispositions to take revenge on the most fundamental terms of human existence, as a person, a constituency, or a putative nation grasps those terms. If and when that happens, an exclusionary, punitive, scandal-ridden, bitter politics is apt to result, regardless of how the carriers represent themselves to others. Here actions speak louder than words.

A world of becoming has considerable evidence on its side, as we shall see; and affirmation of this condition without existential resentment provides one way to act resolutely in the world while warding off individual and collective drives to existential resentment. There are others, as we shall also see. Given the human predicament (explored in chapter 4), no theological or nontheological perspective at this level carries iron-clad guarantees. A crack or fissure running through every final perspective is part of the human predicament as I construe it.

On my rendering, the course of time is neither governed solely by a pattern of efficient causation — where each event is determined to occur by some prior event in linear temporal order — nor expressive of an inherent purpose revolving around the human animal as such. Neither/nor. To put it in different terms, time is neither mechanical nor organic, and its human apprehension is neither susceptible to the method of "individualism" nor that of "holism." We participate, rather, in a world of becoming in a universe set on multiple zones of temporality, with each temporal force-field periodically encountering others as outside forces, and the whole universe open to an uncertain degree. From this perspective, tragic possibility — not inevitability but possibility — is real: tragic possibility as seen from the vantage point of your time or country or species; tragic possibility sometimes actualized through the combination of hubris and an unlikely conjunction of events. Or by some other combination. I even suspect that differential degrees of agency in other force-fields, with which we enter into encounters of many types, increases the risk of that possibility. The universe is not only open; there is an "outside" to every temporal force-field. We are not only limited as agents, but part of our limitation comes from the different degrees of agency in other force-fields with which we interact. The operation of multiple tiers of becoming in a world without a higher purpose amplifies the need to act with dispatch, and sometimes with militancy, in particular situations of stress. The fact that we are not consummate agents in such a world, combined with the human tendency to hubris, means that we must work to cultivate wisdom under these very circumstances. These two dictates, engendering each other while remaining in tension, constitute the problematic of political action in a world of becoming.

William James, Henri Bergson, Friedrich Nietzsche, Alfred North Whitehead, and Gilles Deleuze all advance different versions of time as becoming. Perhaps Merleau-Ponty and Marcel Proust do too, with qualifications. I draw from several of them the idea that it takes both philosophical speculation linked to scientific experiment and dwelling in uncanny experiences of duration to vindicate such an adventure. Both. Luckily, as we shall see, some strains of complexity theory in the natural sciences also support the theme of time as becoming as they compose new experiments and rework classical conceptions of causality. Moreover, in everyday life fugitive glimmers of becoming are available to more people more of the time, as we experience the acceleration of many zones of life, the enhanced visibility of natural disasters across the globe, the numerous pressures to minoritize the entire world along several dimensions at a more rapid pace, the globalization of capital and contingency together, the previously unexpected ingress of capital into climate change, the growing number of film experiments with the uncanniness of time, and the enlarged human grasp of the intelligence and differential degrees of agency in other plant and animal species. Such experiences and experiments together call into question early modern conceptions of time. Many respond to such experiences by intensifying religious and secular drives to protect an established image, as either linear and progressive or infused with divine providence. I suspect, however, that such responses — unless their proponents actively engage the comparative contestability of them without deep existential resentment — can amplify the dangers and destructiveness facing our time. Or, at least, they need to be put into more active competition with a conception that speaks to an array of contemporary experiences otherwise pushed into the shadows.

To amplify the experience of becoming is one affirmative way to belong to time today. Active exploration and support of such a perspective can make a positive contribution to the late-modern period by drawing more people toward such a perspective or by showing others how much work they need to do to vindicate their own perspective. I belong to a growing contingent who think that a perspective defined by active examination of becoming can make positive contributions to explorations of spirituality, economics, political action, poetic experience, and ethics.

As already indicated, periodic sensitivity to a rich drop of time merely sets a threshold condition to entertain the themes advanced here. More is needed to endow them with plausibility. The threshold condition, nonetheless, may be important, for it opens a window to place the theme of a world of becoming in relation to other conceptions of time and it may increase the possibility of positive engagement between bearers of alternative onto-theological images of time. I wish you had been at that party with me.

Is time movement? If so, does that mean time is set in space, as the movement of objects between fixed spatial points? Like planets revolving around the sun in the solar system, if only they too did not actually change in composition, speed, and orbit as time passes. Does the flow of time, on the contrary, express inherent development? Heading toward an end already there implicitly, waiting to be realized? That would give us a profound sense of belonging to time rather than merely acting upon it or being acted upon by it. But it would also subtract an element of real creativity from the world of becoming. It would make creativity more apparent than real, while for many, creativity in multiple zones of time now seems more real than apparent. Is there real creativity in culture and human agency but not in the rest of nature and the cosmos? How would that work? Or, is creativity confined to a god, while everything else moves at the bidding of forces that exceed it?

What if time is becoming, and the future of the universe—and the multiple, interacting, and partially open temporal systems through which it is composed—is really open to an uncertain degree? What if it is really open to metamorphosis? We would then belong to time but not exactly be in it, since we, too, as individuals, families, friends, constituencies, states, and world-historical periods, participate in the vicissitudes of a world of becoming that exceeds us. The ocean waves, the heartbeat, the face, the skin, the arm muscles, the sky, the sand, the breeze, the head inside that box—many of which are portrayed flatly by that picture on Barton's wall, would each participate in different tiers of temporality too, tiers that pass by each other sometimes and intersect at others. Let us, to modify received terminology a bit, call each tier a temporal force-field and call time the bumpy process that gathers disparate tiers together. As when a large wave, set on one tier of temporality, knocks a man and woman over on the beach. Or a bad joke, bubbling up from nowhere when the bottle points at the girl of your dreams, leads to a kiss in which two sets of lips barely graze each other. Or an intensification of sunspot activity, further enhanced by its own powers of self-amplification, generates electrical impulses that overwhelm military computers on the earth, triggering panic among contending military elites replete with their own dynamics of self-amplification.

If multiple tiers of temporality periodically intersect (through chemical, electrical, intentional, gravitational, magnetic, hormonal, or other means) in a world of becoming that is open to some extent, we belong to time in the largest and most fundamental sense of the term. Some pregnant experiences, indeed, may prime us to explore the character of our participation in time, and we may then extrapolate cautiously from those explorations to scientific, theological, and philosophical speculations about its larger, bumpy compass. At fecund moments, we may come to suspect that we experience time in itself in drips and drops. Upon pursuing this or that extrapolation we might probe new experiments in science, literature, politics, and philosophy that touch it. Experience, speculation, and experiment, each placed into dissonant interdependence with the others.

It seems unlikely that any extrapolation, bolstered by the experiments that science, philosophy, literature, film, and art respectively deploy to test it, will demonstrate time as becoming. Or do so for an alternative image, either. Perhaps the idea of a world of becoming, however, can be made plausible to more people and accepted by others as a worthy competitor for attention, if we draw upon multiple resources to express it. Perhaps we can then re-enter the domains of ethics, politics, economics, and spirituality, inflecting each field in the light of those explorations. The agenda is to move from salient experiences of time as duration, the very experience that must be pushed to the background when the dictates of action are strong, to reflections in several zones of life, and then back again, moving back and forth until we reach a reflective equilibrium that carries a degree of plausibility.

Even such a method is not sufficient. For much in us, and in many people around us, resists belonging to time as becoming. Many seek to commune with radical transcendence — either in the shape of a personal God or as the timeless, magnetic power of Being itself — as a mode of being beyond time. Others invoke secular modes of explanation and evaluation that cut this image off at the pass in a different way. Perhaps it is wise to evince respect for such extrapolations while also contesting them. For the quest for eternal salvation and the possibility of human mastery over nature are both challenged by a world of becoming. And it is important to see, as we shall explore, that some theologies of divine transcendence express an idea of becoming too. Existential sources of resistance must be encountered as we pursue that reflective equilibrium. For belief and affect are intertwined in a world of becoming, with neither being entirely reducible to the other. That means to alter our beliefs on this terrain will also require working on affective attachments invested with a received image of time. We experiment upon the registers of belief and affect together, to see whether some distinctive attractions of a world of becoming can be marshaled. For many philosophers, writers, scientists, and theologians already embrace this or that version of becoming.

Experience, experiment, reflection, cultivation of spiritual sensibility, and resolute action are five dimensions that cannot stray far from each other in such an enterprise. The fourth has too often been cast into the shadows by secular philosophies that focus upon belief and argument alone, with adverse political and cultural effects. My agenda is to link the pursuit of reflective equilibrium to questions of existential attachment and political action, allowing each pursuit to inform the other.

I embrace a story of becoming linked to experimental intervention in a world that exceeds human powers of attunement, explanation, prediction, mastery, or control. And to invite you to do the same, without contending that I can drag you there by the force of argument alone. Participation in a world of becoming teaches modesty about the powers of argument even while appreciating its pertinence.

———————

Heraclitus advanced a view with at least vague resemblances to that embraced here. So in one sense it is as old as the hills, hills worn down by time as other mountains surge up in the aftermath of earthquakes and volcanic eruptions. Some of his pithy formulations are presented in the Interlude, as counterpoints to modern formulations. There may, nonetheless, be generic experiences of contemporary life, as already suggested, that render such a thesis potentially more credible to more people today. Perhaps these very same conditions also render that possibility more disturbing to yet others. And perhaps those who resist these disturbances must thereby mobilize more energy than ever to ward them off. Is the rise of contending religious and secular fundamentalisms across the world connected to late-modern experiences of time that disrupt things in both received theological and scientific faiths? That disrupt some elements of the Enlightenment too? If so, it may be even more important than heretofore to place the question of time high on the agenda. It is a timely question. Perhaps we must either redeem traditional conceptions of time in a new way or show more people how and why it is wise to consider time as becoming in a universe that is open to an uncertain degree. "Even the thought of a possibility," Nietzsche says somewhere, "can shatter and transform us." The possibility he noted was the threat that you faced eternal damnation if you denied the God of monotheism. In this case the possibility to think is that we participate in a world of becoming. This idea may be as timely today as those of eternal damnation and a final judgment were to Christians for centuries, or as the Newtonian idea of time as essentially reversible was to many scientists between the seventeenth century and the First World War.

"Today" — meaning during the protraction of a century or so — a growing group of scientists, philosophers, poets, film directors, and cultural theorists explore the issue of time, each adding a layer of reflection pertinent to the others. I seek to draw selectively upon such work in this book to help make my case. I then pursue several of the themes far enough to address the implications for political theory, cultural life, and politics.

The book itself is best read as a set of essays that seek to infuse and augment each other. A theme is enunciated early and connected to specific issues, to be rejoined and enlarged later in the context of other issues: connection as infusion and impingement alike; and repetition with variation. To the extent such an approach works it seeks to enact through its mode of presentation a bit of time as becoming.

Chapter 1, "Complexity, Agency, and Time," brings complexity theory in physics, biology, and neuroscience into conjunction with a world of becoming. Ilya Prigogine, the Nobel Prize-winning chemist, and Stuart Kauffman, the biologist who helped found the Santa Fe Institute in Complexity Theory, provide much of the initial impetus. They are joined and augmented by Alfred North Whitehead, who anticipated these themes in the 1920s, as we explore the meaning of complexity theory, its conception of open systems, the temporal relations between open systems, its revision of widely received ideas about the meaning and distribution of agency, and its methodological theme of connectionism as a corrective to individualism, holism, and organicism. This chapter also complicates recent stories that set "closed" philosophies of immanence against versions that are open to a transcendent force or being. There are in fact several dimensions along which a philosophy of immanence can be open or closed. And the same goes with respect to a philosophy of transcendence.

Chapter 2, "The Vicissitudes of Experience," places Gilles Deleuze, Michel Foucault, and Maurice Merleau-Ponty into discussion on the complexity of perception. It also brings recent findings in neuroscience into conversation with all three. Against some Deleuzians who find Deleuze's work to be incompatible with (any version of) phenomenology, I argue that both schools can inform and correct each other. Merleau-Ponty's late engagement with Whitehead's conceptions of nature and time already drew the two perspectives closer. When we address the materialities of perception in the detail that Merleau-Ponty provides, it becomes all the more pertinent to engage Foucault and Deleuze on how new patterns of discipline and impersonal control permeate late-modern life. These issues are magnified by the accentuated role of TV and New Media today. As we process these themes it may become more apparent how and why the implicit modes of belonging to the world Merleau-Ponty found ensconced in the cultural grammar of embodiment itself have now become stretched and strained in distinctive ways. Such strains may have long been in play, but they take on a distinctive tone and weight in the late-modern world. Placing Merleau-Ponty into discussion with Gilles Deleuze on the need to "restore belief in this world," we explore the question of existential attachment to time during the late-modern era. The idea is that unless such attachments are enhanced, several modes of philosophical analysis, theological creed, and political movement will be susceptible to infiltration by collective drives to existential revenge.

Chapter 3, "Belief, Spirituality, and Time," carries these themes into a close engagement with the work of Charles Taylor, whose recent book, *A Secular Age*, has occasioned considerable discussion and controversy. I attempt to show that while Taylor's thesis of transcendence linked to a new version of secular politics is defensible, it is also noble to defend a spirituality of radical immanence in a world of becoming. Seeking to track the spirituality Taylor presents, one that renders itself open to contending faiths as it marks out its own space, I make the strongest comparative case I can for a philosophy of immanence in a world of becoming. Included in that discussion is an exploration of the role the will and human freedom play in a philosophy of radical immanence. To pursue these claims I need to show how the conception of immanence advanced here departs from the versions Taylor represents on the way to criticizing them. I also argue that a debate about "beliefs" is not enough in the secular world of "multiple options" Taylor characterizes so effectively. We also must come to terms with the existential spiritualities infused into different beliefs, most notably with discernible drives to hubris and existential resentment embedded in some econo-political movements. I test myself with and against Taylor by asking him whether it is appropriate to resist some lived practices of immanence and transcendence alike if and when they are filled with modes of hubris and existential resentment that place the late-modern age at greater risk than would otherwise be the case. And I ask him whether it is possible to forge a new pluralist assemblage composed of minorities of various types who diverge on belief and creed while sharing positive affinities of spirituality across those differences.

The Interlude places quotations from several thinkers of becoming in recent philosophy, literature, theology, and science into conjunction, allowing ancient formulations by Heraclitus to punctuate several of them. The hope is to foment creative leaps across the times, zones, and levels at which the statements are pitched. To do so by allowing oneself to follow their order of placement the first time around and then leap-frogging that order the second time. Does such a method replicate a dimension of thinking itself? It does if thinking requires both jolts to thought and trains of thought to proceed. What about temporal discontinuities?

Chapter 4, "The Human Predicament," compares the Hindu visionary Sankara, the Christian prophet Paul Tillich, the proponent of a theology of becoming, Catherine Keller, and the nontheistic purveyor of becoming, Friedrich Nietzsche. Henri Bergson and Søren Kierkegaard also make brief appearances. On my reading each thinker perceives a distinctive human "predicament" rather than merely presenting a human condition. The relation of time to that predicament is also important to each. Moreover, each seeks to ward off the negative response to existence that Nietzsche calls *ressentiment*, Tillich calls estrangement, and Sankara calls the ignorance of egoism. Each connects the experience of time, the awareness of mortality, and the human predicament, and each seeks to respond positively to the dangers this set of connections carries with it. How do we engage a world replete with overlapping and contending conceptions of the human predicament? Does the fact that the predicament is susceptible to multiple renderings form part of it? This chapter also augments chapter 2 by pursuing "the powers of the false" in a more robust way.

Chapter 5, "Capital Flows, Sovereign Practices, and World Resonance Machines," draws several of these themes and inflections into an encounter with a distinctive feature of contemporary global life. It starts with Hegel's *Philosophy of Right*, paying particular attention to his account of the conjunctions among market arrangements, their assumption of the self-reliant subject, the production of poverty, and the drive to colonization. The intersections between these sectors, he contends, fostered "a rabble" within the compass of nineteenth-century state capitalism. A rabble does not emerge from poverty alone, but from the conjunction between it and emergent standards of subjectivity folded into the institutions of everyday life in a capitalist society. This Hegelian theme is then adjusted and extended in the next two sections, paying particular attention to changes in sovereignty and state organization of power between Hegel's time and today. Eventually, we may be prepared to examine how the globalization of capital, corresponding adjustments in state practices of sovereignty, and the territorial distribution of religious majorities coalesce to foment a contemporary world resonance machine of antagonistic forces. This novel machine does not exhaust the global condition, but it does play an important role in it. It both draws upon and exceeds markets and sovereign power. The machine, you might say, is a global emergent in a world of becoming in which some force-fields move much faster than heretofore. The chapter closes with exploration of how to revamp multiple roles in ways that might contribute to the recoding of this world resonance machine. The idea is that role performance, beliefs, desires, actions, and the larger assemblages in which all are set can resonate back and forth, so that a change in any also enters into the character of the others.

Chapter 6, "The Theorist and the Seer," pursues more relentlessly a theme noted in passing in other chapters. This time the focus is on how to enter into moments of suspension to allow creative thoughts to gestate when a new fork in time emerges. If we participate in a larger world of becoming, times periodically arrive when an established mode of explanation, extrapolation into the future, received moral principle, or habitual response to the global condition is somehow out of synch with a surprising turn. What are the best ways to prime thinking and sensibility in such a condition? This chapter devotes itself to that question, suggesting that it is critical for thinkers to move back and forth between two registers of temporal experience: to dwell in fecund periods of withdrawal from action at some times and to intervene in ongoing practices at others. A series of exemplars is summoned to identify how such movements back and forth might proceed. They include Tiresias, the Greek seer, and two characters in the Jerry Lewis film, *The Nutty Professor*. The chapter closes by exploring a concept of causality pertinent to becoming and how dwelling in hypersensual situations may have, in fact, drawn several thinkers to which this study is most indebted to the theme of time as becoming.

The Postlude offers a highly condensed expression of the perspective advanced in this book.

What, though, are the lures that tug and pull the text along? On the defensive side it is the anxiety that the clash between received conceptions of secularism and transcendence on one side and vivid experiences of time that challenge, as it were, *both* images behind our backs combine today to foment contending modes of dogmatism. Numerous features of late-modern experience call historically entrenched images of time into question, but several theological and secular discourses of the day slide over or demean those experiences. This is a dangerous combination.

Positive lures are also in play. They express, I suppose, a series of hopes: that the idea of becoming can help us to grapple with the place of creative self-organization in both human and nonhuman processes, that coming to terms with force-fields of multiple types with different degrees of agency moving at different speeds can help us to negotiate more wisely relations between the human estate and the larger world, that the spiritual debates of late-modern life can be deepened as some of us expand our appreciation of how we, too, participate modestly in creative forces that constitute the larger world, and that the militant modes of action that may be needed today will be filled with more wisdom and modesty if they are informed by these processes. On this reading, a world of becoming distributes affective and creative power widely rather than either condensing the latter into a single divinity or concentrating both in the human estate. The hope is to foment ways to belong to time and to act resolutely in the world under conditions that place several secular and theological images of time, ethics, and territorial politics under pressure. That hope is pursued only to a limited extent in this book. The underlying idea is to render the conception itself as plausible as possible while at a second level coming to terms without existential resentment with the fact that no single conception is apt to captivate everyone who encounters the issues of mortality, politics, and time. One response to this predicament is to add an alternative to those most widely discussed and to foment a positive ethos of reciprocal involvement between carriers of different conceptions of time.

Debates between secular thought and the three monotheisms are pertinent but insufficient to our time. The idea, however, is not to bury these perspectives; that would be at odds with a pluralist temper. Nor is it merely to appreciate each without challenging it. That would suppress pluralism too. It is to press each and all to compete robustly with another image, to allow the lure of a world of becoming to compete as robustly as possible with each. We bring good tidings in a world replete with both tragic possibility and positive possibilities of resolute action. Does a growing minority sense, with varying degrees of articulateness, that we participate in a larger world of becoming with numerous sites of creative power? If so, it may be timely to augment that appreciation. I also suspect that the quality of the human sciences will improve to the extent that such a view is articulated.

These are some of the lures that pull me, though my ability to articulate them is surely exceeded by their drawing power. Lures are like that, creating poles of attraction that pull you along. Some readers may be drawn to this story, others may reject it, others may fold it into their own thinking in a different way than I do, and still others may accept it as a contestable image of time worthy of finding a place in contemporary debates. During a time when the world is being diversified along more dimensions at a faster pace than heretofore and when territories that most resist diversification must introduce new modes of defensive aggressiveness to carry out that resistance, the need is to pluralize lures and to ennoble the ways we defend them comparatively. Could time as becoming replace the lure of radical transcendence that pulls so many today or the contending (but now nearly defunct) secular lure that "religion" will progressively dissipate as the human power to know and master the world grows? That seems unlikely. But the chance that such an image could captivate a large and dispersed minority may grow as we delineate it closely and come to terms more robustly than before with the inability of any lure so far in the history of the species to exert universal appeal.

CHAPTER ONE

Complexity, Agency, and Time

The Complexity of Open Systems

There has been a tendency in cultural theory, philosophy, and political theory to bypass work in biology and neuroscience, even though we humans have ourselves evolved from other species and come equipped with genes, blood, hearts, muscles, brains, sexual organs, feet, and even hands for typing, a practice that depends upon unconscious habits wired into the body/brain system through training and repetition. (No one I know can recite the order of the alphabet on the keypad they use so efficiently.) There are diverse, even contending, sources of that tendency. The reductionism of biology and neuroscience has been one. The difficulty of engaging them from the outside has been another. The desire to provide cultural theory its own foundations has constituted a third. Related to this, the desire to protect a theology of transcendence has provided a fourth. These disparate pressures push in the same direction. They spawn modes of cultural theory that do not come to terms closely enough with the biocultural organization of perception, the layered complexity of thought, multiple modes and degrees of agency in the world, innumerable intersections between nonhuman force-fields of several types and cultural life, the role of multi-media micropolitics in organizing nonconscious registers of intersubjective life, the critical role that cultivation of the visceral register of being plays in ethical life, the connections between natural and cultural time, and other issues besides.

The arrival of complexity theory in the physical sciences places these reasons and excuses under new pressure. Complexity theory, as I receive it, moves natural science closer to the concerns of cultural theory as it surmounts reductionism. It advances several distinctive themes that touch received theories of explanation, interpretation, agency, ethics, and time in the human sciences.

First, because of periodic confluences between novel changes in the environment and "pre-adaptations" that cannot be identified in advance, much of biological evolution cannot be predicted. A pre-adaptation is a biological feature that plays one role or is redundant at one time, but upon a strategic change in the environment now becomes important and promotes a new function. Thus, early fish had lungs that evolved into swim bladders, a novel functionality that allows fish to adjust their buoyancy to the water level, as the amount of air and water in the bladder is adjusted. Without the lung, fish would have evolved in a different way; with it there was no way to predict in advance that it would evolve the way it did. It is impossible to predict its evolution apart from detailed knowledge of other changes in and around it at a later date.[1] Innumerable such pre-adaptations are retrospectively discernible in cultural life, such as the bills of exchange that evolved into pivots of capitalist systems, the Calvinist quest for signs of predestination that evolved into capitalist tendencies in northern Europe to industriousness and accumulation, the creative (and destructive) use of high speed computers by a financial elite to exploit slower market transactions by the largest mass of investors, the Spinozist inspiration to Einsteinian theory, the receptivity of the visceral register of human intersubjectivity to multi-media coding by TV, the creative adaptation of the liberal doctrine of human rights into rights of doctor assisted suicide and same sex marriage, and the transfiguration of the human knowledge of mortality into a series of faiths that promise life after death. Since pre-adaptations are known after rather than before the fact, we already encounter a source of unpredictability and uncertainty in the evolution of nature/culture.

Second, because of "Poincare resonances" that come into play when a previously stable system is thrown into disequilibrium, there are potentials for self-organization in some natural systems that also exceed our powers of prediction before they find expression. Ilya Prigogine suggests that such resonances were already in play in the period immediately following the Big Bang, generating one temporal flow out of several potentialities available, a direction that has affected everything else since.[2] When a simple physical system faces a new situation of disequilibrium, the pattern of resonance that arises seems to generate forks that can issue in more than one vector of development. The direction selected affects everything else that later emerges, without determining everything else in a simple, linear way. Brian Goodwin suggests, for instance, that such modes of self organization "at the edge of chaos" play a role at strategic intervals in species evolution.[3] The turn actually taken at a bifurcation point is interpreted by some under the star of chance or contingency. Perhaps. I suspect that it is wise to read such turns as modes of emergent causality that are neither reducible to chance, nor to explanation according to a classic concept of causality, nor to probability within a known distribution of possibilities. The actual turn sometimes exceeds any probability heretofore organized into the matrix of recognized possibilities. Some modes of opacity are due to incomplete information and others to processes that are intrinsically complex, when we recognize new conditions of intensified disequilibrium but cannot project with confidence the new turn that will be taken from that point.

I claim that the American evangelical-capitalist resonance machine arose in a similar way, though the fact that its generators included sophisticated human subjects interacting across different subject positions during a period of accentuated uncertainty makes a real difference to the account. At a pregnant moment of new uncertainty, when many social scientists projected the expansion of secular development, a constellation of disaffected white workers, evangelicals, and neoliberal corporate leaders responded creatively to an evolving situation in a way that enabled a new econo-political constellation to emerge. It was irreducible to the separate parts — the perceived self-interests of each constituency — from which it emerged. Its advance grew out of prior spiritual affinities (pre-adaptations) across partial differences of interest and creed between the constituencies. Such a set of spiritual pre-adaptations is most readily identified retrospectively, though those who worried about how new movements of pluralization were closing out white blue collar workers did sense dimly that a potential realignment of some sort could be in the works.[4]

As we shall see in a later chapter, similar developments are discernible in global politics today. The demise of the Soviet Union and the Cold War has combined with concomitant changes in the three religions of the Book to open new destructive patterns of resonance between cross-territorial constituencies.

Third, because every spatio-temporal system constituting the universe is open to some degree, and because each regularly maintains connections with other heterogeneous systems and periodically forms connections to others, another source of potential disequilibrium stalks stable systems. For instance, the tier of chrono-time on which an asteroid flow is set could intersect with the rotational pattern of the earth, creating a collision that affects future life on the face of the earth. Or the trajectory of global capitalism and that of climate evolution could intersect, altering the intensity of the latter and changing the pressures for capitalist development. Or a world financial system with some degree of autonomy could collapse, creating new pressures for war or capitalist reform that were not discernible before that event occurred. Stuart Kauffman, indeed, conjectures that a collision between three open systems helped to generate preconditions for life on earth. "It may be that myriad small organized molecules and even more complex molecules, fell onto the young earth to supply some preconditions that then mixed with the electrical force-fields and soupy stuff on early earth [to form life]."[5] Each of these open systems—molecules, electrical force-fields, and the soupy earth—was propelled by its own tendencies, but the improbable conjunction between them may have been responsible for the origin of life on earth. Of course, many will doubt that such an improbable event could have occurred in this way, as much as some of us doubt the story of a divine creation of life.

Pre-adaptations unstateable in advance, intersections between partially open systems of multiple kinds, and novel capacities for self-organization within a system triggered by infusions from elsewhere periodically operate in and upon each other, generating turns in time out of which a new equilibrium emerges, transcending our ability to articulate it in advance. That means that recent developments in complexity theory carry implications for the image of time we bring to the study of nature and culture and particularly to the multiple imbrications between them.

Some advocates of complexity theory in the natural sciences see this. Ilya Prigogine, for instance, a Nobel Prize-winning founder of chaos theory, argues that time preceded "existence" at the inception of our universe, meaning that the chaos preceding the big bang was itself temporal in character. The universe we inhabit, not necessarily the only one that could have evolved, continues to be "heterogeneous and far from equilibrium." This leads him to postulate an image of time as becoming, a temporal flow that is irreversible in ways that upset the Newtonian model of reversible processes, replete with an element of uncertainty in what becomes and periodically the source of new events and processes. It is the relations between disparate processes set on different time scales that impress him the most.

> "We are in a world of multiple fluctuations, some of which have evolved while others have regressed. These fluctuations are the macroscopic manifestations of fundamental properties of fluctuations arising on the microscopic level of unstable dynamic systems . . . Irreversibility, and therefore the flow of time, starts at the dynamical level. It is amplified at the macro-

scopic level, then at the level of life, and finally at the level of human activity. What drove these transitions from one level to the next remains largely unknown, but at least we have achieved a noncontradictory description of nature rooted in dynamical instability."

The flow of irreversible time is eternal: "We have an age, our civilization has an age, but time itself has neither a beginning nor an end."[6]

Stuart Kauffman evinces a similar view. He draws upon the elements listed above to identify real creativity in the trajectory of natural and cultural processes. Attempts to expunge the creative dimension from natural processes are legion, either in pursuit of a linear, deterministic science or to protect the image of an omnipotent God who monopolizes creativity. But they rest upon speculative leaps or unproven articles of faith. Kauffman is willing to make such a leap in the opposite direction. Why go in that direction? Well, dominant assumptions postulate a radical break between nature and culture that is more and more difficult to sustain. The radical break between humanity and other processes — the "anthropic exception" — is introduced to explain how we have capacities to understand natural regularities but the objects we comprehend have no power to participate in a world of becoming at all. Moreover, the alternative conjecture opens a door to urgently needed modes of collaboration between practitioners in literature, the natural sciences, and the human sciences, as we explore complex interconnections between the human estate and nonhuman processes. This conjecture also carries considerable promise in several fields of inquiry in the natural sciences, most particularly biology and neuroscience. And finally, following this trail may promote new possibilities of cross-fertilization between devotees of divine transcendence who concentrate creativity in God (not all devotees of transcendence do so) and devotees of a world immanent to itself who, while joining them in resisting closures in the Gallilean tradition, admit differential degrees of real agency and creativity into a variety of natural-social processes.

Degrees of Agency

Does such rethinking imply that all differences between "nature" and "culture" are to be erased? Do natural processes contain as much agency as cultural processes? An amoeba as much as a human? A cloud system as much as a state? No. But it does encourage us to rethink the dicey problematic of agency, to convert a dichotomous view that bestows agency upon humans only—or in many cases upon humans to some degree and God to an infinite degree—into a more *distributive* image of agency.

As we pursue this trail, it is pertinent to recall that traditional images of human agency in the monotheistic traditions—revolving around the idea of free will—are themselves replete with ambiguity and paradox. The human will was presented by Augustine, the most profound philosopher of early Christendom, to separate human beings categorically from both unfree nature and an absolutely free God. His image of human free will is set in a fixed tri-archy consisting of nature without evolutionary possibility, a human estate with severe limits, and a God. Before the Fall, the perfectly free act of human will was a perverse act of rebellion; after the Fall, human freedom becomes confounded. We can now will evil by ourselves but cannot will the good unaided. The latter is possible only when human agency is infused with divine grace, that is, with what those outside the Augustinian tradition would call heteronomy. If you try to will the good unaided, another, lower part of the will intervenes, fighting against the first priority. That is to say, the vaunted idea of a free will wheeled out in early modern life to counter mechanical theories of nature and culture is *a will essentially divided against itself after the Fall*. It is free from mechanical determination, but its *internal* freedom is profoundly compromised. Even Kant is eventually pressed to move close to the Augustinian image of a will divided against itself.[7] Later philosophies of a mechanical universe either tend to drop the idea of will from human life or to introduce an "anthropic exception" that is not otherwise examined. It is this exception, it is said, that allows us to explain and control nature; the question of the relation between our bodies and the rest of nature is left in limbo.

My judgment is that no fully adequate conception of human agency is available today. Each theory comes replete with problems and mysteries that render it contestable. But a shift from the tri-archy—nature without agency, humanity with imperfect agency, God with perfect agency—to a heterogeneous world composed of interacting spatio-temporal systems with different degrees of agency carries considerable promise. The agenda is neither to reduce humanity to the rest of nature conceived as lacking all creative power nor to supplement a human will divided against itself with divine grace. It is to appreciate multiple degrees and sites of agency, flowing from simple natural processes, through higher processes, to human beings and collective social assemblages. Each level and site of agency also contains traces and remnants from the levels from which it evolved, and these traces affect its operation.

One charge leveled against such a conception of distributed agency is that it presupposes a conception of linear progress with one breath that it denies with another. But that misses the point. The hierarchy of agency projected here does measure it according to the standard expressed in the human estate; that is, you might say, the partial species provincialism embodied in this account. And it does suggest that some forms of agency precede and enable human agency. But the development of agency often proceeds in a topsy-turvy way, as we have suggested with respect to the origin of life from non-life. Most pertinently, a philosophy of becoming projects no encompassing temporal logic guaranteeing that the retrospective trajectory identified at this point will continue in the same direction. It might change radically, as it did from the vantage point of dinosaur species provincialism when an asteroid shower destroyed dinosauric conditions of maintenance. We say that time is irreversible, but we do not equate irreversibility automatically with progress.

A second charge, more commonly asserted, is that a distributed conception of agency is "anthropomorphic": it projects onto nonhuman entities traits, capacities and feelings that only humans possess. The charge of anthropomorphism did enable the classical European conception of laws of nature to break free from an earlier, enchanted view. But today it functions like a straitjacket. It reflects the convergent upshot of contending assumptions about the world now open to challenge. The contending assumptions are that human beings are made in the image of a creator God and endowed with unique capacities and that nonhuman nature is governed by ironclad laws of determination without agency. These two contending images converge to define anthropomorphism as the fallacy by which human traits are illegitimately assigned to other species and some non-living processes.

With the emergence of complexity theory, however, these injunctions against proceeding from the human estate to consideration of degrees of agency in other domains lose some power. Now it becomes plausible to construe human agency as an emergent phenomenon, with some nonhuman processes possessing attributes bearing family resemblances to human agency and with human agency understood by reference to its emergence from nonhuman processes of proto-agency. For if human agency is an emergent phenomenon rather than an eternal trait, precursors with different degrees of complexity are likely to be found. And other modes of agency that escape the designation of "precursor" are too. If that is the case, the door is open to explore whether force-fields, implicated or not in the evolution of the human species, express this or that degree of agency.

Stuart Kauffman questions the familiar injunction against anthropomorphism by identifying processes in lower organisms that bear family resemblances to human agency. He says that "the agency that arises with life brings values, meaning and action into the universe," and stresses that "agency reaches beyond humans."[8] So, first, agency has evolved into being, meaning that there could now be several degrees and modes of agency. And second, a minimal threshold of agency involves the intersection of intention, value, meaning and action. These elements evolve together.

A bacterium on this reading possesses *some* characteristics of agency so defined. It is attracted to sugar; it pursues it as an end; it adjusts its behavior to pursue its end; and it feels satisfaction when it achieves the end intended. Unlike a ball rolling down a hill, it is appropriate to use a simple variant of teleological language in speaking of a bacterium swimming up a glucose gradient: "Teleological language becomes appropriate at some point in the tree of life. Let us stretch and say it is appropriate to apply it to the bacterium. We may do so without attributing consciousness to the bacterium. My purpose in attributing actions (or perhaps better, protoactions) to a bacterium is to try to trace the origin of action, value, and meaning as close as I can to the origin of life itself."[9]

If Bonnie Bassler, a molecular biologist at Princeton, is correct, bacteria exhibit a degree of collective agency as well. When a certain threshold of bacteria accumulation is reached, say, in the human organism, "bioluminescence" occurs, the bacteria begin to communicate actively through chemical signals, and new collective actions are undertaken. She calls this "Quorum sensing" and thinks of it as preliminary modes of sensing, behavior, and communication from which complex modes of human communication have emerged.[10]

I will call the bacterium a proto-agent, in both its individual and collective modes, to distinguish its activity from mechanical causation and human agency, and also to suggest connections with the latter. It is doubtful that our own agency would have developed without such precursors. In appreciating it as a proto-agent and dark precursor to human agency, we may become more sensitive than otherwise to nonhuman forces, to the multiple layers of performance implicated in human agency and to the sources of drag or inhibition that attach themselves to the latter. It is hard to think or act creatively if a large gathering of bacteria have mobilized to launch an attack on your throat or bladder, and it is also impossible to function without the numerous types of bacteria that inhabit the body.

To locate differential degrees of agency at multiple sites not only supports the theme of evolution; it also points to the complexity of our interactions with multiple systems with their own levels and degrees of agency. Such processes make a difference to the world through intersections with each other and us. For instance, a flu virus evolves from bird hosts to human hosts; a strain of virus or bacteria acquires resistance to human drugs; a stem cell becomes a blood cell as it migrates to the appropriate environment and then becomes cancerous when the surplus it contains beyond its functional role as a blood cell encounters virulent strains in the bloodstream. When you think about the vitality of "actants" in larger assemblages that make a difference to those assemblages, modes of vibrancy below life that take on some aspects of micro-agency become important. According to Jane Bennett, "assemblages are ad hoc groupings of diverse elements, of vibrant materials of all sorts . . . The electrical power grid offers a good example of an assemblage. It is a material cluster of charged parts that have indeed affiliated, remaining in sufficient proximity and coordination to produce distinctive effects . . . The elements of this assemblage, while they include humans and their . . . constructions, also include some very active and powerful nonhumans: electrons, trees, wind, fire, electromagnetic fields."[11] Whitehead and Prigogine agree with this latter point, exploring the vitality of nonorganic elements whose modes of behavior change as they become parts of larger assemblages even as they *also* continue to express a vitality or excessiveness that is not entirely governed by the assemblage.

Perhaps we can now turn to human agency. Human agency involves much more than proto-agency, but it is equally important to bear in mind that limits to human agency flow from the proto-agency of other systems and the strains and limits built into the jerry-built character of human agency itself. There is no consummate agency anywhere, partly because each mode of agency is compromised by limitations attached to its happenstance evolution and partly because each periodically encounters nodes and levels of agency from elsewhere. With such considerations we both curtail the hubris expressed in the "anthropic exception" and explain by other means some of the limits and ambivalences Augustine housed in the inheritance of original sin.

What, though, *are* these other attributes of human agency? Well, a human agent not only has feelings, intentions, and susceptibility to satisfaction and dissatisfaction. Unlike the bacterium, consciousness is the crowning point of its expressive tendencies to action. To identify consciousness as the end point of activity already underway (rather than its starting point) is both to appreciate its importance and to challenge theories of consciousness that make the link between consciousness and agency definitional. Additional capacities are also discernible. You can forge alternative possibilities of action and decide between them.[12] You can also reflect on a previous pattern of action and try to alter it in the light of this second order reflection. If the attempt to alter the settled disposition falters — think of the micro-agentic powers of the desire to smoke, to engage in illicit sex, to brag, or to remain innocent of the complexity of the world — you can apply tactics to yourself self-consciously to loosen up some of the lower order drives (I will discuss what some of these tactics are in chapter 5). You can also invoke ethical considerations to inform your second order deliberations, and so on, almost endlessly.

Even at some of these levels of complexity, it is not clear that agency is entirely restricted to human beings. According to Giacomo Rizzolatti — the neuroscientist who discovered mirror neurons and triggered a revolution in neuroscience that is still unfolding — monkeys with culturally infused mirror neurons and without complex linguistic skills read the intentions of other monkeys and other living beings rather well. They then incorporate some of those intentions into their own repertoires of action.[13] They can also adjust their behavior toward others according to the initial reading of those intentions. They are invested with a degree of cultural agency before and below language. Even a dung beetle adjusts a first order desire to move a piece of dung when it meets a barrier, if not by changing the end, at least by altering the means to it.

Perhaps it should be said, with Sophocles and Hegel, that complex agency involves more than a connection to meaning, goals, and action; it also involves a relation between at least two beings with such powers. I embrace that threshold condition. My tendency is to say that proto-agency meets the conditions Kauffman specifies, that minimal agency meets a higher threshold in which responses to more complicated situations are forged, and that complex agency additionally requires the involvement of two or more agents. Complex agency involves a capacity to deepen sensitivity to others of varying degrees of agentic complexity. It also involves the capacity for self-consciousness, the ability to master the environment to some degree, and the ability to work tactically on the self in response to external pressures and your own reflective responses. Thus, to form desires involved with the desires of others; to reflect on those desires; to form second order desires from those reflections; to be able sometimes to act on a second order desire out of, say, ethical considerations; to act tactically upon yourself to recode to some degree culturally embodied tendencies that so far resist second order desires; and to cultivate new sensitivities to human and nonhuman agents of multiple sorts — all these skills, capacities, and sensitivities are involved in complex agency.

Agency, finally, is linked to creativity, to the formation of novel modes of behavior that were not extant before. Without purporting to give a complete account of creative agency—indeed I am not sure how to do so—creative change in the world sometimes arrives through inter-agental concatenations that exceed the previous reach of either party. We participate in creation, more than being masterful agents of it, partly because it surges through us as well as from us and partly because the confluences of forces from which it emerges often exceed the reach of any single party. Put another way, agency and creativity involve each other, and neither is entirely reducible to the other.

Much of what has been said about individual agents, themselves composed of several micro-agents, can be said about the agency of collective human assemblages that are also involved, internally and externally, with extra-human, open systems critical to them. A state-capitalist system can collectively seek to reform its previous habits of consumption; it can seek to modify the habits and interests that underwrite those patterns; it can use advertising, associational pressure, and erotically charged entertainment to work on cultural habits that resist such changes; and so on. The interaction between those modes of agency and other nonhuman forces makes a profound difference too. Collective agency, like the other modes, involves different levels and sites blending into and limiting each other. Agency is never consummate.

A world of becoming—consisting of multiple temporal systems, many of which interact, each with its own degree of agency—is a world in which changes in some systems periodically make a difference to the efficacy and direction of others. Moreover, since human beings themselves are composed of multiple micro-agents collaborating and conflicting with one another, it is wise to think of both individual and collective human agency as a complex assemblage of heterogeneous elements bound loosely together. Alcoholism, for instance, once its drive to satisfaction is installed in brain synapses, acts as a micro-agent, tempting some centers of human agency and resisting others. That is why it is equated with the devil in many circles. Indeed, from my perspective, the sense of a world of multiple agents expressed through the idea of a devil does not need to be expunged from the universe so that only human beings or God are said to possess the qualities of agency; rather, the idea of the devil needs to be *translated* into an appreciation of the multiple modes of agency in the world that it already expresses darkly.

To gather some of these points about agency and inter-agency assemblages together, consider a recent encounter between a biologist and yeast. We know bakers are often sensitive to yeast, as they feel the dough to ascertain when it is ready to rise. Yeast, a unicellular fungus, generates vibrations that both express its inner states and are potentially discernible to us to some degree. Its rate of cellular vibration falls within the range audible to humans, but its amplitude falls below our sensory capacity. Our everyday agency is thus confined by this limit in our capacity to hear, as well as by corollary limitations in the other senses. Jim Gimzewski, a biochemist, recently amplified the vibrations of yeast cells so that humans can hear them.

The sounds are calming at first. But upon pouring alcohol on a yeast culture, the vibrations and resulting soundscape acquire new intensity. The yeast emits signs of warding off pain. In an interview with Sophia Roosth, Gimzewski asserted that "it screams. It doesn't like it. Of course, yeast produces alcohol as in beer production, but if you put strong alcohol like Absolut vodka on it, if you like, then it screams. It screams. It doesn't like it."[14] The yeast has a capacity to feel and to respond to its feelings.

Does Gimzewski exaggerate? Perhaps. But he does identify a protean effort to ward off suffering. Gimzewski thereby opens us to modes of experience, feeling and proto-agency in the world that most of us had heretofore missed. It is comparable perhaps to experiments with crocodiles in which sound amplification makes us aware of a mode of communication between them that had exceeded our natural ability to hear it. We had previously, with typical humanistic hubris, treated the crocodile as incapable of collective communication. Our capacities of agency with respect to the agency of crocodiles now become enhanced by artificial means. In that case, inter-crocodile communication is the goal of those vibrations; in the case of yeast, the goal seems to be to ward off suffering. The yeast "feels" and "responds". A new inter-agency relation is disclosed through a creative experiment. And new thresholds of human sensitivity are also tapped.

You may resist this extension of "feeling," saying that feeling is by definition only what complex, conscious agents exhibit. But Gimzewski's experiment, in combination with Kauffman's reflections on the agency of bacteria, may open the door to move beyond the hubris of exclusive humanism. Consider Alfred North Whitehead's claim that our current definitions of feeling and associated terms reflect a subject/object duality that has become more and more difficult to sustain. Whitehead, the twentieth-century logician and philosopher of science, was shocked to the core as a young man by the demise of a Newtonian universe he had treated as apodictic. He spent a lifetime revising his cosmology to render it more amenable to a post-Newtonian universe. Pursuing the post-Newtonian intuition that "the universe is a creative advance into novelty," and that a moment of duration in any zone of being "is a cross section of the universe," he proceeded beyond the subject/object dualism of Western Enlightenment thought.[15] He did not seek to break the idea of subjectivity altogether by treating processes as objects fully susceptible to laws of prior determination. (That would open the conundrum of the anthropic exception.) Nor did he pursue the Kantian route by which the laws of nature are constructions necessarily imposed by us upon nature through (subjective) categories of "understanding" that we cannot consistently deny.

Working through and beyond Descartes, Newton, Hume, and Kant (all of whom are discussed in his major work), Whitehead loosened and redistributed common sense ideas of feeling, interpretation, perception, experience and agency. He found fugitive dimensions of each to be appropriate to numerous processes in the world extending well beyond the human estate. With respect to feeling, for instance, he plumbs dimensions that extend deeply into organic life:

> Thus the primitive experience is emotional feeling felt in its relevance to a world beyond. The feeling is blind and the relevance is vague . . . In the phraseology of physics, this primitive experience is 'vector feeling,' that is to say feeling from a beyond that is determinate and points to a beyond that is to be determined. But the feeling is subjectively rooted in the immediacy of the present occasion; it is what the occasion feels for itself, as derived from the past and as merging into the future. In this vector transmission of primitive feeling the primitive provisions . . . appear as wave lengths and vibrations.[16]

Those vibrations (or resonances) again. They are always in play and accelerate when a novel production is in the works. By placing Whitehead into conjunction with Kauffman and Gimzewski we begin to discern the profound connection between expanding our appreciation of multiple modes and levels of agency, feeling, experience and subjectivity and coming to terms with an immanent world of becoming in which the future is not entirely implicit in the past. Do these three scientist-philosophers also encourage us to become more sensitive to everyday life experiences, focusing more attentively on multiple shades of feeling and modes of agency in and around us? Do they problematize received theories of "subjectivity" and "objectivity," pressing us to pay more heed to the layering of agency, to its distributive character and to the potential complexity of inter-agentic relations?

Consider a formulation by Nietzsche that flouts the radical "subjectivism" so often attributed to him by critics and places him into close communication with Kauffman and Whitehead. After criticizing the Kantian version of the constitutive subject, he says in note #636 of *The Will to Power* that, "This world picture that [scientists] sketch differs in no essential way from the subjective world picture: it is only construed with more extended senses . . . And in any case they left something out of the constellation without knowing it: precisely this necessary perspectivism by virtue of which every center of force — and not only man — construes all the rest of the world from its own viewpoint, i.e., measures, feels, forms, according to its own force." And shortly thereafter, "My idea is that every specific body strives to become master over all space and to extend its force . . . But it continually encounters similar efforts on the part of other bodies and ends by coming to an arrangement ("union") with those of them that are sufficiently related to it: thus they then conspire together for power. And the process goes on — "[17]

There are differences between Kauffman, Nietzsche, and Whitehead. For example, my impression is that Whitehead's universe, from the vantage point of the human species, is more benign in its probabilities than that of Nietzsche. Or does Whitehead merely make his points in a softer language when he speaks of "this cosmic epoch" by comparison to other possible ones? It is hard to say.

But when you place these three into conversation it becomes clear that the charge of (human) subjectivism many would bring against them misses the boat. Rather, other traditions give too much priority to the human subject as either a constitutive subject, or a mirror of nature, or made uniquely in the image of God, or a perspectival, arbitrary subject imposing multiple (and contending) readings on a world of objects. For the nonhuman world itself, these three contend, is not reducible to a world of objects. It is composed of multiple systems marked by differing degrees of agency: each mode enters into complex conjunctions with others, and a temporary equilibrium (for seconds or centuries) involves interstabilization among several open systems with differing degrees of agency. A pivotal shift at some point within the stabilized system, or a new conjunction with outside forces, could renew the process of dissolution and resolution. For instance, when a monetary system in which some elements have been fluctuating below human attention issues in a crisis of subprime mortgages, quickly radiating out to other systems such as the employment market, state policy, consumption possibilities, and angry electoral constituencies.

Exclusive theories of human agency vary significantly in the degree to which subjectivity is governed by universal standards or filled with cultural variation. But the biggest mistake made by theories of exclusive human agency is to constitute the rest of the world as if it were a set of mere objects. Nietzsche, Whitehead, and Kauffman all correct that illusion. When that adjustment is made the real complexity of the world comes more fully into view.

The obverse charge to that posed by exclusive humanism could be that, while acknowledging degrees of agency in other force-fields, I have reverted to a classic cosmic hierarchy that places human beings at the top. This issue, too, deserves attention. My effort *begins* from a mode of species provincialism that treats human agency as a measure for other modes. However, it then resists translating that starting point either into a fixed, transcendental subject that rises uniquely above everything else or an evolved species that cannot enter into relations with nonhuman agents that further stretch its appreciations of them and opens up new questions about its own limits. Thus recent experiments with bacterial, crocodile, and yeast expression and communication stretch the confines of our habitual starting point, as would also be the case if we encountered a species that mixed into our capacities of language and reflexivity sensitivities of smell, touch, sight, and parallel processing that greatly exceed ours. Indeed, it is already likely that some human beings sense yeast vibrations before they are rendered audible by artificial means. And Buddhist monks who engage in lucid dreaming surely sense resonances and vibrations that slip below the threshold of attention, conscious or subliminal, of most other human beings. Some of the latter vibrations even affect the rest of us below awareness. Consider the experiment with organ music in which vibrations that excite the skin below the level of audibility are first retained in a church performance and then blocked. The evidence suggests that sub-audible responses to the first set of vibrations find expression in feelings of awe and wonder that are lost when the sub-audible vibrations are dampened. Our potential sensitivity to the world may thus exceed the range of "sensory experience" as that phrase is commonly interpreted.[18] To cultivate it further is to come to terms more richly with multiple modes and degrees of agency that compose the world. Cultivation of enhanced relations with modes of agency that exceed our current powers in this way or that can contribute new powers to thinking in a world that exceeds the modern myths of the masterful human agent, the self-interested agent with a fixed preference schedule, the universal moral subject, and the arbitrary, exclusive human carrier of nihilism.

So, though a preliminary hierarchy is projected with respect to degrees of agency through the constraints of species provincialism, some of the closures in that sense of hierarchy are potentially open to new modes of sensitivity and experimentation that can qualify or enrich it in distinctive directions. We do not know in advance what those limits are.

To adopt the perspective of a world of becoming is to assume a two-pronged approach to agency. At some times and for some purposes you explore how other modes of agency have served as precursors to human agency as they also enter into its layered character now. At other times you focus on how multiple fields with different degrees of agency help to constitute the larger world of becoming in which we are set. Both perspectives are indispensable.

Beyond Individualism and Holism

A world of becoming set on multiple tiers of temporality also exceeds the methodological imagination of both "individualism" and "holism" in the human sciences. A reductive individualist, in a rough and ready sense, tries to isolate distinct building blocks from which a larger order can be constructed. Many individualists probably played with LEGO blocks as young boys. The LEGO blocks may be sense data; they may be human individuals with fixed preference schedules; or, stretching a bit, they may be socialized individuals whose associations are strictly chosen once they reach maturity rather than being already folded to some extent into the visceral register of biocultural life. A theorist could be defined as an individualist in one of those senses.

A holist is one who treats the parts of a system to be sustained by the larger whole that constitutes them. The heart is nothing without the larger organism in which it functions; the conscious self requires an intersubjective web of language to be; an anthem is situated within a nation that gives it meaning, and so on. Such statements, true enough as so far stated, are then pressed further in holism. Let us see how this is so by reviewing a thinker who poses an alternative to both organic holism and reductive individualism.

In *A Pluralistic Universe* William James challenges, in the name of a world of becoming, the holism that governed most philosophy in the United States and Europe of his day. He says "the pluralistic view which I prefer to adopt is willing to believe that there may ultimately be no all-form at all, that the substance of reality may never get totally collected, that some of it may remain outside of the largest combination of it ever made, and that a distributive form of reality, the *each*-form, is logically as acceptable and empirically as probable as the all-form commonly acquiesced in as so obviously the self-evident thing." A little later he adds "radical empiricism allows that the absolute sum-total of things may never be actually experienced or realized in that shape at all, and that a disseminated, distributed or incompletely unified appearance is the only form that reality may yet have achieved."[19]

In these statements James resists organic holism. He contends that there is no "all form" either already intact or towards which everything is inherently tending. His notion of radical empiricism, defined against both logical empiricism and holist/teleological theories, says that when we sink into experience from time to time we make closer contact with a temporal slice of a larger world of connections punctuated by breaks and altered trajectories. He wagers that such pregnant experiences, made available by the temporary suspension of action-oriented perception, provide the initial impetus from which the philosophy of a pluralistic universe can be forged.

To pursue such a line he must also break with methodological individualism. Indeed, the implicit suggestion in his text is that these two opponents love to debate each other far too much, because the problems each faces keep shuffling people back and forth between these two frozen options. The need is to articulate a third possibility. Focusing first on the desperate search by empiricists of his day for disconnected "qualia" he says, "turn your face toward sensation, that flesh-bound thing which rationalism has always loaded with abuse . . . What, then, are the peculiar features in the perpetual flux which the conceptual translation so fatally leaves out? . . . The essence of life is its continually changing character; but our concepts are all discontinuous and fixed."[20] James overplays his hand a bit in his comment about "our concepts," since he himself crafted some that attenuate the tendency to closure he identifies. It is better to think of narrowly defined, discontinuous concepts as an illusion pursued by those already committed to methodological individualism. His key point, however, is that experience itself — during those moments when you suspend action and are acutely sensitive to its flow — discloses a flux in which elements from the past flow into the present and both of those fold into future anticipation. Without anticipation, in which elements in the protraction of the present are lured by future possibilities, experience would be dead. Experience itself consists of temporally interfolded elements, though these folding activities are not at the center of attention during action-oriented perception. Nonetheless, action-oriented perception itself would dissolve if such preliminary processes of interfolding did not operate at a subliminal level. Perception would lack a past to draw upon and aspirations or fears to inform it. Even David Hume's vaunted "habit," introduced to explain how we perceive causal connections that cannot be shown to exist objectively, would collapse if experience lost this temporal dimension.

Take visual perception, the sensory experience most commonly associated with discrete data. It consists of an encounter between intersensory memory and a new situation, as when you see the face of a very old man on the screen, implicitly folding into that image a memory of what it would be like to touch that face. It is called a haptic image, a visual image embodying the memory of touch. The image would be much different if the gritty element were eliminated. The same thing happens with smells, for instance, when you encounter an image of dung with steam floating up from it: touch, smell, and sound, all give texture to vision. Touch, sound, smell, and vision are inter-involved in experience.

To a radical empiricist, experience already comes replete with temporal connections, with a past pressing into the fugitive protraction of the present and a set of ingressions straining toward the future. And it cannot be divided neatly into that part which belongs to a subject and that which belongs to the world. James writes,

> In the real concrete sensible flux of life experiences co-penetrate each other so that it is not easy to know what is excluded and what is not. Past and future, for example, conceptually separated by the cut to which we give the name present and defined as being the opposite sides of that cut, are to some extent, however brief, co-present with each other throughout experience. The literally present moment is a purely verbal supposition, not a position; the only present ever realized being the "passing moment" in which the dying rearward of time and its dawning future forever mix their lights. Say "now" and it *was* even while you say it.[21]

Whitehead agrees, adding only that it is possible to refabulate received concepts sufficiently to render those temporal connections more vivid. Wittgenstein and Nietzsche would add another sentence to that claim, suggesting that since language itself has evolved and is richer than the formal definitions we give, many terms already harbor within them a fecundity that supports the thesis of William James. When Nietzsche says somewhere, for instance, that "there are no facts, only interpretations," he knows that many readers will understand the meaning of "interpretation" to refer only to human

subjects with different renderings of the same world. But he means to say—
as the earlier quotation from *The Will to Power* already suggests—that the
world beyond human subjects, too, is composed of multiple forces of differing degrees of agency that interpret, crudely or subtly as the case may be, the
environment upon which they act. These different levels and modes of "interpretation"—perhaps we should call them most elementary modes of
proto-interpretation—interact to foment a world that exceeds all of them.
Postulation of a world of inert facts is the product of a human subjectivity
filled with hubris.

James, then, is neither an individualist nor a holist. He is what I will call a
"connectionist." Those sharp cuts or reductions we add to experience to
make action-oriented perception more effective are artificial abstractions,
corresponding to what Whitehead later calls the fallacy of misplaced concreteness, simplifying a reality that is already more complex in experience.
And yet, pressing against the alternative thesis of organic holism, the connections are typically loose, incomplete, and themselves susceptible to potential change. They don't add up to a complete whole, and given James's
conjectures they never will. The connections are punctuated by "litter" circulating in, between, and around them. Viewed temporally, which is the
superior way, connectionism presents a world in the making in an evolving
universe that is open to an uncertain degree. Even our most elementary
experiences are temporal, in that the protraction of the present incorporates
the wayward past reaching toward an uncertain future. Such experience,
James is ready to wager, provides a superb entry point from which to probe
the larger universe. Recent developments in complexity theory, I suggest,
support that idea experimentally with the aid of concepts and artificially
enhanced tools of experience and experiment that were not available to
James.[22]

Hume's critique of induction and causality does not apply to James and
Whitehead. For, as Whitehead emphasizes in discussing Hume, both he and
James discern connections where Hume postulates separate, clean percepts.
These two, however, do encounter another version of the problem of induction at a different point. For in a world of becoming, the new periodically
comes into being in ways that defeat attempts to generalize from past regularities to a reliable future. Connectionism overcomes the simple problem of
induction while introducing a more profound one that haunts life periodically; it encourages us to infer from connected experience, while remaining
alert to possible surprises that may overturn some of those inferences. For

example, it is hard to accept the Humean concept of perception in a world where the powers of experience have been augmented by artificial means. It is also hard to accept a predictive ideal of science when new phenomena repeatedly emerge that do not seem predictable in advance of their occurrence.

I, too, am a connectionist, exploring loose, incomplete, and partial temporal connections in a world of becoming. The versions of complexity theory with which I am familiar would not make sense unless they too embraced connectionism over individualism and holism. Without temporal connections, experience could not be. It would be mere noise. But it is also partly because there are vibrations, bits of noise, and litter in each system that do not fit perfectly into it that new things can come into being, ruffling an established set of connections or throwing them into crisis. And it is because of multiple force-fields in a world of becoming that new intrusions periodically impinge upon a specific force-field, sometimes activating the litter in it in a new way.

To me, a world of becoming replete with loose and partial connections does not merely apply to the web of language, or to processes of human communication below language, or to musical experience, or to human thinking, or to artistic movements, or to political movements, though it does apply to all these. These experiences, rather, provide premonitions and anticipations from which connections in other domains can also be pursued. Connectionism applies in diverse ways and degrees to large and disparate processes such as the evolution of the universe, biological evolution, civilizational change, disease transmission, culture/body/brain networks, technological change, and the history of capitalism.

That is one reason why James, Whitehead and complexity theory need each other. The first two figures point to fecund experiences of dwelling that link us to a larger world of becoming, and both Whitehead and the proponents of complexity theory devise concepts and experiments that speak to the larger processes upon which James bestowed so much trust. I am not saying that the combination proves a philosophy of becoming to be true, merely that it renders it plausible enough for close consideration and possible embrace.

Take capitalism. It consists of moving elements such as the relative freedom of capital, contractual labor, the commodity form, and market/anti-market forces. But this complex (or "axiomatic" as Gilles Deleuze would call it) is both incomplete by itself and connected to other force-fields upon which it depends or which may intrude upon it. These include climate patterns, weather systems, animal-human disease jumps, the availability or depletion of clean water, fertile soil, oil, and other "resources," educational systems, scientific activity, adventurous inventors, medical practices, religious evolution, collective spiritual priorities, consumer trends, asteroid showers, and many other processes. All these partially open systems are linked in varying ways and degrees to the evolving system of capitalism. To treat capitalism as an (ideally) closed system periodically disrupted by "externalities" would be to commit the fallacy of misplaced concreteness. The very idea of an externality suggests an illegitimate intrusion into a system that would otherwise be self-sufficient and internally balanced. Indeed, neoliberal economic theory is compromised fundamentally by its tendency to isolate "the market" as *the* consummate or unique self-balancing system. But the world consists of innumerable force-fields with differential powers of self-maintenance, many of which interact periodically to augment or destabilize one another. When this feature of the human condition is admitted, the need to radically reformulate neoliberal economic theory becomes clear.

This means that you can't define capitalism as a pure system, either in the sense advanced by some versions of neoliberalism or in that advanced by those versions of Marxism that reify the base/superstructure relation. It means that when a new possibility or crisis emerges, you must often experiment to ascertain where and how to engage it. It never occurred to Marx, Keynes, or Milton Friedman, for instance, to address the relation between capitalism and climate. That is fair enough for the first two, but Friedman wrote after that issue had been posed. Nonetheless, if each had folded into his theory a greater appreciation of the relatively open and incomplete character of capitalism in a larger world of becoming, the advocates of each theory would have been more alert to changes in other force-fields that can impinge profoundly upon the operations of capitalism. Connectionism, inter-involved systems of multiple sorts, and a world of becoming help to define each other. Capitalism is exempt from none of them, in my view.

Immanence and Transcendence

I confess the philosophy/faith of a world that is immanent to itself. It includes the themes of complexity, distributive agency, connectionism, open systems, and time as becoming. I think Stuart Kauffman, Ilya Prigogine, Friedrich Nietzsche, and Gilles Deleuze share with me such a position, broadly defined. To affirm radical immanence is to confess the contestable faith/conviction that the evolution of every open system in the universe and the interconnections between them occur without the hand, intervention, guidance, or inspiration of a divinity. We also advance the view that, while each temporal system is marked by pluri-potentiality as it forms intersections with others, there is no final purpose governing time as such.

The philosophy of a world immanent to itself does not correspond to the philosophy of "closed immanence" that Charles Taylor discusses and criticizes in *A Secular Age*.[23] Closed immanence to Taylor means, in its most extreme version, the idea that all mystery can eventually succumb (or give way "in principle") to scientific explanation. It means, in a larger sense, any philosophy of time and world that closes off faith in a personal, salvational God that transcends the immanent world. I reject the first, while the second description does describe my stance. I further insist that both my position and the stance Taylor embraces are contestable, meaning that arguments and inspiration can be given on behalf of each but so far no advocate of either has been able to provide sufficient considerations to convince many of those outside its fold. Taylor and I may share that latter sense.

I also want to suggest, however, that the way Taylor applies the term "closed" to a philosophy of immanence is misleading. A philosophy of radical immanence, for instance, is closed to faith in a personal divinity. But it is open, first, to an eternity of time whose scope exceeds every specific force-field, second, to exploration of different degrees of agency, feeling, and creativity in several nonhuman force-fields, third, to exploring two registers of temporal experience within the human estate, and, fourth, to the idea that a modicum of mystery is apt to accompany some key assumptions in this perspective as well as others. Closed along one dimension and open along four others . . .

Several theo-philosophies of transcendence play up the uniqueness of the human estate too much for us; they are also closed to time as becoming. Thus, Taylor, I suspect, is closed to time as becoming, and he plays down modes of non-divine agency beyond the human estate. He may also reserve real creativity to God alone, while we distribute it to different zones of the universe and the relations between them. Yet, he may join us in seeking to bring two registers of temporal experience into closer proximity: the punctual time of everyday perception and the experience of duration available when action-oriented perception is suspended. Indeed, mystical traditions in each of the three monotheisms have long explored the second register.

Alfred North Whitehead joins Taylor in supplementing immanence with a field of transcendence, but his transcendence is more impersonal than the

God of Abraham confessed by Taylor. And his God changes over time. Whitehead, more than Taylor, pursues the eternity of time as becoming and is exquisitely open to exploring differential degrees of agency and feeling beyond the human estate. The latter theme, indeed, forms a key to his philosophy of process, a philosophy that projects a world of multiple, inter-acting open systems of different viscosity morphing at different speeds.

Does a philosophy of radical immanence, however, deny that there is an outside to experience? Not in one important sense. On the reading endorsed here every specific temporal field periodically comes into contact with other force-fields that have heretofore been outside it. Or, put another way, there is always an outside to a particular field of immanence, even if the outside is not invested with divinity. Philosophies of immanence and transcendence diverge in significant ways, but several versions of each project an outside.

There is another sense of transcendence that is important to the spiritual-ity pursued here. That is transcendence as an intensification of everyday experience so as to amplify sensitivities, open the self or constituency to experimentation, or augment experimental ties across lines of difference. These two dimensions of transcendence within a philosophy of radical im-manence will be explored and tested further as this study proceeds. But it is necessary at the outset to resist authoritative descriptions of immanence as necessarily closed and a philosophy of transcendence as simply open. It is equally important to correct the misperception that a philosopher of imma-nence cannot dwell in a suspended state periodically to render experience more sensitive.

Various modes of argument, evidence, and experiment can be marshaled on behalf of immanent realism in a world of becoming. We have already encountered a couple, and I will present others in later chapters. But to *prove* this philosophy/creed would require proving the impossibility of radical transcendence. Most immanent realists, as I read and commune with them, think it unlikely that we will prove our philosophy definitively, or that de-votees of impersonal transcendence or a personal God will do so. A com-parative element of contestable faith enters each camp, even though new events and arguments may conjoin to put pressure on this or that version of either. We define the term "faith" in a way that touches but does not corre-spond completely to some transcendent readings of it. Faith to us means a contestable element in belief that extends beyond indubitable experience or rational necessity but permeates your engagement with the world. It does not mean the receipt of a divine grace that infuses devotees with a confidence that cannot be communicated to others without such an infusion. Immanent and transcendent traditions probably define faith in overlapping but different ways.

The first sense of faith, the one compatible with a philosophy of immanence and with some commitments to transcendence, is pertinent, however, since it distinguishes the theme of immanence endorsed here from hubristic philosophies of closed immanence, as it opens a window to connections between us and some devotees of transcendence. These deposits of faith can shift as new evidence, inspiration, and experience surge forth to put pressure on them. Such a shift will have some things in common with a conversion experience, as it did for Whitehead when he gave up the Newtonian synthesis and the distinctive God attached to it in pursuit of process philosophy.

But why bother to state such a faith? Because faith, argument, and evidence typically become mixed into each other, it seems wise to state your existential wagers on this front actively and openly, to the extent you can. For each disposition does make a difference to how you engage the world — whether, say, you adopt a morality of command or an ethic of cultivation, whether you mine worldly experience alone to strengthen attachment to existence or seek strength from beyond this world, whether you seek to amplify sensitivity to other modes of agency in nature beyond the human estate or focus on either the human estate or its relation to God, and so on. Such modes of articulation can also open each wager / faith to engagement with pertinent modes of evidence, inspiration, and argument from other faiths / creeds, including their accounts of the experience of duration. To articulate the mode of immanence that moves me, for instance, can open people like me to close engagement with developments in complexity theory, opening up new avenues to enhance sensitivity to the world. It also opens us to comparisons that highlight the comparative contestability of the stance we embrace. Articulation, finally, reduces the extent to which each existential stance *merely* flows into life on its own, like the growth of underbrush in a tropical jungle. Such plants do regularly sprout up within and among us as we grow up, because of the layering of culture and density of human embodiment. Knowing this, it is ethically important to explore which plants to cultivate further, which to adjust, and which to try to pull up by the roots before they capture you entirely.

I will later suggest that given the comparative contestability of each such doctrine and the enlarged number of faith minorities now residing in several territorial states, it is both more important today to articulate publicly the philosophy/faith that infuses your participation in public life and ethically honorable to come to terms with the degree to which it remains contestable on comparative terms. I think James, Whitehead, and Nietzsche would agree with me on these points. And I imagine Taylor does, too.

––––––––––

Establishing alliances among devotees of (various kinds of) immanence and (various kinds of) transcendence who care profoundly about the earth, diversity, and equality, is a noble pursuit. Among contemporary theo-philosophers of transcendence there are numerous intellectuals with whom to seek such connections across difference. Charles Taylor, Fred Dallmayr, William James, Catherine Keller, and Hent de Vries are among the Euro-American devotees of the Transcendent who testify on behalf of such possibilities. Thinkers such as Bhrigupati Singh and Veena Das, who explore the links between Hindu thought and Wittgensteinian philosophy, do so as well as do others such as Talal Asad, who considers similarities and differences between Islam and Christianity. Many concede that they, too, are so far unable to prove faith in radical transcendence to many sane people who confess a different creed. And they seek positive alliances across these lines of difference. Many advocates on both sides have dropped the conceit according to which a philosophy is nothing unless it provides sufficient arguments on behalf of its "system." They, too, blur the lines between philosophy and theology, and between science and faith, while giving argument a role of importance in all four.

In everyday politics such alliances may become more viable as well. Young evangelicals in America have recently begun to shift away from the political closures of older evangelicals. If recent polls in the media are accurate, a larger number of evangelicals of all ages now pay attention to the issues of global warming and inequality. There are also pregnant signs with respect to Islam and Catholicism. Some Catholic leaders have renewed a commitment to economic equality, and the power of Al Qaeda could wane as the policies of Euro-American regimes change toward predominantly Islamic regions.

A political resonance machine appropriate to the urgency of today will be composed of multiple constituencies from several subject positions — including class, race, age, gender, creed, and religion — who seek to amplify gratitude for being in their own faiths and to fold that ethos into the way they address pressing issues of the day. It will apply internal and external pressure to several states, corporations, religious institutions, and international organizations at the same time. To define the acceleration of pace, the globalization of contingency, the dangers the current organization of capitalism poses to the precarious balances favorable to human life and species diversity, and the veritable minoritization of the world to be defining marks of our time is to discern why such an assemblage is needed.

So, complexity in the natural and human sciences, differential nodes of agency and feeling in the world, connectionism over individualism and holism alike, radical immanence with distinctive modes of transcendence appropriate to it, a world of becoming, two registers of temporal experience, contestable elements of faith in different cosmologies, and the pursuit of new lines of political alliance across multiple modes of creedal difference — one aspiration of this book is to weave each of these themes into the others.

CHAPTER TWO

The Vicissitudes of Experience

Nature, Culture, Immanence

I seek to come to terms with the materiality of perception by placing Merleau-Ponty, Michel Foucault, and Gilles Deleuze into conversation with each other and with recent work in neuroscience. The first conversation is sometimes obstructed by the judgment that Merleau-Ponty is a phenomenologist while the latter two are opposed to phenomenology. My sense, however, is that there is a phenomenological moment in both Foucault and Deleuze. More-over, the conception of the subject they criticize is one from which Merleau-Ponty progressively departed. He also eventually moved toward a more open conception of nonhuman nature which, he thought, was needed to redeem themes in the *Phenomenology of Perception*. This double movement — revising the idea of the subject and articulating a larger conception of nature compat-ible with it — draws Merleau-Ponty closer to what I will call a philosophy of immanence. Whether that migration was completed or punctuated by a mo-ment of transcendence is a question I will not answer here.

By immanence I mean a philosophy of becoming in which the universe is not dependent on a higher power. It is reducible neither to mechanistic materialism, dualism, theo-teleology, nor the absent God of minimal theol-ogy. It concurs with the last three philosophies that there is more to reality than actuality. But that "more" is not given by a robust or minimal God. We humans can be guilty of many things, but we bear no debts or primordial guilt for being itself, even if there are features of the human predicament that tempt many to act as if we do.[1] Rather, there are uncertain exchanges be-tween stabilized formations and mobile forces that subsist within and below them, as well as between one open system and other human and nonhuman systems that intersect with it. Biological evolution, the evolution of the universe, radical changes in politics, and the significant conversion experiences of individuals attest to the periodic amplification of such circuits of exchange.

Gilles Deleuze and Felix Guattari state the idea of radical immanence this way. First, they challenge the idea of transcendence lodged "in the mind of a god, or in the unconscious of life, of the soul, or of language . . . , always inferred." Second, they affirm historically shifting "relations of movement and rest, speed and slowness between unformed elements, or at last between elements that are relatively unformed, molecules and particles of all kinds . . ."[2] Such a philosophy of "movement and rest" does not imply that everything is always in flux, though its detractors often reduce it to that view.[3] It means that though any species, thing, system, or civilization may last for a long time, nothing lasts forever. Each force-field (set in the chrono-time appropriate to it) oscillates between periods of relative arrest and those of heightened imbalance and change, followed again by new stabilizations. Neither long cycles of repetition, nor linear causality, nor an intrinsic purpose in being, but, as the Nobel Prize-winning chemist Ilya Prigogine puts it, "our universe is far from equilibrium, nonlinear and full of irreversible processes."[4]

There is no denial that we humans—while often differing from one another—*judge* the new outcomes to which we are exposed or have helped to usher into being. What is denied is that the judgments either express an eternal law or bring us into attunement with an intrinsic purpose of being. For immanent realists deny there is such a law or intrinsic purpose. We anchor our ethics elsewhere and in different ways.

Immanent realism is defined by contrast to mechanistic materialism, too. Some causal relations are not susceptible to either efficient or mechanical modes of analysis. There are efficient causes, as when, to take a classic example, one billiard ball moves another in a specific direction. But *emergent causality*—the dicey process by which new entities and processes periodically surge into being—is irreducible to efficient causality. It is a mode in which new forces can trigger novel patterns of *self-organization* in a thing, species, system, or being, sometimes allowing something new to emerge from the swirl back and forth between them: a new species, state of the universe, weather system, ecological balance, or political formation.

Merleau-Ponty moved from his early work on human perception to an image of nonhuman nature that draws humanity closer to the rest of nature than dominant philosophies of early modernity had proposed. A certain pressure to pursue that journey was always there: a layered theory of human embodiment faces pressure either to identify selective *affinities* between the capacities of humans and other living beings and physical systems or to articulate a notion of transcendence that differentiates the human estate sharply from the rest of living and nonliving nature.

Consider some statements from *Nature,* a collection of lectures given by Merleau-Ponty just before his untimely death: "Thus, for instance, the Nature in us must have some relation to Nature outside of us; moreover, Nature outside of us must be unveiled to us by the Nature that we are . . . We are part of some Nature, and reciprocally, it is from ourselves that living beings and even space speak to us."[5] Here Merleau-Ponty solicits affinities between human and nonhuman nature. Does he also suggest that once preliminary affinities have been disclosed it is possible to organize experimental investigations to uncover dimensions of human and nonhuman nature previously outside the range of that experience? And that these findings might then be folded into an enlarged experience of ourselves and the world.[6] If so, when the neuroscientist V. S. Ramachandran, using magnetic imaging and other technologies of observation, exposes body-brain processes in the production of phantom pain exceeding those assumed in Merleau-Ponty's experiential account of it,[7] those findings could be folded into the latter's account along with the techniques Ramachandran invented to relieve such pain. Here *experimental* and *experiential* perspectives circulate back and forth, with each sometimes triggering a surprising change in the other.

Consider another formulation: "All these ideas (vitalism, entelechy) suppose preformation, yet modern embryology defines the thesis of epigenesis . . . The future must not be contained in the present . . . It would be arbitrary to understand this history as the epiphenomenon of a mechanical causality. Mechanistic thinking rests upon a causality which traverses and never stops in something."[8]

"The future must not be contained in the present." Just as the future of human culture is not sufficiently determined by efficient causes from the past, in nonhuman nature, too — when the chrono-periods identified are appropriate to the field in question — the future is not sufficiently contained in the present. Now mechanical causality, vitalism and entelechy, on Merleau-Ponty's reading of them at least, bite the dust together.

But if the future is not sufficiently contained in the present, what enables change over short and long periods? Here Merleau-Ponty approaches an orientation now familiar in the work of scientists such as Ilya Prigogine in chemistry, Brian Goodwin and Lynn Margulis in biology, Antonio Damasio and Ramachandran in neuroscience, and Stephen Gould in evolutionary biology:[9] "The outlines of the organism in the embryo constitute a factor of imbalance. It is not because humans consider them as outlines that they are such but because they break the current balance and fix the conditions for a future balance."[10]

The "imbalance" noted by Merleau-Ponty is close to what Gilles Deleuze calls the "asymmetry of nature," an energized asymmetry that periodically sets the stage, when other conditions are in place, for old formations to disintegrate and new ones to arise. It bears a family resemblance to Prigogine's account of systems that enter a period of "disequilibrium" and to the behavior "on the edge of chaos" that Brian Goodwin studies when a species either evolves into a new, unpredictable one or faces extinction. Merleau-Ponty, in alliance with these thinkers, does not shift from a mechanical conception of natural order to a world of chaos. He suggests that in each object domain periods of imbalance alternate with those of new and imperfect stabilizations.

I take these formulations from Merleau-Ponty to support the adventure pursued here.

The Complexity of Perception

Visual perception involves a complex mixing — during the half-second delay between the reception of sensory experience and the formation of an image — of language, affect, feeling, touch, and anticipation.[11] This mixing is set in the memory-infused life of human beings whose experience is conditioned by the previous discipline of the electrical-chemical *network* in which perception is set and by the characteristic shape of human embodiment and motility. Human mobility is enabled by our two-leggedness and the position of the head at the top of the body, with two eyes pointed forward. This mode of embodiment, for instance, encourages the production of widespread analogies between a future "in front of us" and the past "behind us." Most importantly, the act of perception is permeated by implicit reference to the position and mood of one's own body in relation to the phenomenal field.[12] Experience is grasped, says Merleau-Ponty, "first in its meaning for us, for that heavy mass which is our body, whence it comes about that it always involves reference to the body."[13] My "body appears to me as an attitude directed towards a certain existing or possible task. And indeed its spatiality is not . . . a *spatiality of position* but a *spatiality of situation*."[14]

We also need to come to terms with how perception is *intersensory*, never fully divisible into separate sense experiences.[15] For example, visual experience is saturated with the tactile history of the experiencing agent. The tactile and the visual are interwoven, in that my history of touching objects similar to the one in question is woven into my current vision of it. A poignant example of this is offered by Laura Marks, as she elucidates a film scene in which the composition of voice and the grainy visual image convey a daughter's tactile memory of her deceased mother's skin.[16]

Similarly, language and sense experience are neither entirely separate nor reducible to one another. They are imbricated in a way that allows each to exceed the other in experience: "the sense being held within the word, and the word being the external existence of the sense."[17]

Continuing down this path, Merleau-Ponty indicates how the color of an object triggers an affective charge. People with specific motor disturbances take jerky movements if the color field around them is blue and smoother ones if it is red or yellow. And in "normal" subjects, too, the visual field of color is interwoven with an experience of warmth or cold that precedes and infuses specific awareness of it, depending upon whether the field is red or blue.[18] This field of inter-involvement, in turn, flows into that between color and sound, in which specific types of sound infect the experience of color, intensifying or dampening it.[19] Words also participate in this process, as when the "word 'hard' produces a stiffening of the back or neck." Even "before becoming the indication of a concept the word is first an event which grips my body, and this grip circumscribes the area of significance to which it has reference."[20] The "before" in this sentence does not refer to an uncultured body but to a preliminary tendency in encultured beings. To put the point another way, the imbrications between embodiment, language, disposition, perception, and mood are always in operation. A philosophy of language that ignores these essential connections may appear precise and rigorous, but it does so by neglecting circuits of inter-involvement through which perception is organized.

These preliminary experiences vary across individuals and cultures in ways that are important to an appreciation of cultural diversity. The key point, however, is that some series of inter-involvements is always encoded in preliminary experience, flowing into the tone and color of perception. Phenomenologists, Buddhist monks, corporate advertisers, cultural anthropologists, neuroscientists, TV dramatists, Catholic priests, filmmakers, and evangelical preachers are all attuned to such memory soaked patterns of inter-involvement. Too many social scientists, analytic philosophers, rational choice theorists, deliberative democrats and "intellectualists" of various sorts are less so. An intellectualist, to Merleau-Ponty, is one who overstates the autonomy of conceptual life, the independence of vision, the self-sufficiency of reason, the power of pure deliberation, or the self-sufficiency of argument.

At this juncture Merleau-Ponty's phenomenology encounters the neuroscientist Giacomo Rizzolatti's recent discovery of mirror neurons. To both, social experience is not merely mediated by the web of language, it is also informed by the ability humans and monkeys have to read and mimic the intentions of others before and below language. Thus Rizzolatti explores how culturally coded mirror neurons allow us both to read the intentions of others immediately and to rehearse their behavior enough to install some of those tendencies into our own bodily schemas. Here is one way Rizzolatti makes the point: "the sight of acts performed by others produces an immediate activation of the motor areas deputed to the organization and execution of those acts . . . ; through this activation it is possible to decipher the meaning of the 'motor events' observed, i.e., to *understand* them in *terms of goal-centered movements*. This understanding is completely devoid of any reflexive, conceptual and/or linguistic mediation, as it is based on the *vocabulary of acts* and the *motor knowledge* on which our capacity to act depends."[21] It is important to emphasize that mirror neuron processing does not simply express a fixed genetic inheritance. The neurons themselves become culturally coded through the give and take of experience. Language-mediated experience without this background of less mediated interpretation "would be reduced to a perception 'purely cognitive in form, pale, colorless, destitute of emotional warmth.'"[22] I take Merleau-Ponty to agree in advance with these points, even though his own tendency is to emphasize (correctly I think) how the two modes of experience are mixed together once a sophisticated use of language is accomplished.[23]

Perception not only has multiple layers of intersensory memory folded into it, it is suffused with *anticipation*. This does not mean merely that you anticipate a result and then test it against the effect of experience. It means that perception expresses a set of anticipatory expectations that help to constitute what it actually becomes. The case of the word "hardness" already suggests this. A more recent experiment by neuroscientists dramatizes the point. The body-brain patterns of the respondents were observed through various imaging techniques as the subjects were asked to follow a series of pictures moving from left to right. The images at first glance look the same, but upon closer inspection your experience shifts abruptly from that of the bare head of a man to the nude body of a woman as you proceed down the line of images. People vary at which point the gestalt switch occurs. More compellingly, when asked to view the series a second time from right to left, almost everyone identifies the shift from the nude woman to the man's face further down the trail than they had in moving from left to right. The authors contend that the body-brain processes catalyzed by this series engender dicey transitions between two already embodied attractors. The first attractor retains its hold as long as possible; the second, triggered as you move from right to left, is retained until pressed to give way to another. The suddenness of shift in experience correlates with abrupt shifts in observable body/brain patterns. "By placing electrodes on the appropriate muscles to measure their electromagnetic activity, Kelso could clearly measure the sudden shift from one pattern to another . . . The underlying idea in Kelso's studies was that the brain is a self-organizing, pattern-forming system that operates close to instability points, thereby allowing it to switch flexibly and spontaneously from one coherent state to another."[24]

The "imbalance" that Merleau-Ponty identifies in embryos also operates in the perception of mobile human beings who must respond to rapidly shifting contexts.[25] Perception, to be flexible, is organized through multiple points of "instability" through which one set of memory-infused attractors gives way to another when the pressure of the encounter becomes intense enough. Each attractor helps to structure the actuality of perception.

Perception could not function without a rich history of inter-involvements among embodiment, movement, body image, touch, sight, smell, language, affect, and color. The anticipatory structure of perception enables it to carry out its functions in the rapidly changing contexts of everyday life; it also opens it to subliminal influence by mystics, priests, lovers, politicians, parents, military leaders, filmmakers, teachers, talk show hosts, and TV advertisers.

Another way of putting the point is to say that the actuality of perception is "normative," where that word now means the application of a culturally organized attractor to a situation roughly responsive to it. A visual percept, for instance, contains the norm of a well rounded object, compensating for the limitations of the particular position from which it starts. As Merleau-Ponty puts it, "The unity of either the subject or the object is not a real unity, but a presumptive unity on the horizon of experience. We must rediscover, as anterior to the ideas of subject and object . . . that primordial layer at which both things and ideas come into being."[26] The import of this presumptive unity becomes more clear through the discussions of depth and discipline.

Visibility and Depth

Merleau-Ponty concludes that we make a singular contribution to the experience of spatial depth, even though, as Diana Coole says, "the depth and perspective that permit visual clarity belong to neither seer nor seen [alone], but unfold where they meet."[27] The experience of depth, you might say, incorporates different possible perspectives upon the object into the angle of vision from which it is now engaged. The experience is ubiquitous. If you draw a Necker cube on a flat piece of paper, depth will immediately be projected into it. Upon viewing the image for a few seconds, it becomes inverted, so that a figure in which depth had moved from left to right now flips in the other direction. Upon learning how to produce the flips — by focusing your eye first on the bottom right angle and then the top left angle — it becomes clear how difficult it is to purge depth from experience. The short interval between the switch of gaze and the flip of the angle also testifies to the half-second delay between the reception of sensory experience and cultural participation in the organization of perception. This experiment teaches us that perception must be disciplined to exist and it also draws attention to the fugitive interval during which that organization occurs. René Magritte dramatizes the vertigo that arises when anticipation of depth is stymied in "The Blank Signature." A woman is riding a horse in the woods. But the lines of visibility and invisibility in the painting confound those you anticipate. The horse's back left leg curls behind a tree trunk in front of its torso, and just where the scenic background should slide behind the horse it appears in front of one part of its torso. Now you have a strangely familiar scene in which it is impossible to redeem the depth that experience itself solicits. The Magritte painting dramatizes how the visible, set against a field of the invisible, ordinarily frames the place, import, and depth of an image. The power of depth to insist is further emphasized when you discern how the anticipation of it is realized to the immediate left and right of the woman on the horse. But what enables the experience of depth when perception is unencumbered by such contrivances?

Perception depends upon projection into experience of multiple perspectives you do not now have. This automatic projection into experience also makes it seem that objects see you as you see them. Merleau-Ponty puts it this way: In this "strange adhesion of the seer and the visible . . . *I feel myself looked at by the things*, my activity is equally a passivity."[28] To have the experience of depth is to feel things looking at you, to feel yourself as object. This self-awareness is usually subliminal, but it becomes more apparent when you shift from the process of action-oriented perception to dwell in experience itself. The result is uncanny: to see is to experience yourself as an object of visibility, not simply in that you realize someone *could* look at you because you are composed of opaque materiality, but also because the very structure of vision incorporates into itself the projection of what it would be like to be seen from a variety of angles. This experience codifies, in the anticipatory structure of perception, potential angles of vision upon you and what it would be like to touch, hold, or move the object from different angles. The codification of operational angles of possible action and the background sense of being seen combine to produce depth.

That codification, however, cannot be reduced to the sum of all angles, to a view from *nowhere*. It cannot because each potential angle of vision fades into the diffuse background against which it is set. The codification, then, is closer to a view from *everywhere*, a view projected as a norm into an experience that depends upon implicit reference to it. In an essay on Merleau-Ponty, Sean Dorrance Kelly pulls these themes of anticipation and perspective together. First, the experience of a particular light or color is normative in the sense that "each presentation of the color in a given lighting . . . makes an implicit reference to a more completely presented *real* color . . . if the lighting context were changed in the direction of the norm. This real color, implicitly referred to . . . is the constant color I see the color to be." Second, "the view from everywhere" built into the experience of depth is not a view you could ever actually have, separate from these memory-soaked projections, because there is no potential perspective that could add up the angles and backgrounds appropriate to all perspectives. Backgrounds are not additive in this way. The experience of depth is, rather, "a view . . . from which my own perspective is felt to deviate."[29] Depth perception anticipates a perspective that feels distinct from my actual angle of vision. Perception thus closes into itself *as* actuality a norm it cannot in fact instantiate. Perception *is* anticipatory and normative. The only thing Kelly omits is how the perception of depth is also one in which "I feel myself looked at by things," such that my activity of perception "is equally a passivity." This latter theme, however, has consequences for contemporary politics.

Perception and Discipline

It might still seem that the gap between Michel Foucault and Merleau-Ponty remains too large to enable either to illuminate the other. Did not the early Foucault argue that because of the opacity of "life, labor, and language" the structure of experience cannot provide a solid base from which to redeem a theory of the subject? Did he not say that the transcendental arguments that phenomenologists seek — whereby you first locate something indubitable in experience and then show what conception of the subject is necessarily pre-supposed by that experience — cannot be stabilized when the "doubles" of life, labor, and language both set conditions for experience and fade into obscurity? Yes. But those strictures may be more applicable to Husserl than to Merleau-Ponty, particularly his later work.

Foucault speaks of "discipline" as a political anatomy of detail that molds the posture, demeanor, and sensibilities of the constituencies subjected to it, "in which power relations have an immediate hold on [the body]; they invest it, mark it, train it, torture it, force it to carry out tasks, to perform ceremonies, to enact signs."[30] We note immediately a difference in rhythm between the sentences of Foucault and those of Merleau-Ponty. Merleau-Ponty's sentences convey an implicit sense of belonging to the world, while Foucault's often mobilize elements of tension, resistance, and disaffection circulating within modern modalities of experience.

The initial connection between these two thinkers across difference is that both see how perception requires a prior *disciplining* of the senses in which a rich history of sensory inter-involvement sets the stage for later experience. The critical relation between corporeo-cultural discipline and the shape of experience is supported by the fact that adults who have the neural machinery of vision repaired after having been blind from birth remain operation-ally blind unless and until a new history of inter-involvements between movement, touch, and object manipulation is synthesized into the synapses of the visual system. Only about ten percent of the synaptic connections for vision are wired in at birth. The rest emerge from the interplay between body/brain pluri-potentiality and the action-oriented history of intersen-sory experience.[31]

Let's return to Merleau-Ponty's finding that to perceive depth is implicitly to feel yourself as an object of vision. In a disciplinary society this implicit sense morphs into a more intensive experience of being an actual or potential object of *surveillance* in a national security state. The latter experience was amplified in the United States after the Al Qaeda attack of 9/11, the event in which Osama bin Laden invited George W. Bush to organize the world through the prism of security against a pervasive, non-state enemy, and the cowboy eagerly accepted the invitation. The indubitable experience of self-visibility now swells into that of being an object of surveillance. Everyday awareness of that possibility recoils back upon the shape and emotional tone of experience. Traffic cameras, airport screening devices, Social Security numbers, credit profiles, medical records, electric identification bracelets, telephone caller ID, product surveys, NSA sweeps, telephone records, license plates, Internet use profiles, IRS audits, drivers' licenses, police phone calls for "contributions," credit card numbers, DNA records, fingerprints, smell-prints, eyeprints, promotion and hiring profiles, drug tests, street and building surveillance cameras, voter solicitation, school records, job interviews, police scrutiny, prison observation, political paybacks, racial profiling, email solicitations, church judgments, divorce proceedings, and the publication of sexual proclivities. As surveillance devices proliferate, the experience of *potential* observability becomes an increasingly active element in everyday life.[32]

> A whole problematic then develops: that of an architecture that is no longer built simply to be seen . . . or to observe the external space . . . but to permit an internal, articulated and detailed control — to render visible those who are inside it . . . ; an architecture that would operate to transform individuals: to act on those it shelters, to provide a hold on their conduct, to carry the effects of power right to them, to make it possible to know them, to alter them.[33]

True, Foucault's description of disciplinary society does not deal adequately with differences in age, class, and race. There is today an urban underclass that is subjected to general strategies of urban containment and impersonal modes of surveillance in stores, streets, public facilities, reform schools, prisons and schools. There is also a suburban, career oriented, upper-middle class enmeshed in detailed disciplines in several domains, anticipating the day it rises above them. And there are several other subject positions too, including those who rise more or less above generalized surveillance.

The cumulative message? Watch out. Are you a war dissenter? Gay? Interested in drugs? An atheist who talks about it? A critic of the war on terrorism, drug policies, or government corruption? Sexually active? Be careful. You may want a new job someday, or to insulate yourself against this or that charge. Protect yourself now in anticipation of uncertain possibilities in the future. Discipline yourself in response to future threats. In advanced capitalism, where the affluent organize life around the prospect of a long career, many others look for jobs without security or benefits, and others yet find themselves stuck in illegal, informal, and underground economies, the implicit imperative of the surveillance society is to remain unobtrusive and politically quiescent by appearing more devout, regular, and patriotic than the next guy. The implicit sense of belonging to the world that Merleau-Ponty found folded into the fiber of experience now begins to ripple and scatter.

Neither Foucault nor Merleau-Ponty, understandably, was as alert to the electronic media as we must be today. This ubiquitous force flows into the circuits of discipline, perception, self-awareness, and conduct. It is not enough to survey the pattern of media ownership. It is equally pertinent to examine the methods through which it becomes insinuated into the shape and tone of perception.

Here I note one dimension of a larger topic. To decode electoral campaigns, it is useful to see how media advertising works. According to Robert Heath, a successful ad executive and follower of recent work in neuroscience, the most effective product ads target viewers who are distracted from them. These ads solicit "implicit learning" below the level of refined intellectual attention. They plant "triggers" that insinuate a mood or association into perception, spurred into action the next time the product is seen, mentioned, smelled, heard, or touched. Implicit learning is key because, unlike the refined intellectual activity into which it flows, "it is on all the time." It is "automatic, almost inexhaustible, in its capacity and more durable" in retention.[34]

The link to Foucault and Merleau-Ponty is that they too attend to the preconscious, affective dimensions of discipline and experience without focusing upon the media. Today programs such as *The Hannity Report*, *Glenn Beck*, and *The O'Reilly Factor* infiltrate the tonalities of political perception. As viewers focus on explicit points made by guests and hosts, the constant repetition of background themes can readily be installed as simple fact for listeners who lack exposure to other programs or are already primed to assimilate them. The programs are also laced with interruptions, talking-over, sharp accusations, and yelling. The endless reiteration of these intensities secretes a simple standard of objectivity as the gold standard of perception while insinuating the corollary suspicion that no one actually measures up to it. As a result resentment and dogmatic cynicism are now coded into the very color of perception. The cumulative result of the process itself favors a neoconservative agenda. For cynics typically ridicule the legacy of big government in employment, services, and welfare while yearning for a figure to reassert the unquestionable authority of "the nation." A cynic is often an authoritarian who rejects the current regime of authority. Cynical realists do experience the fragilities and uncertainties that help to constitute perception. But they join those fugitive experiences to an overweaning demand for certainty and authority that overrides them, and they accuse everyone else of failing to conform to the model of simple objectivity they claim to meet. Justification of such a model is thus not sustained by showing how its defenders meet it but by repeated accusations that others never do. A temper that might be called accusatory objectivity is thereby cultivated.

This cynical objectivism is one response to a surveillance society during a time when so many aspects of life also point to the real complexity of perception. Another response, in a world of surveillance, is self-depoliticization. You avert your gaze from disturbing events to curtail dangerous temptations to action and thus heightened visibility. The goal is to avoid close attention or intimidation in the venues of work, family, school, church, electoral politics, and neighborhood life. But, of course, such a retreat can also amplify a feeling of resentment against the cultural organization of life itself, opening up some of these same constituencies for recruitment by the forces of *ressentiment*. Such responses can be mixed in several ways. What is undeniable is that the circuits between discipline, media, layered memories, and self-awareness find expression in the color of perception itself today. Power is coded into perception.

The Micropolitics of Perception

Sensory inter-involvement, disciplinary processes, detailed modes of surveillance, media infiltration, congealed attractors, affective dispositions, self-regulation in response to future susceptibility—these elements participate in perpetual circuits of exchange, feedback, and re-entry, with each loop folding another variation and degree into its predecessor. The imbrications are so close that it is next to impossible to sort out each element from the other as they merge into a larger complex. The circuits fold, bend, and blend into each other, inflecting the shape and texture of political experience. Even as they are ubiquitous, however, there are numerous points of dissonance, variation, hesitation, and disturbance in them. These interruptions provide potential triggers to the pursuit of other spiritual possibilities, where the term *spirit* means a refined state of the body in an individual *and* existential dispositions embedded in institutional practices.

What are the dissonances? A past replete with religious ritual clashes with an alternative representation of God in a film, church, or school; an emergent practice of heterodox sexuality encourages you to question established habits in other domains; the interruption of a heretofore smooth career path disrupts previously submerged habits of anticipation; a trip abroad exposes you to disturbing news items and attitudes seldom finding popular expression in your own country; neurotherapy fosters a modest shift in your sensibility; a stock market crash disrupts assumptions about the self-stabilizing tendencies of the market; a new religious experience shakes and energizes you; a terrorist attack folds an implacable desire for revenge into you; a devastating natural event shakes your faith in providence.

The anticipatory habits of perception are not self-contained. Rather, dominant tendencies of the day periodically bump into new events, minor dispositions, and submerged tendencies. The instability of the attractors and conjunctions that make perception possible thus also make it a ubiquitous medium of power and possible transfiguration.

What might be done today to open the anticipatory habits and sedimented dispositions of more constituencies during a time when media politics deploys scandal, disinformation, distraction, and accusation to divert attention from the most urgent dilemmas of the day?

Television could be a site upon which to run such experiments. A few dramas do so. I would place *Six Feet Under* on that list, as it disrupts conventional habits of perception and occasionally works to recast them. But the closer a program is to a "news program" or a "talk show," the more it either enacts virulent partisanship, adopts the hackneyed voice of simple objectivity, or purports to do the one while doing the other. What is needed are subtle media experiments, news and talk shows that expose and address the complexity of experience in a media saturated society. *The Daily Show* and *The Colbert Report* take a couple of steps in the right direction, calling into question the voice of simple objectivity through exaggeration and satirization. Their stills and close ups of public figures in action reveal how passions infiltrate our perceptual experience below the level of conscious attention. But because we live in a media saturated society much more is needed.

Mark Hansen, in *New Philosophy for New Media*, pursues more subtle possibilities that could eventually find their way into prime time just as the Colbert and Stewart strategies today draw upon innovative techniques of the recent past. They speak to a younger generation already primed by cyberspace to absorb and assess them. In chapter 6, Hansen reviews *Skulls*, an exhibit presented by Robert Lazzarini at the Whitney Museum in 2000. Lazzarini's sculptures are uncanny. They seem like skulls, but you soon find that however you tilt your head or change your position it is impossible to vindicate the anticipation of them. Lazzarini has in fact laser-scanned an actual human skull, reformatted it into several images, and constructed a few statues from the reformatted images. Now no three dimensional image can be brought into alignment with the anticipation triggered by its appearance. "At each effort to align your point of view with the perspective of one of these weird sculptural objects, you experience a gradually mounting feeling of incredible strangeness. *It is as though these skulls refuse to return your gaze.*"[35]

The anticipation of being seen by the objects you see is shattered by deformed images that refuse to support that expectation. You now feel "the space around you begin to ripple, to bubble, to infold, as if it were becoming unstuck from the fixed coordinates of its three dimensional extension."[36] *Skulls*, when joined to Merleau-Ponty's phenomenology of perception, heightens awareness of the fugitive role we play in perception by making it impossible to find an attractor to which it corresponds. These sculptures also dramatize the role that *affect* plays in perception, as they jolt the tacit feeling of belonging to the world that Merleau-Ponty finds lodged in the depth grammar of experience. The implicit sense of belonging to the world is transfigured into a feeling of vertigo. Do such experiments dramatize a sense of disruption already lurking within experience in a world marked by the acceleration of tempo, the exacerbation of surveillance, and the disturbance of traditional images of time? At a minimum, in conjunction with the work of Merleau-Ponty and Foucault, they sharpen our awareness of the multiple inter-involvements between affect, memory, and tactility in the organization of perception. You can now more readily call into question simple models of vision and better appreciate how a disciplinary society inflects affect-imbued perception.

You might even become attracted to experimental tactics to deepen visceral attachment to the complexity of human existence itself during a time when the automatic sense of belonging to this world is often stretched and disrupted. None of the above responses is automatic: an opportunity merely opens. Pursuing it requires moving back and forth between perceptual experimentation and reflection on changes in the larger circumstances of life that enter into affect-imbued judgments and perceptions.

As a preliminary, consider some processes that disrupt the tacit sense of belonging to the world that (especially the early) Merleau-Ponty found sedimented in the pores of experience itself. They include: the acceleration of speed in many domains of life, including military deployment, global communication systems, air travel, tourism, population migrations, fashion, financial transactions, and cultural exchanges; a flood of popular films that complicate visual experience and sometimes call the linear image of time into question; publicity about new discoveries in neuroscience, which include attention to that half-second delay between multi-sensory reception and the unconscious organization of perception; greater awareness of work in the sciences of complexity that transduce the Newtonian model of linear cause into the ideas of resonance and emergent causality; scientific speculations that extend the creative element already discernible in biological evolution to the unfolding of the universe itself; increased media attention to political events that jolt assumptions coded into perception; intense media attention to the devastation occasioned here or there by earthquakes, tornadoes, droughts, floods, hurricanes, volcanic eruptions, and tsunamis; and a vague but urgent sense that the world's fragile ecological balance is careening into radical imbalance.

The signs that these disruptive experiences have taken a toll are also diverse. They include, on the revenging, aggressive side of life, the extreme levels of violence and superhuman heroism in action films, as they strive to redeem simple models of objectivism and mastery under unfavorable circumstances; the intensification of accusatory voices in the media already noted in conjunction with the righteous self-assertion by talking heads of simple objectivism; new intensities of cosmic, civilizational, and national revenge themes in several religious movements; the heightened virulence of electoral campaigns; the freezing in some circles of the tradition of secularism into an unquestionable dogma; and popular desires for abstract revenge that find ample expression in preemptive wars, state regimes of torture, massacres, collective rapes, and the like.

The obverse side of those responses is discernible as well in other practices and constituencies. Today a significant minority in a variety of social positions — including those of class, age, religious creed, gender, and ethnicity — are less convinced of the simple model of objectivity. They respond to the evidence against it by seeking to consolidate attachment to a world populated by sensory inter-involvements, the half-second delay, resonance, attractors, the complexity of duration, time as becoming, and an uncertain future.

Interruptions of Experience

Before we pursue an affirmative response to these conditions, let's look at even more durable sources that feed them. That may deepen our sense of the challenge and provide clues as to how to proceed. The larger sources are perhaps best engaged by bringing a strange couple into communication: Charles Taylor and Gilles Deleuze. For they approach overlapping issues from different starting points. The former focuses on changing "conditions of belief" setting the broad context in which the vicissitudes of late-modern experience are set. The latter examines how "belief in this world" is placed under extreme strain by these and other developments.

In the age of the secular, says Taylor, belief in the transcendence of a personal God, whether Christian or otherwise, has become "optional." Focusing perhaps too much on sources internal to Europe alone, rather than on intersections between Europe, a Jewish minority, the New World, and Islam, he emphasizes how the Reformation defeated the enchanted world that had woven multiple domains of daily experience into a larger vision of transcendence. He links the effect of this change to the partial dispersion of a European monolith once called Christendom, the rise of capitalism as a turbulent engine of production, speed, mobility, and uncertainty, the formation of an official split between private faith and public life (even if the actuality is less sharply defined), and the impressive accomplishments of science in the domains of physics, biology, evolutionary biology, chemistry, and neuroscience. Taken together these developments alter the general "conditions of belief" in which specific beliefs are forged and maintained. The elements listed in the previous section, such as the acceleration of pace and the growing power of the mass media, add additional scope and intensity to those "conditions," though they are not emphasized by Taylor. The result on Taylor's reading is that people in Euro-American societies, and to varying degrees elsewhere too, now find themselves rubbing shoulders with those whose most basic repertoires of belief disturb and challenge their own. Taylor describes this as the extension of choice with respect to belief, though I find that term to focus too much on the cognitive dimension and not enough on combustible affective elements mixed into belief.

One expression and result of these forces taken together is what I will call *the acceleration of pace at which a veritable minoritization of the world is taking place at a faster rate before our very eyes*. Taylor does not concentrate on this effect, though something like it is discernible in his work.[37] By minoritization of the world I mean, in some cases, the more rapid introduction of minorities of multiple types — including religious, spiritual, ethnic, racial, gender practice, and sensual disposition — on the same territorial space. In other cases it means intense pressures to counteract or avoid this result through extreme action, such as building walls between countries, ethnic cleansing, fundamentalization of religious faith, or legal repression of gays. This means that within and across countries, constituencies of diverse sorts regularly rub against each other in churches, schools, neighborhoods, families, cyberspace, the news media, TV comedies, film dramas, political campaigns, military organizations, and the courts, and they encounter the construction of new impediments to such intimacies.

The minoritization of the world, I want to say, is one reason that (what Taylor calls) "belief" now feels more "optional."[38] The multiplication of faith possibilities within the historical terrain of Christendom (such as Judaism, Hinduism, Buddhism, atheism, agnosticism, and Islam, each with its own diversities), the sharpened awareness of Christianity as a minority creed in the world as a whole, the concomitant rise of "exclusive humanism" as a specific "option," and the emergence in some circles of immanent naturalism as a faith / creed that challenges assumptions of both traditional Christianity and exclusive humanism — all this means that experience is pervaded by close encounters, engagements, negotiation, and rivalry between diverse creeds.

Today devout confessions of transcendence of multiple types and modes bump up against each other and the (sometimes) reverent confessions of immanence of multiple types (exclusive humanists, atheist variants of rationalism and logical empiricism, tantric Buddhists, immanent naturalists, etc.). All the parties not only struggle with internal tensions and doubts that always occupy a faith / creed. They persistently encounter other creeds that exacerbate those tensions and uncertainties by posing living counters to them, and they sometimes do so when no specific creed sets the unchallenged center around which a series of minorities are managed, tolerated, or both. Something like this has happened before. But as Taylor says, the rise of "exclusive humanism" as a relatively popular option in Europe and, to a much lesser degree, in the United States, combines with extensive encounters with alternatives beyond Christianity and Judaism to intensify the effect.

Under these conditions each constituency faces the task of affirming its existential creed without becoming overwhelmed with resentment by the fact that it faces living challenges to it at numerous sites and turns. This condition of existence increases the pressure to pour a spirituality of resentment into your faith and, beyond that, either to seek enclaves protected from these pressures or to translate this resentment into tactics of revenge against vulnerable constituencies whose very existence poses a threat to your self-confidence and self-assurance. The time we inhabit, then, exacerbates strains of existential resentment always simmering as a possibility in mortals who must come to terms with the issues of mortality, economic inequality, suffering, sickness, exploitation, and fundamental misfortune. The minoritization of the world, the awareness that you could "choose" another faith, the challenges to self-confidence in your own faith, the temptation to amplify existential resentment, and the drive to blame specific constituencies for this general condition, resonate with one another.

Such a characterization, as stated, is broad and not subjected to the pertinent qualifications. But such a condensation may be needed to show how these diverse pressures affect each other. If we collect the pertinent shifts in contemporary experience — from altered experiences of time to the minoritization of the world — we also sense how such pressures can accumulate for many to disconnect participation *in* the world from an automatic sense of belonging *to* the world. We can see or at least feel the exaggeration in Merleau-Ponty's sense that the layering of embodiment suffices to secure essential belonging. Today what Nietzsche called *ressentiment — a resentment of the most fundamental terms of human existence as you yourself understand them* — too readily becomes insinuated into the pores of experience. The distribution of such a disposition is uneven, but it is not confined to the interior souls of individuals. It can haunt entire constituencies; it can even become embedded to varying degrees in institutions of investment, consumption, electoral campaigns, governing, media reporting, church presentations, Internet debates, and military life.

It is perhaps at this point that Gilles Deleuze can enlarge our grasp of this condition and suggest at least one way to forge the beginnings of a response to it. I refer to Deleuze's claim, one that touches the thought of Charles Taylor in advance in a way that may surprise some, that today we need to find ways to *"restore* belief in this world." Deleuze contends that today, though not for the first time, the distance between involvement in the world and belief in it has grown. Recent developments in cinema simultaneously express these larger developments, amplify them and may suggest preliminary strategies of response that supersede existential resentment. To put it another way, both Taylor and Deleuze think that part of our predicament today is existential, even though neither thinks that the predicament can simply be resolved at this level of being.

Here are a few of Deleuze's formulations about what has been happening, since at least the end of the Second World War:

— It is clear from the outset that cinema had a special relationship with belief. There is a Catholic quality to cinema (there are many explicitly Catholic authors . . .). Cinema seems wholly within Nietzsche's formula: "How we are still pious." Or better, from the outset, Christianity and revolution, the Christian faith and revolutionary faith, were the two poles which attracted the art of the masses.

— The modern fact is that we no longer believe in this world. We do not even believe in the events which happen to us . . . It is not we who make cinema; it is the world which looks to us like a bad film.

— The link between man and the world is broken. Henceforth, this link must become an object of belief: it is the impossible which can only be restored within a faith . . . Man is in the world as if in a pure optical or sound situation. The reaction of which man has become dispossessed can be replaced only by belief . . . The cinema must film, not the world, but belief in this world, our only link.

— Because the point is to discover or restore belief in the world before or beyond words . . . It is only, it is simply believing in the body.

— Whether we are Christians or atheists, in our universal schizophrenia, *we need reasons to believe in this world.*[39]

Deleuze thus speaks to the element of "schizophrenia" to be addressed by both atheists and theists. He surely would not, then, endorse that group of new atheists who think that simply following the logic of traditional science will dissolve the issues involved. Let me follow Deleuze further down this trail: we will consider Taylor's response more closely in the next chapter. I am, of course, not confident that Taylor, Deleuze, or I can forge a response that is sufficient to the issue. But perhaps it is pervasive and deep enough to warrant making some preliminary attempts.

How to restore belief in this world? Some writers, says Deleuze, (e.g., Artaud, Kafka, and Proust), artists (Bacon and Magritte), philosophers (Nietzsche and Kierkegaard), and film directors (Welles, Duras, and Resnais) help us to think through this issue. They begin by first dramatizing a fugitive sense already there in life of jumps and interruptions in experience, by portraying interruptions in smooth narratives. This is very active in film, and such cinematic experience readily becomes coded into the sensitivity of experience beyond the theater. The depth-of-field shots that conjoin dissonant elements of past and future, the irrational cuts through which sound and visual experience confound each other, the aberrant modes of behavior in comedies that convey fugitive experiences exceeding habitual experience, the flashbacks that mark a previous point of bifurcation at which one path was pursued and another was allowed merely to fester as incipient potentiality—these cinema techniques both dramatize features of everyday life already dimly available to us and place them at the forefront of attention for further reflection. The film tactics reviewed by Deleuze anticipate new media experiments presented by Hansen earlier in this chapter. They expose us to experiences of dissonance that cannot readily be submerged again, so that attempts to do so must be more virulent than under other conditions of life.

But such cinematic labors of the negative are not sufficient; they certainly do not suffice to promote positive attachment to this world. Even a "negative dialectic" does not suffice. If things are left there, the embers of *ressentiment* can easily become more inflamed. That is one reason Deleuze is never happy with negative critique alone: the next task is to highlight how our participation in a world of real creativity that also finds expression elsewhere in the universe *depends* on and *draws* from such fugitive interruptions. To put it too starkly (for situational nuances and adjustments are pertinent here), the more people who experience a positive connection between modes of interruption and the possibility of our modest participation as individuals, constituencies, states, and a species in creative processes extending beyond us, the more apt we are to embrace the new temporal experiences around us as valuable parts of existence as such. Certainly, absent a world catastrophe or a repressive revolution that would create worse havoc than the conditions it seeks to roll back, these consummate features of late-modern life are not apt to dissipate soon. The fastest zones of late-modern life, for instance, are not apt to slow down in the absence of a catastrophe that transforms everything. So the radical task is to find ways to strengthen the connection between the fundamental terms of late-modern existence and positive attachment to life as such. This should be accomplished not by embracing exploitation and suffering, but by challenging them as we come to terms with the larger trends.

To state the issue in such bald terms may carry two advantages. It dramatizes the condition so that it is harder to ignore, and it shows in advance how the responses Deleuze proposes to the condition (at least in the Cinema books) fall short of what is needed. They provide merely a start.

One place Deleuze pursues this question is in the chapter of *Cinema II* entitled "Powers of the False." This is the most Nietzschean chapter of that book, organized around readings of several films. The false is not only what is untrue, although that is one dimension of this multifaceted word. It is also, in this context, that which was incipient at an earlier moment, was not enacted when action took a different turn, left a deposit as a gestational force without portfolio, and now jumps from below the threshold of articulation, thought, and consciousness into the adventure of thought, desire, and action. The bump or jolt contributes a creative element to thinking and action, a moment that, because it draws partly upon powers outside our provenance and partly upon what we do with them, is not under the full control of those involved in it. Its agency and our agency become blended together, or better, imperfectly fused, helping to show us that we are never consummate agents even when we participate in creative adventures. All this starts at the thresholds of "the *unsummonable* of Welles, the *inexplicable* of Robbe Grillet, the *undecidable* of Resnais, the *impossible* of Marguerite Duras."[40] These are the moments that spur thinking as an encounter between a forgone past and a new situation, opening a possibility that may eventually belong entirely to neither.

Deleuze thus translates numerous interruptions and dissonances in experience that are too blatant to ignore into positive possibilities, though not certainties. Such a possibility, amidst the dangers and limits accompanying every adventure flowing from it, provides one "reason" to restore belief in this world. We now see interruption as intrinsic to our modest participation in a world of becoming whose powers of creativity also exceed us. Some devotees of transcendence, as we shall see in a later chapter, identify similar challenges and pursue a somewhat different route to this point. Their challenge, too, is to forge positive responses to late-modern conditions of experience and to ward off the existential resentment that can so readily become attached to them and obstruct efforts to overcome exploitation and suffering.

The false for Deleuze can sometimes be a positive power because at those moments when thought is stymied or stuck in the grooves of regularity it acts as a shock, spurring thought on. The false — as incipience — jumps, bolts, bounces or surges across this jagged boundary to invest action itself. It contributes new ideas and energy to action in a world where the periodic emergence of new situations often requires creative invention. As we attend to the powers of the false we are in a better position to restore attachment to this world, to feel how the attenuated link between involvement and belonging itself sets a condition of possibility for our participation in the creative element that operates elsewhere in the world too. We are neither consummate agents on this reading nor protected by the grace of an all powerful God: we participate in modes of becoming that exceed us in a world replete with tragic possibility.

This periodic jump across ruptures shows us the importance of sometimes waiting, dwelling, and allowing new thoughts to emerge, so that we can then test and work upon them further. One reason that film is important, as well as several theological accounts, philosophical explorations, novels, and visual arts, is that this multi-sensory medium shows more people in several walks of life how we already participate in such bumpy processes and how they may now be unavoidable to life as such. It renders our participation in them more vivid. I would cite *Waking Life* as a recent example of that insight, as the audience communes with wavy cartoon figures blending and folding into each other in the wayward existential musings of a man whose brain has six minutes to work after his heart has stopped. This film valorizes together the bumpiness of thought and attachment to this world. *Eternal Sunshine of the Spotless Mind* provides another instance, and so perhaps does *I ♥ Huckabees*. But the most illuminating of recent films in this regard may be *Time Code*, a film with four frames on the screen at the same time, shot with four handheld cameras. The periodic interactions between the anonymous ensembles set on different trajectories are punctuated by a series of minor earthquakes that jolt each ensemble in different ways at the same moments, triggering creative responses of different sorts that then feed into the ensemble relations.

Belief in a world punctuated by dissonance and the periodic need for creative action has to be "restored" because the sense of belonging to it is not automatic. It is not simply there "implicitly." Such a belief, as Deleuze knows, involves an element of faith. The faith can be either in the powers of immanence or in some version of transcendence, for both speak to an outside that exceeds our capacities of encompassment. It may not matter *that* much which direction you take at this point, as long as the debate continues and belief in this world is restored enough to fend off the temptation to resent profoundly the very vicissitudes of experience as such.

There are strains in Merleau-Ponty that resonate with the theme I draw from Deleuze, especially formulations in his last book on nature cited at the beginning of this chapter. By the end of Merleau-Ponty's life, the critical differences between him and the work of Deleuze, then just underway, were largely matters of emphasis and dramatization, except perhaps for the question of how securely a sense of belonging is lodged in experience as such.

There are also partial points of convergence between Taylor and Deleuze, as we have already seen, though the starting points of faith from which they proceed differ radically and the attention to the vicissitudes of time as such is more developed in Deleuze. But there is a critical difference between all these thinkers and many others who think either that there is no real issue here, that a return to traditional secularism will resolve it, or that it can be resolved only by restoration of universal belief in one God.

By "belief in this world," neither Deleuze nor I, again, means that the established distribution of power, exploitation, and inequality now in place is to be protected, though some critics love to jump to this conclusion. Such arrangements make people suffer too much, and they rest upon the repression of essential features of the contemporary condition, including the minoritization of the world occurring at a more rapid pace. Exploitation and domination are things to contest and oppose, as Deleuze did actively while embracing the points reviewed above. The restoration of belief in this world provides an existential resource to draw upon as those struggles are fought energetically and creatively. Nor do we mean that it is always illegitimate to resent your place in the world. Resentment is often a needed impetus to action, even if it carries the danger of becoming transfigured into *ressentiment*. It is existential resentment we worry about most, the kind that is apparent today in practices of capitalist greed, religious exclusivity, media bellicosity, authoritarian strategies, sexual narrowness, and military aggression. We mean, first, positive affirmation of the cosmos in which human beings are set, as you yourself understand that cosmos, second, coming to terms in a positive way with the enduring modern fact of interruptions in experience and the faster pace at which minoritization occurs, and third, accepting the contestability of your existential creed without profound resentment of *that* condition.

Each faith constituency must seek a positive response to these latter conditions in its distinctive way. We here advance merely one possibility that may appear credible to a minority, as it ponders distinct elements of experience and enters into active exchange with other minorities. We know, of course, that such invitations do not always work. Military might and repression do not always succeed in their ends either.

In this chapter, I have tried to chart reverberations between several associated forces and trends: the subtle organization of perception below conscious attention; new practices of state surveillance; the acceleration of pace in several zones of life; distinctive experiences of time that are more widespread and pervasive than heretofore; a veritable minoritization of the world occurring at a more rapid pace; late-modern pressures to resent this world as minoritization proceeds and the sense of implicit belonging is shaken; and the potential powers of the false to both unleash creative action in new situations and to enhance attachment to this world. The task has been to condense a series of elements so that we can better grasp how they interact. Each demands more reflection and experimentation on its own; several will receive that attention as this study proceeds.

CHAPTER THREE

Belief, Spirituality, and Time

The Fecundity of Hesitation

No one has asked me to direct a film. That is understandable since I lack the skill to do so. But, still, it is frustrating. There are activities that need to be seen or at least visualized to appreciate and internalize them. Recent work in neuroscience, for instance, suggests that visualization of an activity in the right mood is effective at installing it on the lower frequency registers of affective-cognitive life.[1] Mystics have known this for centuries, but the neuroscience evidence is nice to have too. Anyway, after watching _The Da Vinci Code_, a film I attended with high hopes, I again felt the urge to direct a film, for the theo-politics forming the ostensible object of this film faltered.

So let's imagine a sequel, one to visualize as we proceed. It stars Angelina Jolie and George Clooney. After a steamy scene, re-enacting the passion that threw Jesus and Mary Magdelene together the first time, the adventurers ponder again the diverse forms Christianity has assumed. They ask not only how variable it was during that long, rough period between the sayings of Jesus and the late 380s when the priority of the crucifixion, resurrection, and the trinity were set in stone by the church and Emperor Theodosius. They also ponder what it might become during a time when several world religions again intensify conflict within and across territorial regimes. They sense that a plurality of creeds will always bloom in a world of becoming, unless several are crushed. And they are impressed with how the acceleration of pace in several zones of life today exacerbates these tendencies.

They sense, with Charles Taylor, that the secular conception of homogeneous time in which that first adventure was set formed part of the problem. So they read and recite sections from Bergson and Proust to each other at night, allowing Bergson to teach them the importance of dwelling occasionally in pregnant moments in which layers of the past and future anticipation reverberate, and allowing Proust to provide hints about how to prime themselves to sink into such moments if and when they start of their own accord. (It is an art house film.) One night they ponder the life of Jesus before going to bed.

As the protagonist Sophie dreams that night about the world of her putative grandfather and grandmother to the nth degree, the screen flashes to Jesus, standing in the midst of an unruly crowd. This dissident rabbi sometimes calls himself "the Son of Man"—almost as if any man could have sired him. He communes with the restive crowd in words translated into English from the earliest written version of the gospel: "'Rabbi, this woman was caught in adultery, in the very act. Moses in the Law demanded us to stone such women to death, what do you say?' But Jesus stooped down and with his finger wrote on the ground. And as they continued to question him, he stood up and said to them, 'Let whoever of you is sinless be the first to throw a stone at her.' And again he stooped down and wrote on the ground."[2] The judgment is distinctive. Perhaps even more notable is how it arrives. As Jesus stoops and draws dreamily on the ground with his finger, he may allow the indignity of his earthly conception, the shame born by an unwed mother, the plight of his people under the yoke of empire, the danger of the vengeful crowd, the Mosaic code he and they have absorbed, the acute danger facing the accused woman before him, and his own unconventional relation to Mary Magdalene to mingle in a crystal of time. A new maxim crystallizes, as these layers of memory, pressure, and concern reverberate in a distinctive situation. Care for the world, informed by exquisite sensitivity to an unpredictable moment, merely set conditions of possibility for it.

The sequel to the movie presents further adventures by the sensitive couple, but we must remain content with this clip for now.

Such a creative moment in the life of Jesus does not mesh neatly with those modern doctrines of time, secularism, and exclusive humanism reviewed by Charles Taylor. It does not because it focuses on a fecund moment of dwelling in duration that punctuates the secular time of everyday perception, judgment, and action. During such a moment, multiple layers of the past resonate with things unfolding in the current situation, sometimes issuing in something new as if from nowhere. The new is ushered into being through a process that exceeds rational calculation or the derivation of practical implications from universal principles. It remains to be seen whether such a process can be as well understood through an immanent philosophy of becoming as through a theology of transcendence.

Becoming and Transcendence

The event could be endowed with transcendent meaning. Most devotees of Christianity read it that way. Fair enough. But I think it can *also* be folded into the tradition of immanent naturalism to which Taylor alludes, as long as that tradition is protected from the reading of Nietzsche Taylor brings to it. I have reviewed differences between his reading of Nietzsche and mine elsewhere, and will not rehearse them here.[3]

Instead, I draw upon a wider band of immanent naturalists who represent time as becoming in an open universe without divine transcendence. When Taylor contrasts a philosophy of pure immanence to one that goes through immanence to transcendence, he often distinguishes them by calling the first closed and the second open.[4] There are immanent naturalists who fit that description, contending that in principle everything is perfectly explicable through universal laws. I am interested in a version of immanent naturalism that projects an open temporal horizon exceeding human mastery and irreducible to both closed naturalism *and* radical transcendence. Indeed, a theology of transcendence *can* be open with respect to God and closed with respect to time as becoming or to the projection of differential degrees of agency in the other force-fields with which human culture periodically interacts. My notion of immanence, however, *is* open on those last two fronts, even as it does not project an image of divinity. It is not too helpful, then, to speak in this context simply of being "open" or "closed," without specifying the possibilities with respect to which the openings and closures occur.

In that sense Taylor may move too fast when he endorses Weber's view that with the rise of secularization the world became disenchanted, leaving behind the image of an expressive world replete with multiple signs from God. World of becoming consisting of multiple force-fields with different speeds and degrees of agency does not fit neatly into either the old enchanted world *or* the disenchanted world generated by the combined forces of nominalism, Calvinism, Newtonian science, and secularization. A world of becoming can be enchanted in some ways, even if it does not express divine meanings that are partly revealed and partly hidden, and even if it is not a providential world. For a world of becoming is marked by surprising turns in time, uncanny experiences, and the possibility of human participation to some degree in larger processes of creativity that both include and surpass the human estate. So Taylor's duality between enchantment and disenchantment needs to be complicated and pluralized.[5]

I also pay attention to minor figures in the recent history of monotheism who hear a whisper of transcendence in the uncanny experience of duration as they, too, advance an image of time as becoming. I engage them to help draw out the version of immanent realism, duration, dwelling, and becoming I confess, to test its power against Taylor's account of exclusive humanism, and to place it into contestation with the vision of transcendence he confesses, one that may be closed — I am not entirely sure — to time as becoming and the projection of differential degrees of agency beyond the human estate.

Consider two groups: the first, the immanent naturalists, includes (to varying degrees) thinkers such as Democritus, Epicurus, Lucretius, Spinoza, Thoreau, Deleuze, Prigogine, and Foucault; the second, philosophers of immanence in a world of becoming with a trace of transcendence, includes Bergson, James, Whitehead, and perhaps Proust. Both groups emphasize the value of dwelling periodically in fecund moments of duration to help usher a new idea, maxim, concept, faith, or intervention into being. All the modern thinkers on both lists are also philosophers of time as becoming, posing a world in which time is neither circular, nor linear, nor purposive. Time periodically folds the new into being in a universe that is intrinsically open to an uncertain degree and in which this or that force-field flowing "outside" the purview of another may abruptly introduce new pressures into it. Becoming, an open universe, multiple dimensions of the outside, all these work upon each other according to such a philosophy/creed.

In a world of becoming, emergent formations are often irreducible to patterns of efficient causality, purposive time, simple probability, or long cycles of recurrence. This occurs in part through periodic intersections between different force-fields, as neural, viral, bacterial, geological, climatic, species, electrical, chemical, and civilizational force-fields set on different tiers of chrono-time infuse (or infect, disrupt, charge, energize, invade, etc.) each other, in part through the periodic emergence of new and surprising capacities for *autopoiesis* when such collisions occur, and in part through the patterns of reverberation between these collisions and capacities for *autopoiesis* during fateful periods of accentuated disequilibrium in one or two force-fields. I mean here to distinguish chrono- or clock-time — the difference measured by a clock between, say, the length of a human life and that of a hurricane — from durational time — those periods of phase transition when reverberations between two force-fields set on different tiers of clock-time change something profoundly. A force-field can be explored through either temporal perspective. When you attend to its length as measured by a clock, you attend to chrono-time, again, as the difference in clock-time between the length of species evolution and that of a hurricane. When you examine it as a duration, you pay attention to the complex processes by which it persists, mutates, evolves, or connects to other force-fields. Some biologists think that the momentous phase transition from nonlife to life was rather short in clock-time but intense in durational time.[6] For our species, periodic dwelling in a fecund moment of duration can occasionally issue in a creative insight, as the story of Jesus reveals so forcefully.

On a related note, a philosophy of becoming calls attention to a host of messy states and processes "intermediate" between subjects and objects, or better put, not readily assimilable to either prefabricated container. There is dust, soot, flour, steam, mist, fog, a vague premonition, a pile of trash, clouds, drizzle, green mold, placenta, a lava flow, a wetland, a flood zone, volcanic ash, a daydream, déjà vu, seasonal transitions, rotting flesh, an oceanic flow, viscous fluids, porous membranes, shifting weather patterns, a melting ice cap, and so on, almost endlessly. These are zones of indiscernibility between those vaunted subjects and objects of which the world was recently said to be composed. They also call into question fantasies of human mastery over a world of solids. Many provide sources of fecundity from which new things and processes periodically emerge: some biologists link the origin of life to a warm, soupy mess, others to the simmering of a volcano. And the emergence of a fecund thought is closer to a viscous fluid flowing through a membrane than to the clean contours of a recollected image. All these messy fecundities are part of what William James calls "litter" in the world, those aspects of being and becoming that he says so many philosophical systems ignore, or try to absorb into a higher purpose, or treat as *merely* transitional states.[7] Litter forms an essential aspect of the world in a philosophy of becoming; attention to it helps to instill modesty into the human estate, reduces the species drive to give itself a unique place in a divine plan, and tames fantasies of full knowledge or mastery of the world.

A world of becoming is not a world of flux in which each force-field constantly morphs into something radically different from its previous state. None of the philosophers of becoming engaged here embrace such a view, though their critics occasionally receive them that way.[8] There are, however, cruel visionaries who do pursue such a world. Thus, in Angela Carter's novel *The Infernal Desire Machines of Doctor Hoffman*, an evil doctor concocts a town in which all processes morph at breakneck speed, even faster than viruses do in our world.[9] It thus becomes impossible to experience a desire long enough to enact it. Desiderio, the hero of the story, eventually finds a way to defeat the diabolical doctor; however, both he and the author also resist a metaphysics of stable essences as they sense the corollary dangers that accompany a world of long, slow time. Each is thus a thinker of becoming transcending the pure flux of Dr. Hoffman.

What, more precisely, is the difference between the world of Doctor Hoffman and a world of becoming? Well, there *are* periods of relative stability and equilibrium in most temporal zones or force-fields in a world of becoming: a virus survives; a human life endures; a solar system evolves slowly; a geological formation persists; a season lasts; a climate pattern stays; a civilization retains a high degree of stability; a species endures; a body-brain circuit is reiterated; a faith evolves slowly.[10] But, particularly when one mode of endurance is touched, infected, electrically charged, magnetically altered, directly battered, or intentionally moved by another moving at a different speed on another tier of chrono-time, a more dramatic change may be in the cards: when an asteroid shower destroys dinosaurs and sets the stage for the rapid evolution of human beings; when a region dried up by a shift in climate lapses into civil war over scarce resources; when floating resentments in one region of the world enter into a dramatic encounter with belligerent patterns of entitlement in another; when a period of capitalist growth accelerates a process of climate change that has a momentum of its own and that then recoils back upon the self-sustaining capacity of capitalism; when a virulent virus jumps from birds or pigs to human beings and then mutates again as it rides around the world through air travel; when a group of devout Christians encounters Buddhism and finds itself tipping toward conversion; when a tick senses movement and scents the flesh of a human walking under a tree and falls on it after eighteen years of immobility. Or take a radical increase in sunspot activity that intensifies electrical fields and overloads computers on the earth, that military leaders then creatively interpret as an attack by non-state terrorists, setting into motion a new spiral of state/non-state terrorism.[11] Yes, in this last example, and several others too, the formulations draw attention to differences of type between fields. But these instances work best as examples of events in a world of becoming when the field-intersections spur creative bouts of self-organization in one or more of the systems involved, as in the self-amplification of sunspot activity and the panic of a military elite feeding on itself.

As already indicated, some philosophers of duration and becoming affirm a world of radical immanence, a world in which the new periodically surges into being without the aid, obstruction, or protection of a divine force. Others focus on duration and becoming as they confess a *limited* God, a God whose intelligence and power is set within the eternity of time. Each tradition could honor Jesus by offering a distinctive interpretation of his calling and mode of inspiration. In doing so, each would emphasize the importance of sensibility, spirituality, and collective ethos to faith, art, culture, economic life, and politics.

Taylor would absorb the first set of thinkers characterized above — such as Lucretius, Thoreau, Deleuze, Prigogine, and Foucault — into a tradition of immanent materialism, in contrast to the Abrahamic tradition of transcendence that he admires most.[12] This contrast is acceptable to me, though I prefer the phrase "immanent naturalism" or "immanent realism" to play up the absence of divinity and play down obstinate assumptions about closure that still cling to the word "matter" in the train of a long history of debate between Christian transcendence and mechanical materialism. I use the qualifying word "naturalism" when emphasizing the absence of divinity in the notion of immanence developed here; I use the qualifier "realism" when emphasizing the judgment that the processes of resonance, mutation, self-amplification, and self-organization reside (to different degrees) in these force-fields themselves and not merely in our "subjective" perception of them. The latter description in my judgment has encouraged investigators for too long to project all creativity, self-organization, and even resonance onto themselves while draining it from other aspects of the world.

Does my acknowledgment of an element of subjective speculation inside immanent realism render the thesis incoherent? No. There is a difference between acknowledging a speculative element in the theory and deciding — unnecessarily — that this means the theory must concentrate all subjective and creative power in the human estate.

Consider two senses of the word "transcendence." By *radical* transcendence I mean a God who creates, informs, governs, or inspires activity in the mundane world while also exceeding the awareness of its participants. By *mundane* transcendence I mean any activity outside a nonhuman force-field or human awareness that may then cross into it, making a difference to what the latter becomes or interacting with it in fecund or destructive ways, often without being susceptible to full representation before the crossing or explanation by means of efficient causation after it. I do not confess radical transcendence, though I have not disproven it. I confess radical immanence replete with multiple, often fugitive encounters with mundane transcendence.[13] On my reading there is an outside of immanence, but it does not translate into a divinity. To use Taylor's terms, my version of immanent realism is open to the outside, even though it omits a place for a personal divinity.

There is also another point of contact and difference between radical transcendence and the notion of immanence supported here. There is a dimension, let's call it "the immanence of transcendence," by which productive conjunctions between disparate traditions engender a positive intensification of life, as when a group of secularists encounter Spinoza. Such amplifications can enlarge a sensibility of presumptive generosity to others, including those devoted to radical transcendence. Too many devotees of radical transcendence, perhaps impressed with the productive power of transcendence as they experience it, miss this spiritual intensification as we experience it. This is a shame, for it is precisely at this juncture that generous devotees of both traditions can foster positive political assemblages.

You can be a devotee of radical transcendence (the version I eschew) without adopting a providential image of history. You can even embrace the idea of time as becoming. Both William James and Henri Bergson adopt the latter combination. Each embraces a *limited* God who participates in a world of becoming without having created it from scratch or governing it the way an omnipotent deity would. To each of these thinkers the transcendent God is itself transcended by a world of becoming. Both thinkers seek, at key moments, to dwell in mystical experience in order to enhance his ability to be a vehicle through which something new and noble is brought into the world.

Can we who believe in immanence with *mundane* transcendence also dwell productively in the experience of duration? Yes. Upon priming yourself, you dwell in fecund moments to see whether something new and pertinent blooms forth through you, particularly when encountering suffering or troubles for which established codes of divinity, rights, morality, and identity have not prepared you adequately. You might start by meditating, or taking a walk in the woods, or reviewing a problem and clearing your mind of trivia before going to sleep, or engaging yourself in a fertile conversation, or attaching a recently invented computer to your head in order to intensify lucid dreaming once it starts on its own, or any number of other ways. If, as the layered past communicates with the new encounter, you help to usher something new into the world, it will be filtered through the experience of duration; it will be touched by the sensibility you bring to the experience of dwelling; and it will later be influenced by the reflexive intelligence you and others bring to bear as you refine it in relation to established codes, principles, understandings, and creeds.[14]

To an immanent realist, such experiments sometimes involve complex passages during which the previously unthought — not quite shaped like thought — bumps or surges into an ongoing pattern of thought under the pressure of shock, need, or abundance, altering or energizing thinking in this way or that. It may jolt an established train of thought, encouraging it to take a new turn. Something like this can happen, I think, if and when you place Hesiod's *Theogony* alongside the "apodictic judgments" from which Kant starts his transcendental arguments about morality, subjectivity, time, and the like. The shock of juxtaposition unravels the apodictic or necessary character of the Kantian starting points, without eliminating them as *possible* starting points for further reflection. As you pursue such an experiment you begin to feel that those starting points, rich with multiple possibilities, have historically been *dramatized* in a specific way, under pressure from centuries of Christendom embodied in cultural experience. You can now, if you wish, identify other possible starting points of argument to pursue alternative renderings at odds with the Kantian system. Shock therapy is indispensable to thoughtfulness, if the shocks are not so large that they overwhelm it.[15]

That which undergoes such a bumpy passage from the unthought to thought is not known or represented before it appears, because it did not possess the shape of the representable before the crossing began. It was at first, perhaps, merely *sensed* and later an *emergent* idea or theme, confounding those who demand that all such passages be smooth. Such a crossing may even be comparable to the passage of carbon from nonlife to life, with the latter being irreducible to that from which it emerged.

Such a set of views is what I mean by the philosophy/faith of radical immanence or immanent realism. It advances an image of mundane transcendence, encouraging movement back and forth between the incipient and new consolidations during a period of accentuated disequilibrium in this or that domain. In a world of becoming (as construed through this lens) each temporal force-field — the clock-time of a single circuit through the body-brain network, the life of a species, the evolution of a civilization, a child's growth into an adult — oscillates between some periods of relative equilibrium and others of accelerated disequilibrium, with the latter sometimes triggered by a period of intersection with force-fields set on other tiers of chrono-time.

Sometimes a seer dwells creatively during such a crossing, as when the Son of Man drew with his finger in the sand and issued his noble maxim, as when Epicurus conceived the very idea of atoms that swerve, as when Spinoza conceived of body and mind as two dimensions of the same substance, as when Zarathustra first dreamt eternal return as the return of difference and then *affirmed* a world so defined, as when Gilles Deleuze first drew something magical from the encounters between experimental film and the desolate landscapes of post-Second World War Europe and then helped to usher into being a concept of causation through resonance that scrambles the classical distinction between social science and interpretive cultural theory. None of these thinkers is transfixed by violence — as Taylor sometimes suggests of immanent naturalists following in Nietzsche's wake. Nor are they tempted profoundly by it, though there are surely devotees of mundane transcendence in a world of immanence who are. For, as we shall see, no single creed guarantees all by itself the quality of spirituality that enters into it. It is pertinent but not determinative in that regard.

All the thinkers alluded to here transcend the experience of homogeneous time occasionally, even as they recognize, with Henri Bergson, that the operational requirements of action-oriented perception solicit such a linear conception. That is, all distinguish between the experience of mundane time and that of durational time, while concurring that the former cannot simply be dropped in favor of the latter. And all evince a care for this world that resonates to some degree with the sensibility of Charles Taylor without embracing his fount of inspiration. Are he and they candidates to enter into noble relations of agonistic respect?

Sources of Becoming

Consider again a couple of nonhuman examples of mundane transcendence in a world of immanence. When the first bit of DNA broke loose from its host cell and "invaded" another cell, the host cell usually died. But as these barrages continued over time a few invaded cells were spurred into a new burst of *self-organization*. Out of the movement back and forth between the invasion and the creative response, the first nucleated cell emerged. It provided a base from which biological evolution proceeded, that phase transition called *symbiogenesis*. Prigogine, Brian Goodwin, and Lynn Margulis think that such creative movements occur periodically in several natural force-fields; they are irreducible either to efficient causation or to scientific atomism, taken generally to refer to the reduction of complex wholes to simple elements. Each also denies that an ideal observer of the first DNA invasion could have predicted the creative response. The invasion-response fomented real creativity in the world. We immanent naturalists find such events to be as wondrous as many others find the divine creation of the world from nothing. Similarly, when a human being dwells in an evolving situation to see whether a new concept or judgment bubbles forth from the layered reverberations between past and present, that can also be wondrous. For us, such events repeat at a much higher level of reflective power that fertile process of *symbiogenesis* by which the first nucleated cell emerged. The latter possibility evolved from the former passage.

The two processes are not identical. The first involves a mode of *autopoiesis* that does not include a crossing from the unthought to thought. While during the second — the case of human dwelling — something passes from the immanent field of the unthought — that which is not entirely shaped like thought — into an established intersubjective matrix of thought. Reworking modestly an invaluable insight Taylor advanced several years ago, such a crossing *expresses* but does not *represent* that which precedes and enables it. His sources are ambiguous and wondrous because they move you as they are carried into the world even as they are not fully articulable in themselves.[16] Ours are ambiguous, and occasionally wondrous, as they cross from one phase state to another. They infuse our capacities of articulation without being representable in themselves. For, again, the antecedent was not shaped like thought; or in other cases, it was an incipient thought replete with pluripotentiality. It has one shape before the crossing and another after, *something* like the early crossing from the nonnucleated to the nucleated cell. In a world of mundane transcendence there are many wonders.

The articulation of a new idea, judgment, maxim, or concept both changes awareness of the source from which it draws and alters the cultural net it enters, in a large or small way. This is another version of the double process beautifully described by Taylor in *Sources of the Self*.

Deep, multidimensional pluralism cannot gain a secure foothold in predominantly Christian states until faith-imbued interpretations of Jesus by Jews, Muslims, Buddhists, Hindus, and immanent naturalists are allowed to compete legitimately with Christian confessions of him as a divine savior. From the point of view of the last theo-philosophy, mechanical naturalism degrades human beings and values analysis too much over dwelling. And many — though not all — theo-philosophies of radical transcendence render humanity so unique that its connections and selective affinities with various nonhuman processes are obscured. Doing so, they risk disparaging our essential connections to a larger world. The funny thing is that exclusive humanism displays a similar tendency. It, too, pulls humanity too far above the rest of nature, with results for those to see who have eyes to see.

Belief and Cultivation

It is one thing to *believe* in the world as becoming; something additional is needed to *affirm* such a world. To come to affirm such a world it is needful to work on ourselves by multiple means to overcome resentment of the world for not possessing either divine providence or ready susceptibility to human mastery. Taylor is dubious about our creed, though he acknowledges that he cannot give knockdown arguments against it. So in a second movement he recoils back upon his initial judgment, calling upon himself and others to enter into what I would call a relation of agonistic respect with the bearers of such a creed. That is the nobility of Charles Taylor.

The minor tradition I embrace is replete with difficulties, puzzles, and problems, amidst its glowing promise. It pursues a conception of ethics, anchored first and foremost in presumptive care for the diversity of life and the fecundity of the earth. This is an ethic of cultivation that infuses mundane human interests, identities, responsibilities, tasks, and understandings rather than obeying an unconditioned law or divine inspiration above them. Our goal is to intensify or amplify a care for this world that already courses through us to some degree. We deploy arts of the self to help this process along. So when people ask an immanent naturalist how his ethic is "derived" or "grounded," the answer is that it is not derived from a higher command or transcendental subject nor is it grounded in a fictive contract. It, rather, emerges out of a seed of care for this world that is already there when you are lucky, and it then grows by cultivating that seed. One advantage of an ethic of cultivation in a world of becoming is that it can bring this care to bear on new and unexpected situations, combining refined sensitivity with critical reflection on a new situation to revise or adjust old norms whose mode of operation is now up for reconsideration.

We also acknowledge tragic possibility in a world without either divine providence or strong susceptibility to human mastery. We strive to affirm existence itself in a world replete with such possibility and to struggle against the emergence of tragic binds. Moreover, we replace the quest to *discover* transcendent meaning with a readiness *to invest* selective activities with meaning. To the extent we succeed in affirming the world as we confess it to be, those investments will express a modicum of care for diversity, the future, and the earth. They will also make us alert to the late-modern politics of diversification, by which new rights, identities, and goods periodically push themselves into being, disrupting fixed conceptions of divinity, justice, faith, rights, identity, and the good.

As we proceed, we relocate the element of mystery projected by many into radical transcendence into natural and cultural processes themselves, and that element now finds expression in our conceptions of time, causality, duration, and freedom.

A refined ethical sensibility, to us, brings care for the world and a presumptive respect for established principles to moments when we are divided against ourselves. A primary principle of ethics for us is the prescription to cultivate sensitivity to new circumstances and social movements that suggest the possible need to change entrenched habits. To accept that principle is to acknowledge the need to work periodically on your preliminary habits of thought and action by tactical means. But how is that principle "derived?" It is, again, not derived, because we doubt that morality and ethics are grounded in a transcendent command in the first instance or in any of the surrogates introduced later (the contract, the transcendental subject, the counterfactual consensus, etc.) to replace it. It is a thing of this world, drawn from preliminary experiences of presumptive care for diversity and the future of the earth that circulate through relations with others when you are lucky. A generative ethic produces a series of timely principles, responsibilities, and obligations out of conjunctions between it and the current condition.

We also dissent from those Taylor calls exclusive humanists. But not entirely for his reasons. Exclusive humanists may be closed to faith in radical transcendence as he says, but they also tend toward closure on two other fronts: to the idea that there are degrees of agency in other force-fields in the world and to time as becoming. A devotee of radical immanence does not confess faith in the God of Abraham but is open on these other two fronts. Is Taylor's transcendence, perhaps, open to the God of Abraham but closed with respect to time as becoming and to multiple force-fields with different degrees of agency?

From our point of view the division between theological philosophies that appreciate an element of mystery in the world and naturalist philosophies that dissolve it "in principle" provides an insufficient set of credible perspectives. For immanent naturalism is irreducible to either eliminative or mechanical materialism. To the immanent naturalist there is no guarantee that the capacities of human knowledge in an undesigned world will ever mesh entirely with the crooked way of the world itself. So we join theologians in supporting a place for mystery against the hubris of some kinds of materialism, and we join some materialists in suggesting that a theological recognition of mystery invests no set of priests with legitimate authority over everyone. Above all, we seek to cultivate existential affirmation of the world as we confess it to be, so that the insidious spirit of *ressentiment* does not seep into the inner core of our being, dividing us too profoundly against ourselves, and encouraging us to search too actively for collective enemies. In that, we make contact with monotheists such as Charles Taylor, Karl Jaspers, Fred Dallmayr, Catherine Keller, and Martin Buber, who advance similar pursuits.

But what about our conception of freedom? The question of human freedom is often presented in the monotheistic traditions under the category of the will. In its classic formulations the will is filled with divine mystery. Thus, Augustine asserts through a famous experiment with two men who are identical in every respect except that one acts against chastity while the other succumbs to desire, that only a will free from external, efficient causality could explain the difference. "What other reason could there be than his personal decision, given their dispositions were precisely the same, in body and mind?"[17] He then contends that the human will, initially free in Adam to will the good, became inherently divided against itself after Adam's freely chosen fall. Human freedom, at least in some senses of the term, is thereafter limited severely. We can will evil by ourselves, but we can will the good only with the aid of God's grace if and as that grace becomes infused into the will. Often we find ourselves willing something decent with one part of the will only to find another part of it vetoing or overriding that first injunction. This Augustinian sense of the will divided against itself speaks to a dimension of human experience. So, any attempt to explore freedom while decriminalizing the will—that is, by relieving it of primordial sin and guilt—must respond somehow to the common experience of division.

If you embrace immanent naturalism you do not assert any of the alternatives Augustine, or Kant after him, denies: mechanical determination, an undivided will, or the full control of intentions by fate. You introduce another possibility into the picture to compete with the Augustinian/Kantian tradition, a counter tradition that contains rich possibilities and comparative uncertainties of its own. You rewrite the image of the will. You treat the will as a power that has evolved from other conditions, that continues to contain traces from that lineage within it, that is sometimes divided against itself in a quasi-Augustinian way, and that is both enabled and limited by other force-fields with their own degrees of agency.

The will, on this reading, is neither an eternal expression of suprasensible freedom, nor reducible to the determinations of efficient causality, nor carrier of an original taint of sin. Rather, it is decriminalized in the first instance, as part of a larger effort to overcome the culture of existential resentment that so easily grows up within and around such renderings of this basic human power.

The will is now conceived as an *emergent*, bicultural formation; it bears traces of that from which it emerged but is irreducible to its precursors. Just as life is not devalued because it has evolved from nonlife and is now irreducible to it, and as the human species need not be devalued because it has evolved from other species, the will is not devalued because it is a partial, sensual formation installed in beings who were not predesigned to be agents of free will. As a formation it is simultaneously experienced in daily life, imperfect in shape, needed culturally, and at risk, as it were, for criminalization by those who demand universal faith in an omnipotent God who holds the first human responsible for the rift in being.

The will, so conceived, consists of two dimensions: a) incipient, ideationally imbued tendencies to action that well up as you respond to events, and b) a limited capacity to veto or redirect some of those tendencies as they approach the tipping point of action. The neuroscientist Benjamin Libet, who has measured the half-second delay between the incipience of body/brain activity and its consolidation in action, suggests that the will is reducible to that nano-moment when you can veto a tendency to action already on the way.[18] To me, however, the will consists of both dimensions together, sometimes in conflict with each other: culturally imbued tendencies to action and a limited power to veto or redirect a tendency as it unfolds. The will *is* thus two sided, as the brain is, but not criminalized at its core because of that.

Each dimension of the will is open to some degree of self-correction or modification over time. You can adjust incipient tendencies, when reflection or the shock of new experience renders this advisable, by tactics of the self that work upon culturally imbued, embodied predispositions to action below the reach of direct intellectual command. That is, you consciously apply tactics to yourself to help recode some preliminary dispositions to action below direct intellectual regulation. These tactics of the self play a critical role in an ethic of cultivation. You can also work on the capacity to exercise veto power by periodically re-engaging the relation between the specific situation in which you find yourself and presumptions of practical judgment already installed in your memory bank.

So the will is both an expression of freedom and periodically fraught with internal division without either being linked to primordial guilt or lifted above organic life. It is a complex thing of this world, revealing how we participate in our way in a larger world in which real creativity is distributed across and between multiple, open systems. The will is not unique — though it is distinctive. Such a conception is not free of mystery or uncertainty, but, as we have already seen, that does not render the conception dismissible.

As these examples show, our agenda is not free of paradox and uncertainty. We replicate in our way the elements of paradox, mystery, and division encountered in other traditions. We do not promise that we will eventually be able to dissolve all of those uncertainties and mysteries; we merely assert that our renderings are capable of competing with others, and that they do not sacrifice the complexity of experience in order to offer a sleek account of it. This is yet another point we share with many advocates of radical transcendence: we resist reductionism and the eager elimination of ambiguity from our engagement with the human estate.

Creeds and Existential Spiritualities

From the vantage point of a philosophy of immanence set in a sensibility of care for this world, the most pressing need today is to negotiate deep, multidimensional pluralism within and across territorial regimes. That may be close to Taylor's pursuit too, though inspired by a different fundamental source. By deep pluralism, I mean the readiness to defend your creed in public while acknowledging that it so far lacks the power to confirm itself so authoritatively that all reasonable people should embrace it. By multidimensional pluralism, I mean a political culture in which differences of creed, ethnicity, age, first language, gender practice, and sensual affiliation find expression in a productive ethos of political engagement between participants. Deep and multidimensional pluralism set conditions of possibility for each other today. The first because it expresses presumptive care for the fundamental sources pursued by others; and the second because it helps to ventilate the internal practices of church and secular associations.

What is most noble about Jesus, to us, are his method of teaching and his capacity to dwell with care and creativity in protean moments from time to time. He cultivates exquisite sensitivity to movements of world. My sense, again, is that deep, multidimensional pluralism in the western world in which Christendom has prevailed will arrive when a wide array of voices can articulate publicly their readings of the word of Jesus without drawing rebuke for treading on ground outside their purview. As others periodically provide public interpretations of the Christ story, we bring ours to them for critical response. As they present Epicurus, Lucretius, Spinoza, Nietzsche, and Deleuze to us, we reply. When Christians, Jews, humanists, Muslims, Hindus, Buddhists, and nontheists can participate publicly and legitimately in such exchanges, deep pluralism will be on the way. It is not that such exchanges must be constant, but that they must find expression when they are pertinent to a major issue of the day. Some, of course, see such an ideal of pluralism as a mere projection from the academy to the larger cultural world. Fair enough. I see it as the most promising response to the late-modern condition in which a veritable minoritization of the world is taking place at a rapid pace, before our very eyes. The academy, in fact, is an excellent perch from which to discern this larger phenomenon.

The issue is critical because with the increasingly rapid cross-territorial flows of capital, media communication, and population movements, the world is not simply becoming more "homogenized," as some commentators love to say. It is quickly becoming a world of multiple minorities, organized along several dimensions, who will either negotiate creative ways to co-exist and interact with respect on the same territories (and across territories too), or increasingly confront each other in bellicose struggles for hegemony. We inhabit a world in which most territorial regimes find themselves under intense pressure either to negotiate a multidimensional diversity of faiths, gender practices, sensual affiliations, family structures, primary languages, and ethnicities in more noble ways or to erect new barriers against these very negotiations. The construction of new territorial walls is merely one visible sign of the latter process. In many states, the putative majority, said to make up the center of "the nation," is more often a symbol of what many wish were the case rather than a description of the actual world. In the United States and Europe, for instance, the productive ethos of engagement previously negotiated between Catholics, Jews, and Protestants, when each was at its best, now needs to be widened to encompass other faiths and extended to other dimensions of diversity pressing for acceptance. If I understand Taylor correctly he concurs in advance with several things I have just said, though the touchstones of faith from which he starts are different.

Here I need to test another point of tension or concurrence between us — and another site of struggle within myself. Taylor is admirable in pointing to the predicaments inside a variety of modern traditions. But what forces help to determine whether those predicaments are explored by devotees as they seek relations of agonistic respect with other traditions or, at the other extreme, are repressed as some factions demonize other traditions? We concur that the latter politics is destructive and dangerous, and often rears its ugly head. We also concur, I think, that the outcome of such a struggle could be fateful for the late-modern era. But what are its cultural sources? And how should they be engaged?

Class, age, race, ethnic, gender, and creedal "subject positions" are pertinent, certainly. But they do not *suffice* to explain political stances, and not only because of the cross-cutting affiliations that sociologists study. Another source is the different *existential sensibilities* between people who share a racial identification, class position, linguistic tradition, or formal creed. The existential dimension is so critical that its cultural variations deserve to be schematized. In forming such a matrix, I do not suggest that belief and spirituality are fully separate, but rather, that affect and belief are always inter-involved with neither entirely reducible to the other. As when a belief is shared with others but held with a different degree of intensity. Or when two parties differ in creed but evince an affinity of spirituality across that difference. Or when you feel a surprising thud in the gut as a proto-belief previously hidden in this nook or cranny is suddenly challenged. Beliefs themselves are layered, with refined beliefs rather susceptible to articulation and more visceral ones often too crude or ambiguous to be articulated until a tipping point carries you in one direction or another. Things are more complicated than a matrix can express, but my point now is to suggest through fabulation how important the intersections between creed and sensibility are.

In the matrix I have in mind there is no place called "unbelief." Every existential stance is infused with belief, though often operating at several levels and punctuated by doubt. Moreover, different existential dispositions can be attached to the same formal creed. So this matrix places an array of creedal *beliefs* across its horizontal axis and an array of existential *sensibilities* across its vertical axis. It is where they touch that is important. The distribution of belief flows from faith in a personal, singular God on the right side to belief in the eternity of becoming on the left, with several stances in between such as belief in a limited god, or a spiritual power without personal traits, or a mechanical world without divine transcendence. On the vertical axis are differences in existential sensibility, with care for this world forming the end point at the top and existential resentment at the bottom.

On the upper right side of this matrix are saints who embrace God and love of this world; on the upper left side are seers who embrace the immanence of becoming and love of this world; on the lower right we find those who mix existential resentment into belief in an omnipotent God; on the lower left those who deeply resent the world precisely as a world of becoming. There are, of course, numerous points on the vertical axis, too, with most of us being inhabited by a degree of ambivalence or inclining in one direction at some points in life and another at others. It is easy to locate my earthy rendering of Jesus on the upper left and the transcendent reading of him adopted by many on the upper right. But what about the Christ portrayed in the book of Revelation? Until someone teaches me things I have yet to discern I locate this vengeful figure at the lower right end of the matrix.

It is also relatively easy to locate Lucretius, Augustine, Spinoza, Arendt, Kant, and Taylor on this schema. After an exhaustive, symptomatic reading of his writings, for instance, I would locate Taylor in the upper right box, inclined toward the high end on the vertical scale of love of this world and about a quarter of the way down the right to left axis between transcendence and immanence.

The point of such a schema is to suggest how important it is for both individuals *and* constituencies to cultivate strategies to overcome resentment of the most fundamental way of the world, as they consciously or unconsciously believe it to be. For the self is a complex social structure, with numerous nooks, crannies, and subterranean relays. And so are constituencies. Some theists may secretly resent the world because they suspect on one level that it deviates from the belief they explicitly support, or because their God demands too much of them. Some nontheists may do so because one part of them believes the God they deny will condemn them, or because they wish they could believe in a salvational God. Numerous other possibilities subsist as well.

But today it is a fundamental responsibility of individuals and constituencies to seek to affirm the most fundamental way of the world as they themselves confess it to be, as they come to terms without resentment with the deep contestability of their own vision. The contemporary struggle between deep, multidimensional pluralism and a cultural division into warring camps depends on it.

How to do this? That is the difficult question. You might struggle with yourself to shift your doctrine to find a better comfort zone through which to respond with presumptive care to new minorities whose presence disturbs you. Or you might work artfully on your visceral dispositions to deepen care for the future of the earth and the diversity of being. Difficulties will be encountered.

There are powerful theological and psychological pressures to deny the feeling of resentment against the most fundamental terms of existence as you officially embrace them. Under such a regime, existential resentment is apt to find expression in the bellicosity and exclusionary character of your political stances. That is why Nietzsche, for instance, found it important to read behavioral *symptoms* as well as doctrinal *confessions*, with Jesus faring well on the first scale and Paul much less so. It is why Augustine was pressed to do so, too, in his readings of Manicheans, Pelagians, and Infidels. Even Kant found himself compelled to distinguish the "ravings" of "enthusiasts" from more generous modes of spirituality. Any of these thinkers may have been faulty in the symptomatic readings he offered. But my point is that, however we might wish to avoid such readings, they insinuate themselves into our dispositions and actions, and the current historical juncture makes it politically and ethically incumbent to explore them. It has always been so, to different degrees at different times. Commentators who purport to avoid such judgments eventually express them in the terms of art they adopt;[19] they may, for instance, represent another perspective in dismissive terms prior to giving a critique of the position so represented.

Today, in the United States and to varying degrees elsewhere too, one crooked line of political division is between those who fold a large quotient of care for the future of this world into their desires, identities, creeds, consumption practices, political loyalties, and economic doctrines and those who infuse a drive for revenge against difference and the weight the future imposes upon the present. One set of capitalist elites and resentful secular males enters into alliance with a subset of evangelical Christians: the connection between them is intense. Each constituency deflates its differences of belief from the others to accentuate the *affinities of spirituality* between them. Egged on by the media, they form a veritable resonance machine, in which the creedally inflected spirituality of each constituency complements and amplifies that of the others. What they share is a disposition toward existence that diminishes care for the diversity of being and our future on the earth. The right edge of the capitalist class vindicates itself by pretending that the free market takes care of itself, even as it heightens the income curve, creates self-defeating modes of consumption, intensifies global warming, and generates financial crises that threaten all of us. The extreme edge of the evangelical right looks to a second coming in which the future of the earth as we now know it becomes unimportant (check out the *Left Behind* series, which has sold 60 million copies, as well as a huge number of DVDs in its wake). Both sides deflate the importance of global warming, resist pluralization, and support bellicose military policies. To some, the Iraq war promised to hasten the desired event; to others, concern for the future would disrupt overweening demands for special entitlement now; yet others are drawn toward this constellation of hubris and *ressentiment* through a series of demeaning economic and social experiences.

Each spiritual constituency amplifies dispositions in the other, until an econo-political resonance machine emerges that is larger and more intense than the sum of its parts. Some who are now ensconced within the evangelical-capitalist machine might be encouraged to flee from it, if more of us paid close, public attention to the role that the contagion of spirituality plays in keeping it alive.[20]

It may be said that these dicey issues can be bypassed by addressing differences in belief and policy alone. The assumption that this is so reflects those brands of intellectualism supported by some branches of secularism and exclusive humanism. I used to adopt such a position myself.[21] Today, I doubt, along with Bergson, James, Nietzsche, and Merleau-Ponty, that it suffices. It is pertinent but incomplete.

Supporters of an ethos of existential resentment are distributed across class positions and creedal stances. Have you listened to publicists on Fox News or the American Enterprise Institute? Or to Paul Wolfowitz, who has moved from being an architect of the Iraq War, to the head of the World Bank, to a position at the Nitze School at Johns Hopkins University? Many privileged elites participate in the evangelical-capitalist resonance machine, working to amplify it. Their sense of entitlement outstrips the real privileges they already have. That is why attention to economic self-interest, elite manipulation, and so on are insufficient to the issue. The point is not that the distribution of existential resentment and attachment lacks familial, social, economic, and political sources and sites of expression. It is, rather, that spiritual dispositions, once set in motion, are endowed with a degree of autonomous energy that can find expression in a variety of practices: from investment, savings, and consumption practices, to the willingness or unwillingness to allow governmental regulation of market practices.

Indeed, the accentuation of the demand to "choose" between multiple options of creedal belief that Taylor tracks in his account of modern secularity makes a contribution to the risks charted here. A large minority, distributed across a variety of subject positions, may profoundly resent the existential weight imposed upon them by the fact that they increasingly rub up against ethnic and faith constituencies of diverse types more often in daily life, electoral politics, and media practices. But if the minoritization of cultural life is proceeding at a more rapid pace today this issue will not go away. It must either be negotiated in more subtle ways or perpetuate culture wars.

Since existential resentment is not a widely confessed disposition, it is most apt to find indirect expression in actions taken, practices followed, and the tenor of alliances formed. Producing, owning, driving, and militantly opposing state regulation of SUVs provided one manifestation of such a bellicose tendency, at least until the recent fuel crisis. People from a variety of social positions converged to protect and enlarge this market, even though everybody could have known for years, if they wanted to, the dangers, fuel costs, resource effects, and results for global warming of these vehicles. But auto producers, cowboy capitalists, liberal and conservative legislators from auto states, a section of the white middle class, and an angry branch of the evangelical movement militantly blocked regulation of these vehicles. Inter-constituency support for SUVs displays a spiritual willingness to sacrifice the collective future to the present: that is the charge. Similar things might be said about militant support for capital punishment, eager embrace of reckless wars, happy support of ruthless politicians, easy tolerance of state torture, casual acceptance of sharp inequality, demonization of non-Christians, and dismissal of critics of unfettered capitalism. I am not saying that the seed is identical in each case; far from it. In some instances it finds initial expression as a belligerent claim to special entitlement, in others a will to existential revenge aimed at particular constituencies, in yet others a spirit of hubris. It is when two or more of these dispositions resonate together that a larger and more dangerous constellation is formed, with each constituency folding the dominant sensibility of its ally into a minor element in its own.

The substance of the positions on these issues is not always the most critical issue, since there are real debates on some of them. It is, rather, the degree of bellicosity with which they are supported, the dogmatism with which the rationale on their behalf is embraced, the burning desire to stoke scandals about those who oppose you, and the easy willingness to make the most optimistic assumption about the future cost of the thing you want now.

An existential disposition has three inter-involved dimensions: a set of beliefs, a spiritual orientation toward this world invested in these beliefs, and a specific degree of intensity. These dimensions hang together loosely, but each retains some degree of separation from the others. And affinities of spirituality can bind constituencies together who diverge in this or that way in their economic and religious creeds. This is both the hope and the danger of contemporary life.

Negotiating the Risks

I agree that it is risky to think and say these things. You run the risk of replicating the very stances you resist. Particularly, if you think, as I do, that those who seek to supplant the evangelical-capitalist resonance machine must ratchet up their own levels of intensity today. Nonetheless, it seems to me that those who prize democracy, deep pluralism, egalitarianism, and the future of the earth must now run such risks in intelligent ways. There is no risk-free way to proceed in the current historical conjuncture. You might even say that the secular tendency to perceive a disjunction between private religious belief and public deliberation has kept too many out of touch with this dimension of politics for too long. It has discouraged many outside official religious constellations from addressing the spiritual dimension of political and economic life.

One way to dramatize the contemporary condition is to say that the difference between the Nixon era and the aftermath of the Bush era is Fox News and the battalion of right-wing think tanks it draws upon to stoke the juices of hubris and *ressentiment*. The two eras display similar tendencies, but the amplification machine forged by the Fox News/think tank/evangelical-capital right is more entrenched and dangerous than that forged by Nixon and his henchmen. Its advocates are constantly searching for new ways to rise from the ashes.

We must interpret publicly the existential symptoms of the most bellicose movements, as we recoil upon ourselves to resist becoming a version of the thing we oppose. One way to reduce that risk is to bear in mind that *no single social category or creedal confession corresponds neatly to the existential disposition you seek to expose, resist, or overcome*. A second is to probe points, places, and constituencies on the margins of the assemblage you oppose to draw factions away from the machine. It is clear that many young evangelicals, for instance, are increasingly dubious about some of the cultural priorities their most visible leaders have accepted for the last thirty years. And the financial crisis of 15 September 2008 may have fomented a similar crisis of confidence and spiritual awakening among a minority of labor leaders and consumers. The real question is why a similar crisis of confidence is not apparent among financial advisers and mainstream economists. The point to emphasize under these circumstances is how an incipient change in the beliefs or spirituality infusing an existing creed comes into its own if it is marked by corollary changes in role performance in church participation, consumption priorities, voting conduct, investment practices, and the like. For belief, spirituality, desire, and role performance are involved with each other, with a change in one helping to consolidate or weaken a change in another. A third way to resist becoming what we oppose is to engage ourselves periodically on this very front, particularly when reading others symptomatically, to examine emerging intersections between our own beliefs, spiritualities, desires, and role performances.

If you are in the middle class, buy a Prius or a Volt and explain to your friends and neighbors why you did; write in a blog; attend a pivotal rally; ride your bike to work more often; consider solar panels; introduce new topics at your church. As you do those things, you may note how an array of hesitant beliefs and desires now becomes more solid and how other tendencies begin to melt away. You may now be prepared to participate in larger political assemblages in more robust ways, joining others whose beliefs, role performances, and desires have also been moving. You can call such a combination micropolitics if you want, a dimension of life that must be joined at many junctures to macropolitics if either is to work in a positive way.

Today it is urgent to forge a counter-resonance machine composed of several constituencies who diverge along lines of creedal faith, class position, racial or ethnic identification, sexual affiliation, and gender practice. It is to enlarge the cohort who give priority to the earth, however they themselves otherwise interpret the most fundamental terms of existence. It is to work on ourselves and others to ensure that we do not resent the most fundamental terms of existence, as we ourselves grasp those terms. This involves affirming a world in which the faith you embrace regularly brushes up against living alternatives that challenge, disturb, and disrupt its claim to universality.

If I read Taylor correctly he concurs, not with the existential creed advanced here, but with the ethico-political need to amplify modes of presumptive generosity with respect to several creeds. He may well also concur with the need to forge a new assemblage — cutting across differences of class, gender, sensuality, race, age, and creed — to foster deep pluralism, egalitarianism, and care for future generations. Where we differ, perhaps, is in the hesitancy Taylor displays to read social movements symptomatically — though he certainly does so with some perspectives, including the Nietzschean — and the urgency I now display in including this task as a dimension of politics. I am unsure how deep this latter difference goes or who is right about it. I sometimes feel divided against myself at this point, while now giving priority to one side of that division.

Interlude

――――――――――

"One cannot step twice into the same river, nor can one grasp any mortal substance in a stable condition, but it scatters and again gathers; it forms and dissolves, and approaches and departs."[1]

"A researcher in natural science at the Petersburg Academy . . . offers a remarkable thought experiment. The rates of sensation and thus of voluntary movements . . . among various animals appear to be approximately proportional to their pulse rates [and longevity] . . . Well then! . . . Assuming that the course of human life were reduced by a factor of one one thousandth and that pulse rate were accelerated one thousand times faster, then we would be able to follow a flying bullet very easily with our vision. If this lifetime were reduced once more . . ., limited to some forty minutes, then we would consider the grass and flowers to be something just as persistent as we now consider the mountains . . . We would be totally unable to observe the voluntary movements of animals, for they would be far too slow . . ."[2]

"Nature loves to hide."[3]

"When, on the other hand, we enormously lengthen and expand a human lifetime, we get quite another picture! Reduce, for example, [the human] pulse rate and sensation threshold by one one thousandth, and then our life would last 'at the upper end,' eighty thousand years: then we would experience as much in one year as we do now in eight to nine hours; then every four hours we would watch winter melt away, the earth thaw out, grass and flowers spring up. Trees come into full bloom and bear fruit . . . Many developments would not be observed by us at all because of their speed; for example, a mushroom would suddenly sprout up like a fountain. Day and night would alternate like light and shadows in but a moment, and the sun would race along the arch of the heavens in the greatest hurry. Were we to accelerate [further] . . . the difference between night and day would entirely vanish . . . and vegetation would continually shoot up and vanish in great haste. Enough then! Every shape appearing to us as persistent would . . . be devoured by the wild storm of becoming."[4]

"The creativity is not an external agency with its own ulterior purposes. All actual entities share with God this characteristic of self-causation. For this reason every actual entity also shares with God the characteristic of transcending other actual entities, including God. The universe is thus a creative advance into novelty. The alternative to this doctrine is a static morphological universe."[5]

"The layered, bumpy, and creative dimensions of thought on the way are closer in shape to several temporal force-fields in nature than classical conceptions of nature are to thinking."[6]

"I had seen Albertine reproduce with perfect accuracy some remark which I had made to her at one of our first meetings and which I had entirely forgotten. Of some other incident, lodged for ever in my head like a pebble flung with force, she had no recollection. Our life together was like one of those garden walks where, at intervals on either side of the path, vases of flowers are placed symmetrically but not opposite one another . . . For between us and other people there exists a barrier of contingencies, just as in my hours of reading in the garden at Combray I had realized that in all perception there exists a barrier as a result of which there is never absolute contact between reality and our intelligence."[7]

"We shall find that there are in nature competing serial time-systems derived from different families of durations."[8]

"It is doubtless this that accounts for that extraordinary energy of unmatched parts in the Search, whose rhythms of deployment or rates of explication are irreducible; not only do they not compose a whole from which each part is torn, different from every other, in a kind of dialogue between universes. But the force with which the parts are projected into the world, violently stuck together despite their unmatching edges, causes them to be recognized as parts, though without comprising a whole, even a hidden one . . . By setting fragments into fragments, Proust finds the means of making us contemplate them all, but without reference to a unity from which they might derive or which might derive from them."[9]

"The cornerstone of my theory is that the conscious mind is a persistently poised quantum-decoherent system, forever propagating quantum coherent behavior, yet forever also decohering to classical behavior . . . Here mind — consciousness — is identical with quantum coherent immaterial possibilities . . . yet via decoherence, the quantum coherent mind has consequences that create actual physical events by the emergence of classicity. Thus, res cogitans has consequences for res extensa! Immaterial mind has consequences for matter!"[10]

"Each task of creation is a social effort, employing the whole universe. Each novel actuality is a new partner adding a new condition. Every new condition can be absorbed into additional fullness of attainment. On the other hand, each condition is exclusive, intolerant of diversities; except insofar as it finds itself in a web of conditions which converts its exclusions into contrasts."[11]

"The sea is the fairest and foulest water; for fish drinkable and life sustaining; for men undrinkable and deadly."[12]

"Physicists believe in a 'true world' in their own fashion: a firm systematization of atoms in necessary motion, the same for all beings . . . But they are in error . . . This world picture that they sketch differs in no essential way from the subjective world picture: it is only construed with more extended senses [with microscopes, etc.] but with our senses nonetheless. And in any case they left something out of the constellation without knowing it: precisely this necessary perspectivism by virtue of which every center of force — and not only man — construes all the rest of the world from its own viewpoint, i.e., measures, feels, forms, according to its own force . . . My idea is that every specific body strives to become master over all space and to extend its force (-its will to power:) and to thrust back all that resists its extension. But it continually encounters similar efforts on the part of other bodies and ends by coming to an arrangement ('union') with those of them that are sufficiently related to it: thus they then conspire together for power. And the process goes on."[13]

"There is no manifestation of life which does not contain in a rudimentary state — latent or potential — the essential characters of most other manifestations. The difference is in the proportions . . . There is not a single property of vegetable life that is not found, in some degree, in certain animals; not a single characteristic feature of the animal that has not been seen in certain species at certain moments."[14]

"They do not comprehend how a thing agrees at variance with itself; it is an attunement turning back on itself, like that of the bow and the lyre."[15]

"The intuition derived from the maximization of mutual information, or coordinated altering behaviors among pairs of variables, in critical networks is that the most complex coordinate behavior can occur in critical networks . . . In more ordered networks the behavior would be more 'frozen' and less complex. In the chaotic networks, slight noise would dramatically alter network behavior . . . Certainly, what happens here is more interesting than the dull behavior found deep in the ordered regime, where most genes are frozen in fixed states."[16]

"The fairest order in the world is a heap of random sweepings."[17]

"I think that we have to understand the historical universe. In traditional science the universe was considered to be a geometrical entity. Now we add a narrative element . . . I want to emphasize that the universe acts as a whole and is evolving . . . In my view gravitation maintains the universe out of equilibrium, but we don't know how. Our universe is far from equilibrium, nonlinear and full of irreversible processes . . . We see stars being born, other stars die, and all kinds of non-equilibrium structures but we do not understand how the universe remains far from equilibrium."[18]

"This world may, in the last resort, be a block universe; but on the other hand it may be a universe only strung-along, not rounded in or closed. Reality may exist distributively just as it sensibly seems to, after all. On this possibility I do insist."[19]

"Let us not concur casually about the most important matters."[20]

CHAPTER FOUR

The Human Predicament

Why predicament? Because we suffer, we die, and we inhabit time even as, when we are lucky, we find folded into the depth grammar of life a durable sense of its incredible sweetness. To be human is thus to have an image of the human predicament, or sometimes two or three competing within and around you. This is at first a set of cultural orientations finding expression (today) in church sermons, novels, prayer, TV dramas, films, family stories, neighborhood contests, radio talk shows, philosophical texts, professional sports, responses to fateful events, and political campaigns. An image of the human predicament informs affect-imbued judgment before it becomes an object of reflection. That is why it can be shocking when your image is opposed by others during a crisis. The first instinct is to condemn the alternative, because it challenges a comforting orientation to the sources and remedies of suffering. The "you" here is both individual and collective.

Why, though, insist on the term "predicament," rather than, say, "condition" to characterize this issue? A modern geneticist may have a conception of the human condition — in which humans are either susceptible to genetic determination or involved in complex interchanges between cultural settings and genetic elements laden with pluri-potentiality. But neither characterization assumes the shape of a predicament. A predicament is a situation lived and felt from the inside. It is also something you seek strategies to ameliorate or rise above. Some secular thinkers resist the word "predicament" because it inclines things toward theological concerns: it contains a plea for redemption of some sort. "Existential condition" would be better, they say, if you must engage the question at all, keeping open to what extent our condition is a predicament from which we need redemption. The word "redemption" worries secularists.

I resist such a secular objection, with some trepidation, for two reasons. First, the term "predicament" encourages us to open more expansive communication between the compartments of philosophy and theology, atheism and theism, and social science and political theory. Those closures, to the extent they persist, paralyze thought. Second, when you press protean thinkers commonly placed on the first side of these three pairs, something like a predicament to be plumbed and engaged often emerges. Some may initially slide over it, but it is there.

For Sophocles, the human predicament consists in the fact that multiple gods — or forces — are either indifferent to human welfare or often hostile to it. Our predicament involves how to negotiate life, without hubris or existential resentment, in a world that is neither providential nor susceptible to consummate mastery. We must explore how to invest existential affirmation in such a world, even as we strive to fend off its worst dangers. Augustine, by comparison, thinks that life is not worth living unless it is subtended by a providential God who promises eternal salvation for some human beings. For him, our predicament is how to negotiate a world in which human freedom is compromised after the fall, the will is essentially divided against itself, the true faith is often under assault, and humans depend upon the uncertain grace of God to will anything positive on earth or to gain eternal salvation.

These competing conceptions share the sense that suffering comes with human life, joy is intermittent and unreliable, mortality is inescapable and the vicissitudes of time leave their mark on us in other ways. Sophocles and Augustine are vivid in portraying suffering, what missteps are most likely, and how the consequences feel.

There are other objections to this enterprise: to focus intensively on the human predicament, it is said, is to bracket how a historically specific hierarchy of human powers, freedom, income, security, or insecurity is maintained. Thinkers who focus on a generic predicament are too slow to engage specific cultural issues. The objection is understandable, up to a point. Some purveyors of a general predicament do push worldly cares into the shadows, except for engagement with the institutions important to the prophets involved. So many economic and political theories avoid this dimension for that very reason, but it is a shame. Every cultural or economic agenda draws part of its sustenance from the implicit sense of the human predicament that informs it. Equally, specific historical experience is very apt to flow into your larger sense of the human predicament. Repeated rebuffs and misfortunes in daily life, for instance, are apt to take their toll on your reading of it. If, for instance, your home territory has been occupied for decades, or, the constituency you belong to has received special entitlements and now finds itself humiliated. Humiliation is fungible, flowing back and forth between specific cultural experience and entrenched readings of the human predicament.

Even economic theories invoke images of the human predicament. One theory may reduce it to a tragedy of the commons, in Garrett Hardin's term. That reduction protects field boundaries between the human sciences — that is, it sustains academic identities; but it may slide over its own ostensible object of inquiry. It is difficult to explain the *intensity* of hostility by many of relative affluence today to adjust patterns of consumption in the face of climate change unless you join an account of the infrastructure of consumption to the deeper identities of those locked into it, and unless you link both to the cultural distribution of existential orientations to the future. Different images of the human predicament now emerge as part of the larger picture. I have recently tried to trace resonances between economic practice and existential orientations in the United States.[1] Here I focus on comparative renderings of the predicament itself, with side forays into their implications for economic and political practice.

Two Registers of Temporal Experience

To address this issue in the late-modern age is to extend the requisite terms of comparative reference, even if you stutter and stammer in getting started. That is why the recent book by John J. Thatamanil, *The Immanent Divine*, is so pertinent to a person with my limitations of range and experience. He compares the thought of Sankara, the great eighth-century Hindu teacher of the Advaita Vedanta, to that of Paul Tillich, the twentieth-century Christian who sought to rework aspects of his tradition as he opened it to dialogue with others. Each, according to Thatamanil, engages the human predicament. Moreover, both criticize "dualism," particularly that of theologies that treat God as a personal being, entirely above other beings. Thatamanil explores these two visionaries comparatively. He also uses both as a springboard to advance a third reading of the predicament to attract escapees from both traditions.

Both Sankara and Tillich are visionaries of "divine immanence," though in different ways. To Thatamanil that phrase expresses appreciation of how divinity is both shorn of personal characteristics and manifest in the grittiness of the world, rather than hovering above it as an external power. "One striking point of similarity is that both characterize divinity not as an infinite being among other beings but rather as being itself, that which gives being to all beings but is not itself one of those beings."[2] Sankara thinks that the wise often proceed from early commitment to a personal divinity to a reading of Brahman as being-itself. Tillich portrays Christianity as a creed that advances through faith in a personal God to ecstatic communion with a divinity that embodies the power of being itself. These latter orientations are difficult to articulate. In fact, you come to terms deeply with each only through a process of training, devotion, and absorption that includes and exceeds verbal articulation. The One is shown but not known.

Amid this similarity between the two is a key difference. Sankara draws you toward a higher state in which attainment of Brahman is steadfast. Tillich finds the connection, even at its highest pitch, to be ecstatic and episodic rather than constant.

So what is the fundamental predicament to Tillich? Part of it resides in false renderings of life that continue to capture many and the estranged responses that follow. For Tillich, it is immature to accept a "supranatural" reading of God, that is, "any conception of divinity that imagines God to be a . . . deity who can and does regularly intervene from without into natural networks of causation."[3] Another deficiency is to live without reference to divinity at all. The authentic predicament is that freedom is bound up essentially with estrangement from the divine force that exceeds us, that we tend to misread our relation to it, and that we can come to terms with the divine force only temporarily and ecstatically. Freedom is estrangement, and estrangement is only susceptible to episodic relief. "Although human life is punctuated by healing events of divine-human reunion, life cannot be characterized as a sustained and incremental movement into healing."[4] To expect more is to sin and to sink into a quagmire of existential resentment that often finds expression in supranaturalist or closed naturalistic renderings. There is even a sense in Tillich, though Thatamanil does not concentrate on this, that estrangement, once resentment of it is overcome, can become a positive condition of freedom.

The human predicament is susceptible to amelioration, but only to a degree. The mature response is to live within the limits it poses in a way that affirms them. To do less is to be vulnerable to one of the angry, resentful orientations to life always on offer. To accept the human predicament is to become a mature self; acceptance can also elevate entire communities of faith to some degree. Indeed, sometimes you can hear in Tillich the idea that embracing estrangement contributes an element of creativity to human life.

There is an additional theme in Tillich that Thatamanil ignores. While there is a generic predicament, collective resentment or acceptance of it varies significantly across time and place. In Christendom between 400 and 700 CE, Tillich says, Christianity encouraged an exploratory approach and sometimes generous encounters with other traditions. But with the rise of Islam in close territorial proximity, Christendom became more militant. Encounters with other creeds became defensive and aggressive at the same time, resulting in a strengthening of the hierarchical and polemical tendencies of the church. "With the strengthening of the hierarchical authority it became increasingly difficult for it to recant or alter decisions made by bishops, councils and, finally, popes. The tradition . . . became an ever augmented sum of immovably valid statements and institutions." Even more disturbing was the intensifica-tion of the polemical factor. "It closes doors . . . ; it increases the proclivity to judge, and it decreases the proclivity to accept judgment."[5] So the generic predicament and specific historical situations surge and flow into each other. There is, you might say, a generic potential to resent the human predicament, which is part of what makes it a predicament. But as the above examples show, the collective intensity of acceptance or rejection is affected by a host of historical factors. Whether you agree with Tillich's specific historical account is less important than to see how historical and generic features work back and forth upon each other.

Sankara's teaching touches the confession of Tillich without duplicating them. The former projects movement from an "ignorant" dualism toward nonpersonal eternity, in this case Brahman. Suffering accompanies worldly engagement. In his own words, we live in a "vast ocean that is filled with the water of suffering arising from ignorance, desire and action; that is infested with huge sea animals in the form of acute disease, age and death; that has no beginning, end and limit and provides no resting place; that affords only momentary respite through the little joys arising from that contact of the senses and objects."[6]

"Ignorance, desire, and action"—such are the tribulations plaguing hu-manity. It is when you rise above the myth of the active, consummate human agent of desire that you approach a high point of communion. As you advance—through engagement with scripture, your guru, ritual, and medi-tation—you move from an ignorance that is unavoidable at the start to sustained contact with eternal constancy. Now the tone and character of life begin to shift. You shuck off worldly ambition and appreciate the joy of communing with Brahman. To rise above the predicament is thus to give up spurious demands for consummate human agency.

Does Sankara, then, find the daily world of desire, suffering, agency, and egoism to be unreal? Not exactly. He is critical of "Buddhist idealists" who call the everyday world a dream that blocks engagement with changeless Brahman. So how does *he* distinguish between contact with the changeless and ego-centered perceptions and desires set in the flux of everyday life? The short answer, I suppose, is that you must inhabit the practices he commends to experience the difference. That is not too surprising. Every profound presentation of the human predicament supports such an injunction at some point or other.

But the question can nonetheless be pursued to a point by those outside that tradition. To make a first approach, it may be illuminating to compare Sankara's distinction between eternity and flux to the inversion of that very distinction in Bergson. To (nearly) invert the relation is still to accept two registers of experience. In the rapid mobility of everyday life, Bergson says, perception expresses the quick organization of simplified, schematized images fitted roughly to the needs of action. This mode of experience is indispensable. We could not get through the day without such simplifications.

Yet, it is unwise to extrapolate from [action-oriented perception] to the fundamental contours of being, time, and belonging, themselves. Another type of experience, subtending and enabling the first, is available. When you sink into the experience of duration, you slide closer to time itself in both its natural and cultural expressions. To Bergson, dwelling in duration carries us to an experience in which each temporal dimension slides and flows into the others. Dwelling is not pertinent to driving a car, shaving, or pursuing an argument with your spouse. But it is essential to come to terms with our fundamental participation in time, ethics, and the world.[7]

Bergson flips the relative standing of flux and constancy pursued by Sankara. But Bergson also identifies a certain ripening of attachment to being as you become immersed in the most fundamental register of experience. Cultivation of this latter experience can then flow into the character of everyday perception, desire, and action, making a difference to them without eliminating them.

Bergson thus keeps both registers of experience alive. It may appear, however, that to approach the bliss of the changeless Sankara commends, you must withdraw resolutely from everyday desire. While you are in communion with being you do not contribute to the suffering of others. But, outsiders persistently ask, is not more activism both possible and needed?

Let's pause at this point. A fast reply to Sankara may obscure corollary quandaries those with a strong sense of agency face when we support activism in the midst of uncertain circumstances, when we celebrate agency and desire without due attention to how the pursuit of reputation, power, and wealth so easily become infused into them. Is there, then, in Sankara, a mode of activism that falls between the stools of quietism and self-aggrandizing desire? Or better, an orientation to worldly action that is neither selfish in the narrow sense nor selfless in its withdrawal from the everyday world? Does the difficulty in negotiating the shoals of agency and quietism constitute part of the human predicament?

Sankara's "quietism" is the most objectionable thing to many western theists and atheists. Thatamanil, however, suggests that such an interpretation exaggerates. It does so because Sankara's words are distorted by the way they appear when folded into our world of contrasts and identities. Overcoming ignorance *is* essential. But attainment of the higher state does not mean that all who do so always resist activism. The approach to Brahman can infuse greater care for worldly suffering into desire and action, and subtract the pressures for narrow, egoistic gratification from them. So says Thatamanil.

I am not (now) competent to decide whether Thatamanil deepens our grasp of Sankara at this point or revises the tradition he admires. Either way, his point is well taken, within limits. His exploration of what grounds and exceeds desire advances us beyond the fixed, narrow egoism that rational choice theory and neoliberalism attribute to desire as such; and it may even ameliorate the prominence of sin in Tillich's account. Thatamanil and Sankara together press us to rethink the shape and tone of desire, problematizing assumptions that we typically bring to the topic, such as, for example, the idea that desire and the experience of a lack must presuppose and engender each other, or the sense that the shape of worldly desire and the principles of moral obligation simply belong to different domains. Does it also encourage closer exploration of that vast middle ground—that excluded middle in much of egoistic and moral theory alike—between desire in its most selfish guise and altruism as action without selfishness? Does it point us toward an activism that instills care for others in it without being reducible to altruism? At this point, I will merely suggest that the urgent, vague topic of desire is jostled and disturbed by Sankara's entrance into the discussion.

If Thatamanil's adjustments are accepted, the differences between Tillich, Bergson, Sankara, and Nietzsche (the latter to be considered soon) now become more matters of real emphasis and inflection than clean lines of separation. Nietzsche, for example, who himself chides Buddhism and Hinduism for quietism (while later facing that same criticism from Hannah Arendt), also finds periodic dwelling to be essential to reflective, expansive action in a world of "becoming." He, too, finds it wise to work on the quality of desire through bouts of creative suspension. Bergson also agrees on both counts. Several accounts of the human predicament contain commendations to oscillate between cultivation and resolute action, while some Euro-American activists who encounter the first injunction become so unnerved by it that they do not hear the second invocation. Could it be that unless ethical life, political activism, consumption practices, and investment decisions are informed by positive modes of oscillation between desire and dwelling they will remain in dismal disrepair? Are worldly theorists and actors ill-equipped to disrupt the self-defeating logic of economic life unless and until they also work on their own modes of desire by strategic means? Does democracy itself require periods of oscillation between everyday desire and profound engagements with the vicissitudes of time? Does the tendency to disparage such oscillation in the name of worldliness form part of the contemporary predicament?

Yes, different degrees of susceptibility to everyday suffering, exploitation, insecurity, and humiliation have a lot to do with the character of desire. The hesitations noted above may be more difficult to pursue in some situations than in others. But many of us are not in those desperate situations, and so the issue remains open for us. It seems like an act of bad faith to reject the issue because it does not speak immediately to the life circumstances of others.

The renderings of the human predicament we have so far perused suggest that the degree to which we either sink completely into everyday perception and desire or punctuate them with hesitations makes a contribution to the quality of agency and desire. This is pertinent in an era when prevailing practices of production, income, consumption, saving, and investment both intensify inequality and pose dangers to the future of the earth.

A Theology of Becoming

So far we have focused on two registers of desire and perception through the eyes of Tillich and Sankara, with a lot of help from Thatamanil and a little from Bergson. Thatamanil himself proceeds through both Tillich and Sankara to a third reading of the human predicament: one indebted to both but reducible to neither. Neither visionary reaches the nondualism he himself promises, Thatamanil says. Both draw the vicissitudes of time into relation with a higher condition of timelessness, maintaining a dualism between time and timelessness. Here is how Thatamanil puts the point: "Unfortunately, both Sankara and Tillich failed to surmount dualism altogether, Sankara left in place a split between an unreal world of change and real and changeless Brahman. Tillich, for his part, cannot imagine that human beings can be free without standing in some ontological sense outside the divine life. A residual substantialism persists in Tillich's theological imagination."[8] So Thatamanil adds another candidate to our renderings of the human predicament, giving us three, so far, unless we also include Sophocles, Augustine, and Bergson.

Thatamanil adjusts both readings to carry them beyond the residual dualism he resists. Drawing upon the theological work of Joseph Bracken, he translates the substantialism of each into a notion of the infinite as activity. The surpassing and grounding element now becomes *activity* rather than *substance*. Henri Bergson now re-enters the fray — though he is not discussed in the book — for he, too, contends that time as becoming precedes and subtends being. The admission of eternity as pure activity, Thatamanil contends, would allow Sankara and Tillich to reduce the difference between the flux of life and the force of divinity without eliminating it. The persisting tendency toward quietism would also be curtailed. The focus would shift to how to infuse individual and constituency desire with nobility rather than whether worldly desire should be overcome by communing with the eternity of being. Moreover, I think, and I assume that Thatamanil agrees, *creativity now becomes distributed across different zones*, finding differential expression in divinity, nature, and culture alike. No force-field either monopolizes time entirely nor the creative element in it. A quotation from the text delineates a couple of these points:

> The forgoing analysis has demonstrated that Advaitins have strong internal reasons to be sympathetic to Bracken's version of nondualism. Likewise Tillichians must also abandon the residual substantialism that lingers in Tillich's theology by adopting this dynamic vision of being-itself as ontological creativity. The greatest benefit would be that such an account can undergird a far more robust prognosis for the human predicament than Tillich was able or willing to provide. A theory of God as ontological creativity can provide a framework in which human beings need not stand on their own ground outside the divine life in order to be free.[9]

It is not clear to me that Thatamanil has "demonstrated" his case, though he does give arguments to support it, nor that accepting it would automatically eliminate all traces of dualism, for dualism presents many faces. His main point, however, is that to translate substance into infinite activity is to draw humanity and divinity closer together. Bergson and James would agree on both counts. A human predicament remains, in that everyday modes of action-oriented experience too often disconnect us from the more radical register of experience that situates us in time as such, in that suffering and mortality remain, and in that several responses to the human predicament make things worse rather than better. Now, perhaps the vicissitudes of time become even more acute, since collisions between different force-fields can periodically throw rough things into the world. But engagement with being through devotion, revelation, and meditation, Thatamanil thinks, can now invest worldly activity with higher nobility. The two modalities fold into each other.

The concomitant risk or potential, one that Thatamanil does not address, is that the desubstantialization of divinity may render faith in it more precarious, hence introducing pressures for existential resentment from another direction. The introduction of becoming as a public philosophy to debate could intensify existential disaffection among several constituencies as it challenges their ideas of divinity as fixed eternity embodied in an omnipotent, omniscient God, and thus threatens hopes for eternal salvation. If this image of the human predicament does run such a risk, should it be offered only as an esoteric doctrine? Should its public articulations be suppressed? Or should it be engaged and debated alongside other images?

These are perhaps Straussian questions. But they arise during a time that itself renders the *question* of becoming more difficult than heretofore to ignore in a public forum. That is part of the contemporary predicament. Several constituencies are ready to entertain it, and ignoring the question may put us at risk too. We pay a price by suppressing the issue amidst the multiple experiences reviewed in chapter 2 that give it life, for ignoring it could give too much license to hubris in the world. And yet, its very expression outrages some. That is the bind, one with no easy or simple resolution.

Let's forge on, mindful of the situation, partly because most people are alert to one side of the bind but less to the risks identified by those working its other side. We will pursue these issues through an engagement between Catherine Keller and Friedrich Nietzsche. Both explore time as becoming, one on a theological and the other an atheological register. To add those two to our list of prophets of the human predicament increases it to at least seven. And counting.

In *The Face of the Deep: A Theology of Becoming*, Keller argues that hints of a world of becoming in Judeo-Christian scripture have been displaced by later redactions, translations, and interpretations. What is (now) the second verse of Genesis captivates her. "When in the beginning Elohim created heaven and earth, the earth was *tohu va bohu*, darkness was upon the face of the *tehom*, and the *ruach elohim* vibrating upon the face of the waters."[10] This verse depicts an unruly world already there when God acted upon it. The earth was form. The *tehom* was saltwater, chaos, and depth, quivering in itself. Pluri-potentiality simmered in it, making it susceptible to creative shaping, and later, to co-shaping by God, itself, and humanity. Even the Hebrew word for spirit, *mrfet*, suggests the idea of vibration, introducing an idea with strange resonances with recent work in complexity theory.

Christian theology, from at least Paul and Augustine to today, typically sacrifices the early appreciation of depth, vibration, and becoming to faith in an omnipotent, creator God who stands above the world (what Tillich calls "supranaturalism"). As a result of that fateful theological decision, institutionally affirmed for centuries, imperfection is sucked out of divine creation, humans are defined as fateful carriers of original sin who brought all imperfection into the world, much of human agency has been absorbed into divine grace, and positive worldly activism has been blunted in some instances and, in others, transmuted into worldly bellicosity. If a perfect God created the world from nothing, all worldly imperfection is either introduced by us through free will or a veil of appearances to be torn away in the future. Free will protects God from participation in the human predicament. Keller does not put these points so bluntly, but I think they are discernible in what she does say.

On the other hand, if a divine hand acted upon a simmering, unformed mess already there, a portion of primordial guilt is lifted from humanity. We face a future that is not determined so much by the past, free will, or divine grace. We inhabit a world of becoming. Both Genesis and biological evolution now occur "at the edge of chaos," with an element of creativity and uncertainty circulating through both.

In a world of becoming, God and humanity are co-present. "The action of God is its *relation — by feeling and so being felt*, the divine invites the *becoming* of the other, by feeling the becoming of the other the divine itself becomes."[11] The feeling of the divine, correspondingly, uplifts us as we pursue the human adventure in a world that is not closed. An "*oscillation between divine attraction and divine reception, invitation and sabbath*" now begins to inhabit desire.[12] The past works upon the future through uncertain vibrations during the protraction of the present. The present always vibrates with a degree of uncertainty. But some "moments" of radical oscillation and perturbation open upon a future that is yet more uncertain, for good and bad. As Keller puts it, "becoming remains incalculable in advance and evanescent in the present. It gets causally interconnected only after the fact. It recapitulates, it decides, it flows beyond itself."[13]

What is the human predicament in a world of becoming? I may extrapolate a bit beyond Keller here. The predicament is one in which we are tethered to mortality and time without the possibility of consummate control over nature or the strong assurance of eternal salvation. For God participates in time too. Mortality may now be a condition even more difficult to accept for many who have pursued eternal salvation, with resentment of it installing dark, war-like orientations into private and public life. On the other hand, the very pressures that place the idea of becoming actively on the register of cultural reflection mean that those who press to secure the universal legitimacy of divine omnipotence or consummate human knowledge have to work harder than before to make either idea plausible, even to those who officially accept one or the other. This combination carries the risk of intensifying dogmatism, in order to protect two dominant modes from erosion under new conditions of being. It also increases the risk of defining those who experiment with the themes of becoming as enemies of God, science, or both.

These dangers, however, are risks and not certainties. The connection between creed and ethos is loose and susceptible to multiple inflections, and most constituencies have multiple strands of belief and sensibility coursing through them, including some of the issues and concerns voiced by Keller. She makes it clear that the God she embraces is one whose (limited) power finds expression through love and whose relation to us is compromised by the adoption of either secular or theological hubris.[14] She accentuates a sense already in circulation that we belong to time and participate to a limited degree in the creative powers discernible in nature, divinity, and humanity alike.

Having translated the unilateral, uncertain grace of an omnipotent God into co-dependency between God and humanity, Keller calls upon us to act in favor of human dignity, equality, and presumptive respect for the protean character of diversity, even as we accept that the vicissitudes of time will produce occasional shifts in the meaning of those terms. The acceptance of becoming also places the faithful in a position to commune with recent work in complexity theory in physics, biology, and neuroscience, as Keller herself does. The sciences of complexity rethink time as they also rework causality, which is one of the reasons that the issue of time is not so easy to erase from the agenda of cultural exploration today.[15]

It is not too surprising, then, that Keller has written another book in which she resists apocalyptic demands flowing from evangelical re-enactments of the *Book of Revelation,* as she challenges the American pursuit of "messianic imperialism."[16] Divinity, creation out of the deep, becoming, co-presencing, risk, worldly participation, new surprises—each component in this theology folds and melds into the others, fomenting a distinctive account of the human predicament and possible modes of response to it.

It is not only faith in an omnipotent God acting upon history that cuts off a world of becoming at the pass. So do Newtonian science, a dominant tendency in Kantian metaphysics, and several secular orientations. What happens, though, as the idea of becoming finds more active expression in theology, science, philosophy, political theory, and popular films, generating resonances across these practices? It becomes more difficult to deflect the issue or to slide time as becoming into the rusty containers of nihilism, subjectivism, and relativism. But, as Keller also knows, theological talk about different images of God can throw many into doubt about their own faith. This is both the gift and risk of Keller's endeavor. Without putting words into her mouth, I think that she knows, as Charles Taylor and Gilles Deleuze also argue in their own ways, that the very "conditions of belief" of late-modern life bring all of us into close proximity with multiple images of God and Godlessness, and that trying to avoid such encounters is apt to bind you to the most dangerous, bellicose God of all. So Keller accepts the risk. She writes in a way that refuses to caricature nontheistic images. Part of the modern predicament is that existential uncertainty increases as you run these risks, and ugly spiritualities emerge if you refuse to do so. The risk is invested in the way of the world itself rather than simply one account of it.

An Atheological Predicament

Nietzsche steps into the uncertainty Keller acknowledges, not to settle the issues involved but to introduce another "conjecture" into the matrix. It is his philosophy of becoming in a self-organizing universe that is most pertinent to us. Many commentators read Nietzsche's eternal return as either an existential or ethical test, or a doctrine of long cycles, or both. A few conclude that he eventually shucked off the account and replaced it with a tragic vision in which time is less important.[17] I concur that Nietzsche *can* be read in these ways,[18] but it seems to me to be most productive to read him as a prophet of time as becoming in a world without God.[19]

Thus Spoke Zarathustra (TSZ) is pregnant in this regard. In it Zarathustra experiments with different readings of time as the text unfolds, until we arrive at a world of becoming. The image is then consolidated in some passages published in *The Will to Power*, in which Nietzsche offers his version of the distinction between the experience of punctual time and becoming. It is perhaps pertinent to note that Zarathustra lives in "the East," and that Dionysus, the god whom Nietzsche appreciates throughout his work, also migrated from east to west. Nietzschean gods are seldom stationary, national gods.

The first dramatization in TSZ, in which Zarathustra debates a dwarf riding on his shoulder who weighs him down with the spirit of gravity, is laden with ambiguity. " 'Behold this gateway, dwarf,' I continued. 'It has two faces. Two paths meet here; no one has yet followed either to its end. This long lane stretches back for an eternity. And that long lane out there, that is another eternity. They contradict each other, these paths. They offend each other face to face; and it is here at this gateway that they come together. The name of the gateway is inscribed above: Moment.' "[20] Here is an image of an infinite time, as past and future stretch in different directions forever. Do they nonetheless meet in an infinite circle? Note that Zarathustra also says that each path "offends" the other at each moment of contact. There is dissonance at the gateway and in the moment. And Zarathustra is sharply dissatisfied when the dwarf responds to his "riddle" with a ditty about the circle of time.

Soon, during the same "Vision and Riddle," Zarathustra lapses into a dream in which a snake crawls down his throat. Amidst great drama, he finally bites off the head of that snake, laughing with joy and wickedness after he does so. Does the snake represent original sin crawling into the human soul? The theme of circular time? Both? It is not that clear. After that moment of creative transgression, Zarathustra soon ripens enough to formulate his vision more sharply. Here are a few things he says later:

— Verily, it is a blessing and not a blasphemy when I teach: 'Over all things stands the heaven Accident, the heaven Innocence, the heaven Chance, the heaven Prankishness.'

— O heaven . . . that is what your purity is for me now, that there is no eternal spider or spider web of reason; that you are to me a dance floor for divine accidents, that you are to me a divine table for divine dice and dice players.

— I taught them all *my* creating and striving, to create and carry together into the One what in man is fragment and riddle and dreadful accident; as creator, guesser of riddles, and redeemer of accidents, I taught them to work on the future and to redeem with their creation all that *has been*. To redeem what is past in man and to re-create all 'it was' until the will says, 'Thus I willed it and thus I shall will it' — this I call redemption and this alone I taught them to call redemption.[21]

Now a reading of the human predicament emerges, joined to thoughts about how to respond to it. The "moment" is a protracted present in which, on occasion, movement back and forth between previously stabilized elements foments significant disequilibrium. This is a time ripe for "accidents." The impetus might be an external intrusion — for any zone including the evolution of the universe, biological evolution, asteroid flows, civilizational variations, a brain injury to a ruler or priest, or a collective change in religious creed can participate in this or that moment. Humans are not the only agents in the Nietzschean world, if by agent you mean in the simplest sense the ability to make a difference in the world that exceeds efficient causality without knowing quite what you are doing. This becomes most clear during periods of disequilibrium when several forces interact in a new way, when the demarcation between agency and cause becomes fuzzy and problematical.

Eternal return as the repetition of long cycles is transfigured into time as becoming; what returns is the fecundity of the moment from which new twists and turns can flow. Augustinian and Kantian doctrines of the human will divided against itself now prove to be insufficient to such an image of time, for they too radically *condense* the principal sources of rupture and dissonance into the interior of the human soul. Nineteenth century scientific conceptions of nature set on a linear trajectory of efficient causes are insufficient too. Zarathustra's announcement of "a dance floor for divine accidents" calls all such conceptions into question. It plays up the element of chance at pivotal moments when several dancers of different kinds are active. It summons attention to "divine accidents" that propel new things into being from time to time. The meaning of the moment, introduced at first through that drama with the dwarf, is now enriched.

Another way to grasp Zarathustra's story is to compare its intersections and differences with that of Kierkegaard (or Climacus). Kierkegaard also focuses on the importance of The Moment. The most profound moment was when "the God" came to earth in the guise of a man; but others arise as well whenever the question of the grant or denial of grace becomes salient. In both Kierkegaard and Zarathustra the dissonance of the moment is given primacy, that which is outside experience can later become terribly important to it, and we participate in a cosmos that exceeds our grasp. So an inexorable element of faith is involved in the way we conceive and live. The meaning of "faith" in Kierkegaard, however, is irreducible to its meaning in Nietzsche. The former contends that faith is not deep until you leap to "the God" whose ways are mysterious to you and that the leap will falter unless it is met by grace. Anything else is a "belief" that could in principle be confirmed or disconfirmed by earthly means. Nietzsche, on the other hand, severely doubts that his concept of the world of becoming will ever be proved or disproved definitively; he invites you to experiment with this "conjecture" as if it might be true and to fold those experiments into your operational faith. That means that you act upon this faith while folding an appreciation of its comparative contestability into your second-order understanding, partly so that the quality of your relations with other faiths can be enhanced. Nietzsche and Kierkegaard thus not only exude different faiths, they secrete overlapping but different conceptions of what it means to have faith: in one case you must receive grace to really make the leap; in the other you work on yourself to accept a world of becoming that is never apt to be proven definitively.[22]

Those Zarathustra admires most are creators, *guessers* of riddles, and "redeemers of accidents": creators, guessers, and redeemers who strive by their actions to overcome resentment of a world of becoming. One key response to the human predicament becomes the nobility to make reflective wagers when the future is uncertain. We bear the weight of the past in us as we project ourselves into the mystery of the future. Those who act without *existential* resentment upon the accidents that befall them so that more gratitude is infused into future acts pose the most promise for the world. Those who demand extra compensations to face life—a moral god, the hope of eternal salvation, the compensatory promise of human mastery over the world—teeter on the verge of resentment unless they fold into those very faiths an expansive love of the world they depict. If they do, they become ripe candidates for what Nietzsche calls a "spiritualization of enmity" between diverse constituencies infused with different faiths.

The shape of the future is unknown in its complexity, but Nietzsche knows enough to say that those who resent its unknowability the most are the least suited to negotiate the temporal dimension of the human predicament. There are, of course, numerous other dangers in a world of becoming, arriving from numerous zones and sources. Such is the shape of the human predicament in Nietzsche.

Have we not set to the side Nietzsche's statements about *amor fati*, and the quietism they seem to support? Hannah Arendt, in one of her readings of Nietzsche, would say so.[23] But we do not set them aside; we incorporate them into a larger network of Nietzschean themes. In the context of Zarathustra's ruminations, a double process becomes discernible. You work slowly upon yourself to accept fate, expressed, say, in the death of a beloved one, or the inheritance of your dad's meekness, or the recent defeat of the political movement upon which you staked your life, or the now more vivid sense of the unavoidability of your own death, or the loss of the providential meaning you once found bestowed upon history. But the inheritance of fate can also be worked upon so that you modify not it but the effect it has on your future actions. You work to draw something noble from fate and to add something to it: to incorporate the courage and generosity of your beloved more actively into future action; to translate the meekness into a polite mode of courage pointing to the future; to roam through the debris of a defeated movement to forge a new possibility; to work ardently to affirm death as a condition of the vitality of life; to inspire others by the way you die rather than to pull them down as you go under. *Amor fati, the affirmation of becoming, and participation in creative forces that exceed us co-determine each other, with each modifying the meaning otherwise given to the others.* It takes the latter two in conjunction to become worthy of the event.

In a world of ungodly becoming, mortality means oblivion; "divine" accidents periodically unsettle political programs; markets periodically lurch into volatility; this or that aspect of nature sometimes erupts in a surprising way; and any such force may interact at a timely or untimely moment with some of the others. In such a condition, universal morality requires radical augmentation by a preparedness to respond creatively and sensitively to new, unanticipated situations.

There are rewards attached to embracing the world as becoming. The vitality of life is experienced actively. You do not live in constant anxiety about whether you have been chosen for eternal life or eternal damnation. You are in a good position to cultivate sensitivity to selective affinities with

other aspects of living and non-living nature. And you periodically participate in individual and collective experiments that stretch the shape of desire
and collective action in new ways, coming to appreciate through action our
modest participation in the creative dimension of the world. To embrace
without deep resentment a world of becoming is to work to "become who
you are," so that the word "become" now modifies "are" more than the other
way around.

Yes, profound misfortune, the decline of old age, or horrific collective
events may render you unable or unwilling to negotiate new setbacks and
uncertainties, but the Nietzschean drive is to stay aloft as long as possible in a
world of becoming without transcendent guarantees and to draw on the
surplus energies available to you to make a positive difference in the world as
long as you can. You do need to draw upon the powers of resentment and
indignation from time to time, as Nietzsche himself emphasizes, but you
seek to do so in ways that do not allow those resentments to slide into
ressentiment. Very little good can come from that.

Part of the human predicament is that the spirit of existential revenge so
readily slips into the pores of cultural life, inhabiting diverse creeds and
institutions. Maybe you officially accept a providential view, but secretly
suspect the Nietzschean conception is correct. That is a good recipe for
ressentiment. There are others. Zarathustra's own ape, for instance, drives
this latter point home to him as it embraces the creed of becoming while
expressing resentment of it in every word and gesture. Zarathustra finds that
he is compelled to "pass by" this *doctrinal* ally who belies his *spirit* so profoundly. The experience of Zarathustra in Part IV with different representa-
tives of the last man also exposes several risks of resignation or existential
resentment.

The positive task is to work, by individual, political, and institutional
means, to overcome resentment of the human predicament, to translate the
experience of time as becoming into a condition you affirm, to fold a spirit of
presumptive generosity for the diversity of life into your conduct, and to act
creatively and resourcefully in a world punctuated periodically by prankishness and accidents. Zarathustra himself, however, does not accept the above
formulations fully. He gives up on politics after some bad experiences with
it, focusing on noble individuals. I suspect that Zarathustra, had he encountered the tightening web of social relations and global dangers we now face,
would rethink that lapse into compensatory individualism. I commend such
a rethinking, at any rate.[24]

Near the end of his journey Zarathustra sinks into yet another uncanny state, at noon when there is no shadow. "Still, still! Did not the world become perfect just now?"[25] Awakening from his slumber, he asks, "What happened to me? Listen! Did time perhaps fly away? Do I not fall? Did I not fall — listen — into the well of eternity . . . ? Did not the world become perfect just now? Round and ripe?"[26] Perhaps Zarathustra has ripened and is now prepared to draw sustenance from a new bout of dwelling. This time, in the reverie of the moment, layered resonances between past and future reverberate through him. He participates in a bit of time as becoming, even as he also acknowledges that the larger compass of past-present-future reverberations greatly exceeds his participation in them. Echoes of Sankara, Tillich, Bergson, and Keller are now discernible.

To affirm a world of becoming is to worry about the excesses of humanism as well as those of monotheism. The former too often supports a consummate conception of human agency; it is not alert enough to multiple modes of proto-agency in other aspects of nature and culture that often exceed, overlap, and perplex us. It thus readily becomes too enamored with its own agency.

For Zarathustra, like Bergson, you need punctual time to get through the day; but you need its periodic suspension to commune with real time. When Zarathustra falls into the blurriness of the moment at noon, new vibrations course through him. Is the shape of worldly desire enlarged by such experience? Nietzsche thought so. He also thought that desire driven only by the experience of lack — the lack of a full self, the lack of providence, the lack of love, the lack of reputation — could, through tactical action and fortunate networks of connection to others, become infused more with the abundance of the "gift giving virtue." When desire contains abundance it is reducible to neither the pole of selfishness nor that of altruism, rather, spirals of presumptive generosity become coded into relations between desiring agents as such. For, as Zarathustra also says very clearly, it takes relations of agonistic respect between diverse modes of nobility for any single mode of nobility to be.

If you embrace a world of becoming in which the shape of desire is important to the quality of collective life, one critical task (among others) is to instill networks of desire with a greater degree of positivity.[27] You do so in part by pursuing tactics of the self in which individuals draw upon tools and small assemblages to affect themselves; you do so more robustly through strategic action on larger networks of desire, and most importantly through resonances back and forth between these levels. Microtactics of the self might involve priming your dream life before you fall asleep, meditation, prayer, neurotherapy, selecting particular films for viewing with others, reading provocative texts, and allowing each of these experiences to engage the others. Micropolitics extends microtactics, though it takes left Nietzscheans such as Foucault and Deleuze to reveal their importance. Joining this church rather than that, acquiring these friends and allies rather than those, participating in this pattern of consumption and investment rather than that, entering into this political movement rather than that, voting in this way rather than that, such actions permeate patterns of desire and extend the stage on which desire operates.[28] To alter the networks in which you participate is eventually to alter the relational mode of desire coursing through you, in a modest or notable way: you now participate in a modified assemblage of desire that includes and exceeds you. When the next round of action by you or your assemblage expresses that altered quality either or both may be poised to take a more adventurous political stance or accept a new level of ethical responsibility than before. You may be ready to listen to a new mode of inspiration to which you were previously tone-deaf. This is how, on the positive side, spirals of interinvolvement between desire, action, ethics, and politics work. They can become negative as well.

The Powers of the False

Is there more to be said about how to consolidate attachment to a world of becoming, received in either a theistic or nontheistic vein? I think there may be, by way of a slight detour. In chapter 6 of *Cinema II: The Time Image*, Gilles Deleuze enters into a conversation with Nietzsche about the "powers of the false." The "false," on the epistemic register is that which deviates from or contradicts the truth. The idea of the false here, however, operates on another register. It is energies that do not fit into a particular regime of equalization or truth, but nonetheless exert a real effect. Say that at a pivotal moment in species evolution, a bifurcation point hovers between two possible directions. The direction *not taken* may later function as an incipience that festers with pluri-potentiality. At a later date this incipience might be activated under new circumstances, entering into resonance with actualities already there. Moving this onto the human register, consider when Proust's narrator slips on a couple of uneven stones and is hurtled back to another moment when a similar thing had happened, barely perceptible at the time under the pressure of another course of action. Now those two disparate moments enter into a new pattern of resonance, opening up a possibility of feeling, thought, or action unavailable until that moment.

The false is that which falls below clean recollection because it was not consolidated enough at its inception to assume the shape of a conscious image. It carries power if at a later date it becomes a trigger below or on the edge of sensory awareness that makes a difference to thought and action. The false sows a seed from which a new idea, strategy, or temper can be ushered into the world in a new setting. It is not, then, merely that which exceeds us (as the "negative," the "lack," the "other," or the insoluble "gap" between concept and thing to which much of social theory in the last part of the twentieth century was devoted).[29] It also helps to propel new turns of becoming at strategic moments. I speak, then, of the *powers* of the false.

How the powers of the false work behind the scenes in the human estate can be brought out by considering a person who has lost that fragile balance between a train of thought and new triggers that move thought and conversation in a different direction. In *Time Regained*, the aging Marcel encounters the Baron de Charlus, the arrogant intellectual he had known as a young man. Charlus is now less coherent than before; he has aphasia. In this new conversation two de Charluses now contend radically with and against each other.

> "Of the two, one, the intellectual one, passed his time in complaining that he suffered from progressive aphasia, that he constantly pronounced one word or letter by mistake for another. But as soon as he actually made such a mistake, the other M. de Charlus, the subconscious one, who was as desirous of admiration as the first was of pity and out of vanity did things that the first would have despised, immediately, like a conductor whose orchestra had blundered, checked the phrase which he had started and with infinite ingenuity made the end of his sentence follow coherently from the word which had in fact uttered by mistake . . . ; his vanity impelled him, not without the fatigue of the most laborious concentration, to drag forth this or that ancient recollection . . . which would demonstrate to me that he had preserved or recovered all his lucidity of mind."[30]

Proust's second sentence consists of phrases that are barely balanced, its form enacting the struggle between the two Charluses. The poise that Charlus has lost between two interacting forces pulling in different directions also discloses elements that must be in play when we maintain our poise. As Proust knows, perhaps better than anyone else, the unconscious triggers of memory that jolt a train of thought—turning it in a new direction—contribute creative potential to human thought and action. The *effects* of such triggers are more discernible when a brain disease upsets the precarious balance between creativity and habit in the quantum brain, even if we are not in a position to *know* the shape of each trigger that unsettles the balance.

Such is the case with the quantum brain and the precariousness of the human condition. Stutter and stammer, as you allow a word or phrase to surface from a trigger that emits it, but not too much or too often. An excess of either stifles the moment of creativity in thought; the lack of either does too.

Because we participate periodically in quantum moments of creation that make a difference to life and the world, we are junior partners in a larger world of becoming. We cannot control or master that world, nor is it designed for us. But we are part of it and make a difference to it. Perhaps the powers of the false now become more audible in the following formulation by Nietzsche than they would have been without this detour through Proust:

> By far the greater number of motions have nothing whatever to do with consciousness; nor with sensation. Sensations and thoughts are sometimes extremely insignificant, and rare in relation to the countless number of events that occur every moment . . . Of the numerous influences operating at every moment, e.g., air, electricity, we sense almost nothing: there could well be forces that, although we never sense them, continually influence us. Pleasure and pain are rare and scarce appearances compared with the countless stimuli that a cell or organ exercises upon another cell or organ.[31]

Some "motions" subsist on the edge of sensory awareness. Others have no presence in it. They make a difference as vibrations even though they are not intense enough to hear. They are expressed only through their effects, and those effects are never pure since they involve a mix between trigger and actuality. They make a difference to how consciousness functions. Nietzsche is thus a philosopher of the "modesty of consciousness," not its loss. Moreover, to him there are multiple degrees and sites of agency in the world. What Nietzsche espouses is both the absence of a final purpose *and* the insufficiency of linear causation in a world where partial agents of many types and degrees periodically intersect with the powers of the false.

When Nietzsche and Deleuze (and Whitehead, for that matter) speak of the "innocence" of becoming, they include the role that the powers of the false play in setting new possibilities into motion previously confined by culturally fixed modes of "equalization." Equalization here means an organization that hives off enough difference to enable itself to be, as it also leaves energetic remainders behind. These remainders set the stage for the powers of the false to come into play as this or that new "moment" arises.

To these three thinkers, then, a world of becoming is not saturated with "original sin," "primordial guilt," or "divine judgment." To drop those elements from the innocence of the world of becoming is to take a step toward embracing the largest compass of the universe as such, to embrace the sort of cosmos (they think) we inhabit. Another step is taken if you affirm and experiment with the *powers* of the false, those energetic remainders that prowl in equalizations and periodically help to forge new explorations. A third step is to explore how human thinking, including that of Charlus before his delicate balance was lost, participates in such processes, how the creative element in thinking is enabled by our participation in a larger world of becoming. A fourth is to cultivate a sensibility that appreciates our participation in the element of creativity and bestows presumptive respect upon the protean diversity of life spawned by it. You strive to intensify one aspect of desire or to fold a new element into it, as you also extend the limits of responsibility that previously set the limits within which you were prepared to restrain desire. You then draw upon that sensitivity when new and surprising things throw some dimension of established habit, judgment, or morality into a quandary.

It seems productive to me, then, to juxtapose Nietzsche and Keller on the issue of becoming. One places it on a theological and the other an atheological register. The differences between them are real, but they may concur on how the powers of the false operate and the need to overcome the resentment of time as becoming. They touch each other, too, in the drive to magnify attachment to this world. Putting them into conversation may enlarge a series of what Keller, during an APSA panel in 2009 in which we both participated, called "theopoetic reverberations."

Both Keller and Nietzsche resist folding too much systematicity into ethics and an ethos of politics. Systematic morality weighs too heavily upon time. The ethical sensibility of an individual (and a positive ethos of engagement between diverse constituencies) must be poised between habits that have stood us in good stead heretofore and periodic sensitivity to the emergence of new issues and problems. There must be a *torsion* between principle and innovation, habit and sensitivity, being and becoming. The first principle of such an ethic is to overcome resentment of the world of becoming, even if your new faith cuts into previous hopes for a providential world or consummate human agency. A second is to cultivate sensitivity to new turns in the world as they arise. A third is to remain attentive to the provisional standing of your own philosophy of time as you engage constituencies imbued with other images. Systematic moralities are too crude, self-enclosed, and lazy for a world of becoming, both thinkers contend, particularly when the pace of life has accelerated in this or that zone. Diverging on the question of God, Keller and Nietzsche nonetheless touch each other in uncanny ways.

Mining Disparate Traditions

We have sketched several characterizations of the human predicament. They vary significantly, but a few pointers and issues may emerge from the sample.

First, the duplicities of ignorance-Brahman, estrangement-ecstatic communion, and existential resentment-gratitude identified, respectively, by Sankara, Tillich, Thatamanil, and Keller/Nietzsche are all dangerous. Each of these thinkers also charts two registers of experience, with the second carrying some possibility of infusing more care for the world into the first. The destructive potential can reach a high pitch if resentment of the most fundamental terms of existence, as you yourself understand those terms, becomes coded too deeply into investment routines, consumption practices, electoral campaigns, church assemblies, political machines, and individual actions; that is, into desire as it operates in each assemblage.

Second, some characterizations of the predicament revolve around engaging resistance to subliminal experiences of time as becoming. This is understandable because a world of becoming places at risk simultaneously the promise of eternal salvation, the moral image of the world, the scientific ideal of consummate knowledge, and the promise of human mastery. *If* we inhabit a world in which the experience of becoming now finds more intensive expression through the acceleration of pace in several zones, media accentuation of natural disasters, the rise of complexity theory, the increasingly rapid minoritization of the world taking place before our very eyes, new adventures in media art, the strange imbrications between capitalist expansion and climate warming, and the interplay between everyday life and experiments in film, then the issue of time may pose sharper challenges to familiar modes of cultural reassurance. The question is whether it is riskier to fend off such experiences in science, politics, theology, film, ethics, media, art, and everyday life or to engage them affirmatively. My wager is to present the case for a world of becoming so that it might be embraced by a larger minority as it enters into communication with established theo-ontologies of everyday life.

Third, all these engagements address the slippery issue of desire. Some may counsel us to rise above worldly desire; others to suspend it on occasion to enlarge the compass of everyday desire; and others to infuse more energy, presumptive generosity, and sensitivity into worldly desire. The human predicament, all agree, is entangled with the shape and quality of desire in its individual and institutional manifestations. Today one critical question is how to fashion a positive frugality of material desire, a task pursued by several of these figures without perhaps being resolved by any. And how to do so in ways that foment the exploratory temper needed to come to terms with surprising twists and turns in time. My sense, at any rate, is that all these thinkers would pose the quality of desire as a central issue.

Fourth, each characterization poses *strategies* to respond affirmatively to the world it acknowledges. These can involve, in the first instance, engagements with priests, gurus, philosophers, sacred texts, ritual practices, and communing with others. Often a movement back and forth between cogitative and meditative practices is commended. In some traditions the thing above all to overcome is deep resentment of the human predicament, *however you yourself depict that predicament*. Indeed, each tradition develops what might broadly be called meditative strategies to deepen, extend, or amplify our attachment to the world, finding such strategies helpful in moving us to more generous or accepting modes of being. You work, in some, to intensify experience of the sweetness of life. Some concur that such affirmative modes of response must find expression in political, cultural, and economic life if they are to make a real difference, though not all emphasize this. For, as some of our gurus see, existential resentment, profound political humiliation, and persistent exploitation can work back and forth upon each other, generating powerful resonance machines of destruction. Strangely, many people with numerous privileges and an inflated sense of entitlement work to exacerbate the most negative machines. If the quality of spirituality makes a real difference to the institutional life in which it is embedded, it now becomes clear why no classic list of "social positions" suffices to explain the constituency basis of destructive and productive political movements. There is an element of prankishness in the social distribution of existential orientations and political identifications.

Fifth, another complication enters the picture as you compare, even in a preliminary way, different characterizations of the human predicament. Each characterization reaches a point at which its meaning and import become blurry, uncertain, or paradoxical from the perspective of those not imbued with it. Indeed, some of those qualities never disappear entirely for its own devotees. We are densely embodied beings, and our existential faiths are lodged in several layers of being, some of which exceed direct intellectual control. Can the discussions of "immanence," "ignorance," and "Brahman" pursued by Sankara be that clear to those who have not been inducted into the appropriate experiences and virtues? Sankara himself thinks that induction and reflection are both needed. So do Tillich, Thatamanil, Keller, and Nietzsche, in their respective ways. Any graduate student who has been exposed to the disciplinary mechanisms by which rational choice theory, Kantianism, Habermasianism, Foucauldianism, Straussianism, or neoliberalism are installed should hesitate before ignoring the ubiquity and risks of induction routines. Kant himself thought that induction was important to draw students to the brink of his philosophy. Think, to take a contemporary instance, how neoliberalism is rehearsed five days a week in America on the *Kudlow Report*, *Your World with Neil Cavuto*, *Hannity's America*, and *Glenn Beck*, while other readings of our economic condition are barely audible to most citizens. These shows blend hubris and *ressentiment* in a distinctive potion that can become highly potent. Think how such a perspective affects the hopes, senses of entitlement, and class contempt of many in the speculative class, as well as a section of the middle class that hopes a stroke of luck will lift it up to the wealthy class.

These last complications add a sixth dimension to the human predicament. While there are several credible candidates to explore, none is so clear and commanding that it is apt to capture the imagination of everyone everywhere not already inducted into it. And there is simply not enough time in life to explore each as fully as its complexity requires. This is merely one of the factors that contribute to the minoritization of the world today. For now, and into the foreseeable future, part of the human predicament is that a plurality of conceptions of it will persist. I have my candidates, others have theirs. Many even pretend that they have demonstrated theirs, or that a combination of devotion and engagement with scripture should seal it in certainty for everyone. To me, these last assertions emit a whiff of dogmatism and *ressentiment*.

During a time when the expansion of capital, inter-territory media communication, and population migration generate a more rapid minoritization of the world, part of the contemporary predicament is how to respond to the obdurate plurality of being in positive ways. The pluralization of the world, in conjunction with bellicose movements that turn militantly against it, forms a critical part of the contemporary predicament.

Today, it is important, first, to articulate comparative readings of the human predicament, second, to affirm the reading that makes the most sense of evidence, argument, and experience to you, third, to cultivate a presumption of agonistic respect for other readings, and fourth, to find ways to embrace without existential resentment the most fundamental character of being as you yourself confess it to be. The "you" refers to intra-individual, micro- and macro-assemblages of desire.

CHAPTER FIVE

Capital Flows, Sovereign Decisions, and World Resonance Machines

Civil Society and Its "Rabble"

Civil society, says Hegel in his magisterial study, *The Philosophy of Right*, is a modern civilizational advance that promotes and demands a high degree of self-reliance, creative enterprise, and self-responsibility among its (male) participants. Its impersonal capacities of self-regulation, exemplifying one version of what will later in this chapter be called an abstract machine, lift it above every previous mode of being in human history. Some may quibble with that last claim, but Hegel himself says that civil society also contains inveterate tendencies to overreach itself, to spawn forces that break its equilibrium, and to resist the internalization of state norms and directives that would otherwise lift its balances to a higher level. These "irrational" tendencies are expressed in the over-specialization of work that narrows the horizons of laborers, in the expansion of consumption needs that accompany the wrenching of people from traditional life, and in the entrepreneurial hubris that arises when the market spawned virtue of self-reliance becomes too inflated.

In another domain, when the production protocols of the market are not well regulated, it fosters a level of production that exceeds the capacities of many within the state to buy its products, creating a crisis of over-production and under-consumption, and expanding the size of the impoverished class. It is bad enough that people suffer under such a regime, Hegel thinks, but that suffering is exacerbated by the fact that the (advanced) mode of subjectivity created by civil society transforms the new bearers of poverty into a "rabble." The impoverished are now the product of a system that blames them for their impoverishment rather than treating it as the curse of fate. They thus become problematic to the world and to themselves. Hegel's presentation of the rabble deserves quotation:

> In this condition [of poverty] they are left with the needs of civil society and yet — since civil society has at the same time taken from them the natural means of acquisition . . . they are more or less deprived of all of the advantages of society, such as the ability to acquire skills and education in general . . . When a large mass of people sinks below the level of a certain standard of living — which automatically regulates itself at the level necessary for a member of the society in question, that feeling of right, integrity and honor which comes from supporting oneself by one's own activity is lost. This leads to the creation of a *rabble*, which in turn makes it easier for disproportionate wealth to be concentrated in a few hands.
>
> Poverty in itself does not reduce people to a rabble; a rabble is created only by the disposition associated with poverty, by inward rebellion against the rich, against society, against government, etc. It also follows that those who are dependent on contingency become frivolous and lazy, like the *lazzaroni* of Naples, for instance . . . The important question of how poverty can be remedied is one which agitates and torments modern societies especially.[1]

This question agitates modern life because the expectation of self-reliance and the consumption needs generated by civil society sow resentment against the market-state regime among those for whom the gap between those standards and the capacities and standing they can acquire is large. The principle of subjectivity essential to civil society thus converts the poor into a rabble. I do not accept the term Hegel deploys ("rabble"), with its own tendency to condemn and dismiss the constituencies whose suffering and resentments are identified. He does have a tendency to relieve institutional responsibility for the cruelties the system promotes because of his claim that it promises to pass through this phase to a higher level. What is needed here — and what I will try to provide in a later section with respect to a new global version of the systemic cruelties Hegel charts in the nineteenth century — is an account that shows how the dominant system and the constituencies plagued by it interact to produce a phenomenon irreducible to either alone. This being said, I do want to underline the way in which the new thresholds of agency, education, skill, and commodity consumption Hegel identified as necessary to participate with efficacy in the nineteenth-century capitalist state combine with the experience of impoverishment to increase disaffection and resentment among the poor and lower-level workers in that regime. Today, the destructive dimension of the relation between civil society, civil religion, and existential resentment is not confined to those in positions of poverty. It circulates more widely within states and across regions linked together by capital/media practices. Such resentments, as we will explore further, can be propelled in a variety of directions.

Hegel's next insight is that civil society must expand beyond the territory of a single state to maintain itself, almost from the start. As imbalances in civil society develop, pressures grow to relieve them by external expansion. State capitalism in the heartland requires colonization of the hinterlands: to secure raw materials, to relieve problems of overproduction and under-consumption at home, and to bring the virtues of civil society and the modern state to virgin territory. The sea provides a wonderful gift from providence for colonizing efforts, Hegel says, providing capitalist states with smooth space upon which to travel and creating a protective barrier between them and colonized regions. The open space remains today, but its protective function has dissolved.

At home, the higher balance needed is incorporated into the virtues of family life, estates that mediate between market and state, a Christian religion that translates the human essence available to philosophy into popular images, states that lift the market to a high level of rationality, and a world-historical state that limits the sovereignty of other states to bring a yet higher rationality to the world market and interstate system.

What, though, enables these semi-sovereign states and the world-historical state to be wise? And what induces other states and regions to accept that wisdom? It is *Geist*, finding its highest expression in philosophy and progressively higher degrees of expression in civil society, the state, and the world-historical state. *Geist* is always in play inside several institutional venues, particularly the state. But it becomes most *visible* in a world-historical state that faces no higher earthly sovereign entity above it.[2] Here, "the higher praetor is simply the universal spirit which is being in and for itself, i.e., the world spirit."[3]

What happens if you accept much of Hegel's description of civil society and the state, while seeking to lift the heavy ontology of *Geist* in which that study is set? This is not entirely an anti-Hegelian question. In his late lectures on aesthetics he seems to pull back from a reading in which *Geist* eventually expresses the coming together of philosophy, econo-political institutions, and human reconciliation; he slides toward a reading in which art uncovers a stubborn element of surplus and messiness in the world that exceeds the image of philosophy extant in *The Philosophy of Right*.[4] In that work he concludes that philosophy itself would become dull and lifeless if it did not periodically draw sustenance from art and if art did not draw creative energy from those stubborn elements of surplus, messiness, and loose energy circulating through culture. Such messy forces are also detectable in *The Philosophy of Right*, but there, at least on my reading, they are mostly folded into a progressive dialectic finding its eventual and highest expressions in the modern state and the world-historical state. To my knowledge, Hegel did not carry these late insights back to his philosophy of the state, at least not to the degree commended by a philosophy of becoming in an open universe. He also excluded nature from the historical dialectic he traced and sought to illuminate: this omission is fundamental. These, then, are the terms of comparison I have in mind when I point to the closures of *The Philosophy of Right*.

In one sense, the remainder of this chapter can be read as speculation about what might have happened if Hegel had pursued the theme of surplus further in cultural life, extended it to nature, and more actively *affirmed* a world of radical immanence in which becoming can be stabilized in this or that zone, for a time, but eventually exceeds being.

What happens to Hegel's picture if you conclude that several of the mediating processes and institutions he cites in *The Philosophy of Right* (gender subordination, the heterosexual family, the three estates, markets, the police, colonization, international law, and a world-historical state) are even more ambiguous than he imagined? They can impose internal and external constraints on capital and markets, *but they can also become permeated with the very energies he expected them to regulate and modulate*. Adopting such a strategy — thinking through and beyond Hegelian interconnections and interpenetrations within a more radical philosophy of becoming, we may discern seeds in the nineteenth century of a contemporary global condition that now exceeds the control of any market system, state, or network of states. Hegel never did show how, once capitalism expanded, a worldwide capitalist system could unfold, capable of resolving poverty, resentments, and anger throughout its enlarged zone of being. He did not even articulate a strategy to resolve poverty (and to transcend the rabble) within core capitalist states. Today there is ample reason to doubt that the world capitalist system is susceptible to planetary universalization without being modified more fundamentally than he imagined. The *Star Wars* films, popular since the 1970s, express both this collective anxiety and the compensatory fantasy of colonizing new planets to escape the binds of Earth. The more recent film *Avatar* presents a much more ambiguous picture.

Today, you might say, global capital, the new modes of sovereignty states struggle to enact as they respond to the expansion of capital, and a regional distribution of alternative religious creeds, function together to engender hostilities that stretch beyond the control of any state, interstate system, or world market. The rabble Hegel discerned within single states in the early nineteenth century has become angry minorities distributed within and between world regions. As I will suggest, these elements, in conjunction with bellicose practices of First World states, combine to produce a new global "abstract machine" that exceeds the control of the global market, state, religious practices, and interstate agencies from which it emerged. Hostile multitudes inside and outside First World states are linked through contagious acts that elude the full control of market and interstate systems while drawing selective energies from them. Hegel's discussion of a rabble generated and demeaned by civil society provides us with hints about how such a trans-state conglomerate has formed and the part the institutions he examined play in consolidating it. These constituencies, distributed as minorities at many sites, are first called upon to meet standards at odds with their conditions of life and then condemned for the responses they tolerate, support, or enact. They are placed in what Gregory Bateson called a double bind, in which the first bind foments volatile resentments and the second denies legitimacy to every attempt to explain the systemic sources of these resentments.

Capitalism as "Interstate" System

Immanuel Wallerstein, writing a century and a half after Hegel, contends that capitalism was an interstate system from the outset, not defined by the primacy of market practices. Anti-market mechanisms were needed to generate profit for particular firms and to fuel the historic expansion of capitalism (with capitalism defined by the competitive demands on each organizational unit to accumulate profit). Initially it took the form of a "large geographic zone within which there [was] a division of labor and hence significant internal exchange of basic . . . goods, as well as flows of capital and labor."[5] It was thus cross-state from its inception. Entrepreneurs in the Mediterranean states entered into exchange with those in others, and the sovereignty of each state was tethered to the aspiration to promote market advantages for corporations housed within their borders. So capitalism was always interstate capitalism. The interstate system soon reached a point when leading states faced pressure to secure resources, goods, and labor from regions of the world in which the state form and the activities of civil society were initially resisted.

As the "interstate zone" of capitalism expanded beyond the Mediterranean basin, capitalism became a world system consisting of relations of uneven exchange between regions (as well as of constituencies within capitalist states). As this happened, pressures also arose to invest one state in the "core area" with hegemony.[6] The hegemonic state, in a way reminiscent of Hegel's world-historical state, is the state that exercises sovereignty most fully, in the ways it determines both its own internal priorities and sets parameters for other states. Other states, by comparison to it, are semi-sovereign. As we shall see and Wallerstein may or may not, even the hegemonic state eventually faces an "outside" to sovereignty.

Though Wallerstein himself does not emphasize this, to talk about a "world capitalist system" does not mean that everything everywhere is drawn inexorably into it. The system propels expansionary drives within and across regions, but it also co-exists with zones and practices partially outside its provenance. Specific cultural priorities, habits of family life, religious belief and ritual, underground markets, new social movements, tax evasion, cross-state political formations, military reticence or adventurism, media humor and drama, scientific research and teaching all possess partial and shifting degrees of autonomy from system governance. To insist that every practice, once capitalism expands its reach, is entirely absorbed into its orbit is to translate the idea of a world-capitalist system into that of a totality. Such an image exaggerates the absorptive power of one system, and discourages exploration of ways to stretch and challenge global capitalism in creative ways. It promotes either a response of managing the system without modifying its trajectory, or of preparing a revolutionary movement, or of waiting passively for it to burst into flames of its own accord. That is, to translate a world-capitalist system into a world totality is to misread what is outside it, to miss those things imperfectly incorporated into it, and to present an apolitical orientation to it.

Wallerstein seems right in one crucial respect: capitalism is never simply internal to a single state, or after its early rise, to a small number of states. Rather, individual states, world markets, and a hegemonic state forge relations of dependence and interdependence with each other. But Wallerstein's analysis, to my eye at least, poses at least five issues that are not engaged sufficiently. First, to what degree does the relation between regions of the world express ironclad imperatives of uneven exchange in capitalism itself and to what extent does this unevenness reflect other power advantages such states possess, such as political drives to hegemony, military advantages, alliances that support certain monetary processes, and so on? Second, what is the independent measure, if there is one, by which an existing mode of cross region exchange can be characterized as symmetrical, asymmetrical, or radically asymmetrical? Third, to what extent and in what ways do other regional cultural formations, particularly religious practices and spiritual dispositions, impinge upon and become infused into capitalist practices within and between regions. Fourth, why does Wallerstein deploy a rather mechanical mode of explanation for the past necessities of capitalist evolution but invoke ideas from complexity theory of fluctuating initial conditions, emergent causality, and zones of unpredictability when addressing future "bifurcations" of the system? If such concepts are applicable to late capitalism, are they not also applicable to its past? Fifth, and related to the previous point, the idea of capitalism as an interstate system from the start does pose a valuable corrective to other theories, but capitalism is now also a world system that spills over state *and* interstate containers. Its modes of production and exchange both exceed state boundaries and interstate relations, and roll back to help shape and confine them. Perhaps it has always been this way, though to a lesser degree than now. These global flows of capitalism are particularly important for the themes pursued in the last two sections of the chapter. It is not that Wallerstein ignores global flows altogether, but that the interstate dimension is weighted too heavily in relation to them.

To introduce these uncertainties into capitalism is to say that it is neither a self-sufficient system nor always able to absorb, on pre-established terms, several dimensions of the outside that it faces. Wallerstein's quest to purge *Geist* from his neo- or left-Hegelian theory—a difficult and important effort —carries with it a corollary need to articulate the specific shape of expressive practices embedded in contemporary capitalist institutions. This suggests that capitalism, in a way that both recalls and exceeds Hegel, faces an outside that is irreducible to *Geist*. On such a reading, Hegel's introduction of a divinized *Geist* provided a strange marker for the multiple forces that impinge upon capital from the inside and outside simultaneously.

Despite these doubts, questions, and reservations, it seems wise to carry forward three features of Wallerstein's account: that capitalism is an interstate system from the start, that its history is marked by asymmetrical modes of exchange within and between regions, and that a hegemonic capitalist state often emerges to help "manage" cross-region relations. We now need to pick up another element to prepare the explorations in the last two sections of this chapter: the shifting role that sovereignty plays in the state as the interstate and global dimensions of capitalism expand.

The Changing Face of Sovereignty

As capitalism morphs and expands, the practices of sovereignty shift too. To chart these shifts it is pertinent to recall that the idea of state sovereignty itself is ambiguous. In this respect it tracks the ambiguity of divine sovereignty in Christianity. Sometimes sovereignty is approached as a legitimate mode of final decision or rule, and sometimes it is seen as an irresistible exercise of power, an exercise that either ignores legitimacy or produces it through the fact of its action. This ambiguity is lodged in the histories of Christian theology and state sovereignty. These two tendencies of sovereignty, as legitimate decision procedure and as irresistible power structure, historically have shifted back and forth as they compete for primacy. Moreover, the more you examine the actual practice of state sovereignty, the more it becomes apparent how its sites of action shift and slide with changes in events. Sometimes the positional sovereignty of an official authority prevails, as when the Gang of Five Republican Supreme Court Justices handed a contested election to George Bush in 2000 by stopping Florida's recount of the votes. The fact that this decision encountered little resistance by those citizens who give priority to counting all the votes allowed sovereignty as positional authority to rule the day. At other times positional sovereignty can be overturned by the irresistible power of official or rogue elements, as when President Jackson and white vigilantes effectively overturned the Supreme Court's decision to give autonomy to the Cherokee in the southeastern United States in the early nineteenth century, as when George W. Bush overruled, through the use of signing statements, specific dictates of the legislation he signed into law, as when NATO effectively overturned otherwise sovereign decisions in Bosnia, as when Hitler's brownshirts brought down an elected government. Sovereignty is an essentially ambiguous and shifting practice, despite what some theorists say about it.[7]

Hegel evinces appreciation of the complexity of sovereignty during the time of capitalism. You can detect in his work a distinction between the *expressive* and *decisional* elements of sovereignty. The monarch is the decisional sovereign, in his system, but when relations between civil society and the state are in order, the scope of sovereign decision is small. The monarch merely dots the i's and crosses the t's of issues relayed to him. More fundamental is the expressive dimension of sovereignty, which consists of pervasive tendencies and pressures that, because they are embedded within and between the state, markets, family, church, occupational organizations, and civil servants, set both the larger conscious context of decision and the unconscious background of the thinkable and tolerable. The expressive dimension limits the decisions of the sovereign by promoting an irresistible context in which decisions are considered. The expressive dimension of sovereignty is both institutionally embedded and further animated by the emergent power of *Geist*. The integrity of the family is protected; the market retains self-regulating powers; the estates are honored; civil servants are heeded; and colonization is pursued. These effects are primarily the result of accumulated cultural forces which converge to create a higher balance between interacting institutions than would otherwise be available. Expressive sovereignty infuses rationality into institutional relations. Institutional interconnections, expressive sovereignty, sovereign decisions, and *Geist* fold and loop into each other. In one of Hegel's favorite terms, they "interpenetrate," signaling how deeply Hegel feels the insufficiency of any analysis couched in external causes between otherwise separate units.

As in the first section on civil society, I seek to preserve Hegel's insights about the importance of interpenetration and expressive sovereignty. I abandon the faith, however, that what is expressed always conduces to the welfare of the state and interstate capitalist system, either immediately or over the long term. In the long term we are all dead. Expressive sovereignty, on this reading, flows from converging institutional pressures into sovereign decisions. This mode of sovereignty sets the background for market performance and sovereign *decisions* as it supports specific terms of exchange, the preliminary definition of friends and enemies, the shape of state-nonstate relations, the place of religion in public life, the role of the family in ethical life, and so forth. It is *not*, however, expressive in the sense that it automatically exudes a higher rationality. A state composed of military, capitalist, and religious fanatics, mutually inflaming one another, can be expressive, dangerous to others, and self-destructive at the same time. That which is expressive, in the sense used here, could support the future of capitalism or produce practices that cause the collapse of the world system. It could decrease asymmetrical exchanges with other regions, even though we cannot say in advance precisely how far the systemic limits of capitalism would allow that to occur. It could respond positively to the veritable minoritization of the world taking place before our very eyes. It could work to turn back the effects that interstate capitalism has had on global warming, even to the point of evolving into a system that is post-capitalist. But it can also point in the opposite direction on each count, toward modes of investment and consumption that intensify climate warming and resource depletion, toward asymmetrical modes of regional exchange that inflame resentments by those on the wrong side of these equations, toward bellicose military policies to preserve regional advantages, toward pronouncements of Christian or civilizational superiority that further activate resentments, and so on. Expressive sovereignty is a powerful force operating within and across institutions: its connection to worldly wisdom, however, is to be assessed rather than presupposed.

Another distinction is pertinent here. The relation between expressive and decisional sovereignty is subtended by that between external and internal sovereignty. The first speaks to internal sovereignty over a territorial populace. The second speaks to relations between states in which most states are semi-sovereign and a few possess greater leeway both in its internal actions and its sway over other states and regions. That is to say, there is always an outside to state sovereignty, an outside that, as we shall see, includes and exceeds the constraints posed by other states and interstate relations.

One defining feature of contemporary life is the way the globalization of capital squeezes the relative autonomy of states and interstate organizations. A common territorial reaction to this squeezing operation is to expand and intensify internal disciplines, to strive to bring sections of the populace more fully in line with these pressures. Under these conditions the expressive dimension of sovereignty morphs into the micropolitics of discipline and other modes of impersonal governance. Michel Foucault and Gilles Deleuze began to chart this metamorphosis a few decades ago. Foucault shows how disciplinary supplements to sovereign decisions are now supplemented by new modes of "governmentality" designed to regulate the probable behavior of large populations rather than to place delinquents in enclosed sites of control.[8] Deleuze builds upon this idea, speaking of how both sovereign decisions and disciplinary institutions are increasingly supplemented by systems of "control."[9] A system of "control," I want to say, often takes the form of a resonance machine. In present-day America, the evangelical-capitalist resonance machine discourages numerous orientations to markets, faith, media pronouncements, foreign policy, and styles of living by pushing a bellicose spirituality into several institutions and encouraging those institutions to resonate together. Like the modes of governmentality Foucault describes, this resonance machine helps to distribute the movement and behavior of large populations more than it compels individuals by law to obey or threatens them with confinement. Both governmentality and control speak to the expressive dimension of sovereignty articulated by Hegel, but they carry it in new directions through additional mechanisms he did not imagine.

I call these processes "channeling apparatuses" to play up how they focus on aggregates more than individuals, move aggregate spiritualities and behavior in some directions rather than others, work often behind the backs of those moved by them, depend upon advanced technologies of publicity, affect modulation, and surveillance, and most pertinently are replete with potential lines of escape, counter-strategies of response, and periodic processes of redirection. A tax strategy, for instance, may be designed to shift aggregate behavior, while it also opens unforeseen loopholes through which it is defeated. The prominence of the SUV in several states emerged from one such loophole, created by the differential regulations given to cars and trucks with respect to mileage standards, emission requirements, and safety standards: call the SUV a truck and you win the game. Or, an evangelical-capital market strategy might eventually erupt into a crisis, creating an angry mass of previously duped retirees, workers, investors, consumers, and taxpayers.

As the global dimension of capital expands, as conflicts between hegemonic states and regions outside (current) core states escalate, and as interregional religious conflicts intensify, corollary processes emerge to tighten the decisional, disciplinary, and channeling modes of state sovereignty. The fact that the United States has the largest prison population in the world provides one index of this tendency. State channeling also grows, including passport rules and tracking, Internet sweeps, street surveillance practices, phone tapping, the creation of rumors to regulate conduct, embedded reporters, retired military media "analysts" paid by the Pentagon to support its wars, systemic links between think tanks and the media, drug sweeps, state decisions that shape the infrastructure of consumption to favor one set of consumption choices, and so on almost endlessly. The expressive dimension of sovereignty today devolves increasingly into disciplinary and channeling networks bolstered by a bellicose religious ethos. And part of the decisional dimension is farmed out to entities that subsist in a shadow zone between sovereign power and the institutions of civil society. As I mentioned, these entities include think tanks, outsourced military forces, retired military generals, embedded reporters, private intelligence agencies, security airport personnel, passport offices, and so forth. Watch out. You are being observed, managed, regulated, infused, channeled, and disciplined from multiple sites.

A Global Resonance Machine

We now are in a position to explore an emergent formation that draws on aspects of several of these elements to forge a larger global network of antagonistic forces. To explore this formation, it is necessary to introduce one more concept, with apologies to Deleuze and Felix Guattari. As I use the idea, an "abstract machine" is a cluster of energized elements of multiple types that enter into loose, re-enforcing conjugations as the whole complex both consolidates and continues to morph. It is an abstract *machine* rather than a mechanism or stable configuration because of the element of instability between its interacting elements, its tendency to move fast, and its periodic capacity to morph. It is *abstract* in that the organization of the moving assemblage is not shaped or governed by a guiding authority. The elements in such a mobile machine impinge upon one another to some degree, infiltrate each other to an extent, and also exceed both relationships in generating loose energies that might be colonized in new ways. An abstract machine involves extensive self-organization among disparate elements, and it sometimes evolves or morphs beyond itself. An abstract machine is a species of what we have called a force-field: it is, however, one in which the flow has accelerated, resonances have intensified, and the capacity to morph is sometimes heightened.

A lava flow constitutes a simple abstract machine: the flow of molten lava, the melted rocks of different types carried by it, the uneven terrain over which it flows, the differential cooling rates of each type of rock when the lava meets water and open air. Each lava flow congeals into a granite formation, the pattern of which is not predictable in advance. Similarly, warm water in the Caribbean, a wide expanse of sea, and fluctuating winds can coalesce into the abstract machine of a hurricane. At a certain tipping point the heterogeneous elements enter into a spiral of self-amplification, creating a hurricane whose exact direction and intensity can baffle the humans tracking it.

Finally, the dynamic assemblage between a species, a gene pool, a rapid shift in milieu, and the entry of new predators can also compose an abstract machine. Once underway, a new machine can accelerate the pace of species evolution. As far as I can tell, evolutionary biologists are unable to predict with confidence when the next species will emerge and what shape it will assume, once some of these elements change. As a general rule, say the authors of this concept, "an assemblage is all the closer to an abstract machine the more lines without contour passing between things it has and the more it enjoys the powers of metamorphosis."[10] A further example is the abstract machine of climate change and capitalist development, with each force-field becoming an element in the larger machine formed by their confluence.

An abstract machine is composed of multiple elements, some of which were hanging loose before its formation, others of which may have been part of a machine that has since dissolved or been overwhelmed, yet others that are given shape by the emergence of the machine itself. No central agent has designed it and none controls it, though multiple and minor modes of control do circulate through it. The machine's rate of movement is relatively fast (a lava flow but not a congealed slab of granite). It periodically enters into new conjunctions with other such machines. Its partial congealment contains an uncertain degree of pluri-potentiality, and it generates patterns of behavior with a degree of unpredictability. Once a machine gets rolling, it is "abstract" because of its self-amplifying character, because its dynamism exceeds the control of humans entangled in it, and because it is susceptible to changes through the interplay between new infusions from outside and responses by extant elements. An abstract machine in which the human estate figures prominently is irreducible to machines entirely outside the human estate. The former introduce complex relations of agency, alliance, affect, and so on somewhat less discernible in the latter. Nevertheless it may be useful to see that abstract machines are formed in the nonhuman estate, the human estate, and, particularly, human-nonhuman relational processes.

Economic markets form only one such type of machine in a larger world composed of numerous interacting and often interpenetrating machines. A market's shifting inter-involvements with abstract machines of different sorts, each itself passing through periods of equilibrium and disequilibrium, suggests how magical the neoliberal story of markets with extreme powers of self-equilibration is. For this machine or open system both generates internal strains and fractures that can accumulate to promote an abrupt shift and enters into numerous, shifting intersections with other machines of multiple types. Neoliberal economic theory, in fact, is most at home with itself when it presupposes a rather fixed conception of nature that capitalism can master with little blowback from the force-fields composing it. As the example of Alan Greenspan, the long-term head of the Federal Reserve, indicates, this feature of neoliberal theory provides the impetus for a political alliance between neoliberals, wary of global warming because of how severely it would upset the assumptions of their model, and the evangelical right, which opposes the theory of human-induced climate change because it would upset their faith that only God can intervene so radically in nature.[11]

Consider the global market in derivatives that grew at an explosive rate between 1973 and 2008. It eventually came to provide speculators with trillions of dollars to make rapid hedge bets on interest rates, mortgages, and exchange-rate differentials, often taking advantage of the slower processes governing states, retirement funds, international organizations, and traditional banks. Its bets focus on these domains more than traditional futures and options tied to hogs, wheat, oil, and corn. Its recent explosion depended upon uneven regional exchanges and speeds, lightning fast instruments of global exchange, expansion of the class of speculators, ideological success within and between states to stifle market regulation, and boosting by international agencies. Once this machine became organized it tested the capacities of regulation by any hegemonic state or international organization. Most agents in it believe that they can quantify and assess comparative risk probabilities, but the rapid assumptions they must make about regime stability, natural processes, resource bases, and the transparency of other participants means that the system is highly volatile and filled with objective uncertainties. The turbulent character of this global system has helped to destabilize the economies of several countries, including Thailand, Turkey, and Brazil by withdrawing currency support at key moments. It has more recently played a major role in the world economic crisis, sparked by the United States. The pace, scope, and opacity of the derivative machine created its potential to cascade rapidly once a few precipitating changes were triggered.

Ideological assumptions combine with market uncertainties and differentials in the speed at which different classes of investors can act to produce the rapid expansion of a world speculative class and to introduce much suffering and violence into the world, in both hegemonic and nonhegemonic regions. "High-frequency trading," for instance, introduces a new class difference into investing, whereby slow institutional investors provide the base for high-frequency traders who work at speeds faster than a second, exploiting those of slower speed as they take risks that could bring everything down. The recipients of such adverse effects cannot easily locate traditional institutions to hold accountable for them. It is difficult to rebel against such a worldwide, dispersed machine after it has been consolidated.[12] Many recipients of this impersonal suffering and loss, then, are ripe candidates to seek new outlets for accumulated energies of resentment.

It is tempting to study this machine further, and I hope to do so at another time. Now, however, I am most interested in the emergence of another global machine connected to this one, as it gathers additional sovereign and spiritual energies into its fold. It might be called a Resonance Machine of Global Antagonism. In this (nearly) global machine, dissonant forces, drawing upon competitive practices of sovereignty, resentments tied to uneven exchange, speculative practices beyond the reach of those affected, and a regional division of dominant religious institutions become condensed into a global resonance machine of cross-regional antagonism. The suffering, anger, and resentments Hegel identified in the lower reaches of state civil society are now distributed selectively within and across regions. These reactions activate significant minorities in different regions, helping to draw them into an abstract machine that exceeds the elements from which it is drawn. Each expression of revenge on one site activates and amplifies those on the others.

Since the close of the Cold War, this global antagonism machine has been consolidated. The elements from which it was formed include loose energies of resistance released by the close of the Cold War, a world divided roughly into regionally based religions with significant internal minorities, uneven economic exchange between regions that correlate approximately with a distribution of religious differences, extreme dependence by hegemonic states upon foreign oil supplies, the rise of a world derivatives system that places the fate of numerous states in its hands while increasing the difficulty of identifying accountable agents responsible for that fate, the accentuated role of mass media in most regions, the hubris of many capitalist elites and dominant states about their ability to control the world, and simmering resentments felt by many on different sites in this machine about the place of mortality and time in the human condition. The hubris, resentments, tensions, and injustices accumulated from multiple sources condense into a global machine of revenge and counter-revenge. The elements in the machine do not exhaust all the spaces and actions they occupy, rather, they form a significant aspect of them, in the way that participants in a single state can be divided by class without the class composition exhausting everything about them or that order.

I call this a global *resonance* machine because the interplay between its elements amplifies global antagonisms in a way that both touches and exceeds the capacities of state and market processes. This global resonance machine does not correspond to the world characterized by Samuel Huntington in *The Clash of Civilizations*.[13] He speaks of two territorial civilizations involved in an escalating set of conflicts that sharpen territorial boundaries, while I speak of practices that exceed these civilizational boundaries and of estranged minorities within and across them. Each antagonistic party in this global machine periodically takes action that inflames the others.

Huntington, in fact, is a warrior on one side of the machine. I track its operation from the perspective of one whose care for those caught in the machine's vortex softens and informs the initial identifications from which I start. Knowing how you are already primed to identify with those closest to you, it is wise to complicate those identifications enough to participate in efforts to tame the larger machine that works to dogmatize and militarize them. "They resent our freedom," one bellicose minority says; "they hate our piety," another intones. On this point, I agree with Talal Asad, who sees significant clashes within both Islamic and Euro-American regions, with some factions in each contributing passion to a machine destructive to both.[14]

This global amplification machine, organized in the interstices of regional markets, religious energies, and sovereign practices, exposes one way in which there is an outside to both decisional sovereignty and markets, an outside that both draws upon these forces and turns back on them to twist them in new ways. It lifts, as it were, the expressive dimension charted by Hegel to a global level, showing us again that the expressive dimension can be both real and sometimes profoundly destructive in shape. Other dimensions of the outside, such as climate change, resource availability, rapid disease transmission, and unruly forces too protean to identify before their effects crystallize, will not be engaged so closely here, though they are pertinent too.

The elements of uneven exchange, uneven resource dependence, existential resentment, creedal division, derivatives, media insurgency, and sovereign modulations spawn popular resentments susceptible to intensification through creative acts: global market priorities that create new modes of suffering and weaken specific regions, suicide bombings that intensify resentments, provocative declarations about the inferiority of this or that creed, media demonstrations, new territorial claims, rogue settlements in occupied territories, tactical defilement of sacred sites, provocative cartoons, nuclear proliferation, the construction of new territorial walls, collective rapes, preemptive wars, sovereign bombing campaigns, state torture, and so on exacerbate a world antagonism machine already in place, propelling it in directions that sometimes surprise the parties involved. This combination of systemic characteristics and singular acts escalates collective drives to abstract revenge on both sides. Responses that depend solely upon neoliberal market philosophy and sovereign decisions can easily inflame the machine further. Surely the invasion of Iraq strengthened support for Al Qaeda, as does the expansion of the Israeli settlements, American forays into torture, the razing of Haditha, and the introduction of the Guantanamo Gulag. All these contribute to a self-amplifying, nearly worldwide machine of antagonistic relations that exceeds the sovereign, market, and spiritual forces from which it draws much of its power. It is, you might say, the consummate anti-cosmopolitan global machine.[15]

This machine expresses and amplifies already existing resentments about human mortality, heightens the visibility of regional religious diversity, highlights different senses of regional entitlement, and reacts negatively to the veritable minoritization of many territorial state regimes taking place at a faster pace than heretofore before our very eyes. The last, ironically, is mostly a product of the global expansion of capital, uneven market shares, new strategies of border crossing, and the enhanced role that the media play in most regions. The irony is that the staunchest defenders of the mobility of capital are wary of the world minoritization it helps to foster. The media are prime catalysts of amplification here, like a hot sea lifting a tropical storm into a hurricane.

Existential resentment pours gasoline on the flames, once the fire has started. The drive to take revenge on the visibility of other faiths that exacerbates the vague sense of uncertainty you feel about your own creed is not primarily an individual or private phenomenon. This was the mistake of secularism, which pretended that faith was confined to a private realm. As contending drives to existential revenge are amplified by the machine, they soon slide back into several zones of institutional life — media practices, voting patterns, family life, military priorities, investment decisions, career aspirations, consumption demands, patriotic fervor, religious articulations, and the reverberations among these institutions. That is to say, the expressive dimension of cultural life, which Hegel sought heroically to enclose within territorial states, now flows back and forth between territorial life and a global amplification machine. Today, the expressive dimension of late-modern life spills into modes and zones beyond the Hegelian imaginary. His insight, which many secularists continue to miss, minimize, or relegate to "irrationalism," was that the expressive dimension of collective life is always with us. His mistake was the belief that a world-historical agency of *Geist* would progressively become absorbed into the world, territorial state system. In fact, the expressive dimension is irrepressible, it often exceeds state and interstate containers, and its character can be either positive or destructive, depending upon the machines through which it is organized.

It is perhaps salient to point out again how my attention to the rolling and roiling interactions between hubris and existential resentment does not carry with it a denial of the positive role that anger, resentment, indignation, and the like can and do play in politics. There is no politics without passion. It is when the trials of life / or the hubris of mastery slide into institutionally embedded drives to existential revenge that things become most dangerous. That is a risk accompanying any and every positive social movement. As we saw in chapter 3, it is also a risk that we should engage self-critically as we respond to new configurations of struggle.

This world machine houses numerous individual, constituency, state, and corporate agents. In a fast-paced world in which most territories face pressures of minoritization and many in numerous congregations ramp up their resentment of the human predicament, the machine foments regional resentments, hostilities, and struggles that flow over the practices of sovereignty and markets alike. The result is an expressive machine, composed of heterogeneous constituencies that interpenetrate and exacerbate each other.

The global resonance machine we have merely sketched could morph into a new one, just as the Cold War morphed into this one during a short phase transition. China or India could supplant current hegemonic states, introducing new pressures and priorities into the world and slicing up the machine. Resource and climate crises could generate new preemptive actions by western states or close them out of needed oil supplies and foreign credit. New social movements in Muslim countries could open alliances with selective western states. A new plague, transmitted far and wide by the rapid modes of transit that grease the world capitalist system, could dry up preemptive wars and insurgent responses. Or several of these could coalesce in a surprising way. Indeed, climate change adds a node to this amplification machine, introducing another form of uneven exchange, pressure points, and limits to capitalist expansion.

A cross-region/capital/media/spiritual machine now creates and exacerbates regional hostilities. Implacable minorities on each side periodically take action that spur those on the other to extreme responses, as both parties insert themselves in the networks of capital flows and state practices of sovereignty. No traditionally organized state, party, or interstate capitalist system effectively controls its course. No single party intended the deadly conflicts spawned by the machine. But several agents exacerbate them, as the Israeli settlements and occupation of Palestine do, as Osama bin Laden did when he attacked the Twin Towers with suicide bombers, as Bush did when he first accepted bin Laden's invitation to create a cross-regional war and then invaded Iraq, as bin Laden did again when he told Americans to vote against Bush in 2004 — knowing that would drive them to vote for the enemy he needs, as Bush, Rumsfeld, Blair, and others did when they increasingly defined a rogue minority within Islam as a general force of "Islamofascism," as suicide bombers do when they kill people in crowded restaurants, as Huntington, Glen Beck, William Bennett, Sean Hannity, and other American publicists do when they define the world in terms of fixed civilizational units that must enter into implacable struggle. And as each drive does in exacerbating the others.

What is the advantage of thinking these conflicts in terms of a mobile resonance machine that absorbs and helps to shape agents of various sorts? I am not entirely sure. But it might encourage a contraction of hubristic assumptions about how to relate to the world. And it might encourage us to think about how to intervene more creatively at more numerous points in the machine. There is, of course, no guarantee of success. That was lost when the theme of *Geist* progressively realizing itself was dissolved into expressive forces of multiple sorts with different degrees of volatility and uncertainty, when the compensatory idea of a self-sufficient world market dissolved, and when an outside to sovereignty and markets was acknowledged that sets limits to fantasies of human mastery. Familiar stories about western civilization, Christianity, Islam, capitalism, the sovereign state, and cosmopolitanism may all receive body blows if you come to terms with such a world amplification machine.

Counter Movements?

During the early stages of Christendom, dissident monks and priests formed collectives in the desert, or inserted themselves as moles into the church hierarchy, or formed new orders that pressed upon the hierarchy. Peasants could cross themselves on Sunday, work for the master, pay their tithes, and avoid the authorities at most other times. Upon the consolidation of capitalism and the modern state, revolution seemed to set one possibility of positive change, electoral takeovers another. During the 1960s and 1970s in Europe and the United States, protests and strikes took aim at both the state and several institutions of civil society. And today, in the United States at least, an evangelical-capitalist resonance machine infuses the institutions of civil society (churches, investment activity, media financial reports, families, associations, consumption practices, corporate boards, schools, etc.), as it also seeks hegemony within courts, the executive bureaucracy, and Congress.[16]

What are possible modes of positive intervention in this amplification machine? Certainly state and interstate actions could make a major difference, even though they cannot dismantle the machine alone. Concerted state and interstate pressure to regulate derivative markets, to roll back Israeli settlements, to promote a new state of Palestine (or even a larger, pluralistic Israel) would help immeasurably. So would the end of preemptive wars and the bellicose image the United States has presented to much of the world during large stretches of time. But these and other actions are also insufficient to the times. Equally important, they require significant constituency changes on the ground to make them feasible. A combination of luck, exhaustion of the most militant constituencies on each side, cultural shaming, and creative action by nonstate actors within and across states is also needed to turn the machine in a new direction. The hawkish minorities on each side must be matched and surpassed by counter-constituencies anchored in multiple sites.

Here I focus primarily on one dimension of such activity, a "triggering" force that carries Hegel's expressive dimension of sovereignty into contemporary role definitions. It is misleading to divide the political world into individuals, constituency organizations, and states. Each individual, for instance, is ensconced in a variety of roles. And each role both informs the individual and is linked to larger assemblages. The connections are relatively conscious when consumption patterns of dress, hairstyle, housing, entertainment, and car choice forge identity niches. Role specific habits of eye contact are less conscious, as in the street rules of middle class eye contact between the sexes in the United States of the 1950s. Yet those habits helped to constitute a pattern of gender relations that found expression in family life, education, dating, sports, work life, voting habits, and church practices. A role is neither reducible entirely to the individuals who inhabit it nor thoroughly assimilable to the larger assemblages that help to shape and manage it. It is the site of strategic ambiguity, periodically susceptible for that reason to creative political deployment.

To consider multiple roles in relation to this global resonance machine suggests how accumulated changes in these practices might make a contribution to turning the machine in a different direction. Certainly, a large number of preachers, imams, rabbis, writers, military leaders, talking heads, and unemployed workers introduced changes into role conduct that helped to organize the current machine. Osama bin Laden's roles as a wealthy man, investor, devotee of Islam, Saudi, and charismatic leader all underwent change when he founded Al Qaeda.

We are, variously, teachers, blue collar workers, writers, film directors, consumers, investors, faith devotees, parents, lovers, voters, Internet users, TV viewers, military veterans, charity donors, members of an age cohort, contributors to retirement funds, homeowners or renters, neighbors, models, athletes, students, advertising executives, geologists, oil drillers, and so on, endlessly. The trick today is to infuse a bit of the warrior ethic into the performance of several of these roles, not in the spirit of Napoleon, Putin, and Bush, of Gandhi, Thoreau, Nietzsche, and Martin Luther King Jr., with the inspiration and strategic sense of each adjusted to the new circumstances of being. The task is to inhabit several roles in more militant, visible, creative, and inspirational ways, as we come to terms with their cumulative effects on the world.

The accumulation of rapid shifts in role performance might introduce new pressures into the world. The goals in ascending order are: first, to induce cumulative changes in individual and group conducts that shift the center of gravity in this or that way and encourage others to do so; second, to push collective role assemblages in new directions; and third, to inspire initiatives that draw energy from activity on these first two fronts to escalate both internal and external pressures upon corporations, states, universities, churches and temples, investment firms, the media, the Internet, and international organizations.

The initial potentialities are numerous. Consumers can, as the need and opportunity arises, alter patterns of consumption with respect to food acquisition, vehicle use, housing, cuisine, clothing, and entertainment, seeking to gear each mode more closely to a near future that reduces oil dependence, improves food production, and curtails emissions, and also to inspire more active and intense support for collective modes of consumption that reduce inequality within and between regions. Investors and participants in retirement investment funds can readjust the priorities of those investments, as they also organize to demand closer state regulation of volatile markets. Congregants within churches, temples, synagogues, mosques, and madrassas can repudiate publically the most ugly pronouncements and actions taken by others in the name of their faith, to shame those who have hijacked their creed for retrograde means, and to press their own congregations to change their energy use, relations with other faiths, and relations to corporations and the state. By doing so they also help to recompose the connection between existential faith and drives to implacable revenge so prominent today. Experts in oil exploration, sustainable energy production, electrical engineering, and automobile production can experiment with new modes of transportation and energy use. Writers, TV producers, actors, bloggers, and film directors can infuse a gratitude for being more actively into their writing, films, and characters, seeking to challenge cynical existential dispositions on the Left that come perilously close to the forces they would resist. Veterans, who have experienced the horror of war up close, can relate that sense of horror to others, while publicizing nonmilitary ways to engage contemporary issues. Reporters and dissident economists can publicize microeconomic experiments in various corners of the world that could be extended, exposing investors, consumers, and producers to a larger range of possibilities than generally recognized. Teachers in schools and universities can teach students how the media work upon them daily at multiple levels of the sensorium, and how they too can acquire sophisticated media skills.

The possibilities are endless. The point of individual and group experimentation with role assignments is simultaneously to make a direct difference through our conduct, to open us to new experiences that might alter our relational sensibilities even further, to unscramble role assumptions assumed by others, to form operational connections with others from which larger political movements might be generated, and to make connections with noble role warriors in other regions and walks of life to enlarge the space and visibility of positive action. A stated change in personal or constituency *belief* is not enough since the layered embodiment of belief and the actual performance of roles are so closely bound together. *A belief is an embodied tendency to performance; concerted practices of performance help to alter or intensify beliefs; and new intensities of belief fold back into future desires, performative priorities, and potentialities of political action.* Such a spiral can produce positive as well as negative effects. For example, an accumulation of resentments against states, corporations, and consumers for their refusal to address global warming could eventually inspire a cross-regional movement to launch simultaneous general strikes in several states.

Such dramatic actions are not apt to take place unless and until the spiritual ground has been prepared and the unity of obstinate elites has been weakened. Effective role adventurism helps. It builds a reservoir of public readiness for more militant action upon and by civil society, state, and inter-state institutions. As some churches modify their behavior toward mosques, and vice versa, the door is open to form a cross-state citizen movement to modify the practices of states and international organizations. As those movements coalesce, support for the most bellicose forces on each side wanes. When those effects are consolidated, corporations, churches, states, and international organizations are placed under yet more positive pressure, or alternatively find it possible to take more risks. If and when such a ma-chine becomes organized, each pressure point begins to resonate with the others, creating a resonance machine larger than its parts.

At the early stages of such a movement, it is important to think tactically about how to proceed, so as to put effective pressure on others through example, inspiration, and shaming. The goal is to build a resonant assemblage by deploying mobile intersections between belief, role performance, desire, and action to prepare the way for more militant sit-ins, highway blockages, selective refusals of participation, and so on, as events unfold. One key to formation of vibrant cross-state citizen movements is to respond creatively to new and surprising events as they arise, drawing upon the fund of readiness built up by role adventurism to engender larger, more militant actions. Such a combination takes a leaf out of the "shock doctrine" of the neoliberal right while diverging from it in every other respect. As Naomi Klein shows, the neoliberal right has been primed for decades to use surprising events as a pretext to install a neoliberal agenda through top-down action.[17] The shock side of its economic doctrine shows how political neo-liberalism is in its essence. It pursues a neoliberal politics of elite control in the service of military bellicosity and regional inequality in the name of freeing a self-regulating economy that it pretends is waiting to emerge. Its politics is top down, war-like, and inegalitarian while its doctrine celebrates the ever receding promise of world markets that thrive most when they are least regulated. We, by contrast, must start in the middle of things and constituencies, pushing out in several directions, responding creatively to new events in a world in which no self-organizing economic system can fulfill the promises of neoliberalism, because the world is composed of mul-tiple, interacting temporal systems, with many containing capacities of self-organization and metamorphosis. Micropolitics on several fronts can render creative mass responses to new events promising because of the close inter-involvements between role performance, intensities of belief, and political action.

Is it not obligatory to expose and resist the system as such rather than taking cumulative actions to move it? Don't such actions necessarily fold back in on themselves, feeding the closed system they seek to move? Some theorists on the Left say such things, but they themselves have too closed a view of the systems they criticize. No system in a world of becoming composed of multiple, interacting systems of different types, with different capacities of self-organization, is entirely closed. It is both more vulnerable to the outside than the carriers of hubris imagine and periodically susceptible to creative movement from within and without simultaneously. Moreover, pure negativity on the Left does not sustain either critique or militancy for long, but rather, it tends eventually to lapse into resignation or to slide toward the authoritarian practices of the Right that already express with glee the moods of negativity, hubris, or existential revenge. We have witnessed numerous examples of such disappointing transitions in the last several decades, when a negative or authoritarian mood is retained while the creed in which it was set is changed dramatically. We must therefore work on mood, belief, desire, and action together. As we do so we also amplify positive attachment to existence itself amidst the specific political resentments that help to spur us on. To ignore the existential dimension of politics is to increase the risks of converting a noble movement into an authoritarian one and to amplify the power of bellicose movements that mobilize destructive potential. To focus on the negative dimension alone is to abjure the responsibilities of political action during a dangerous time.

To review, none of the role interventions listed above nor all in concert could *suffice* to break such a global resonance machine. Luck and pregnant points of contact with salutary changes in state actions, other cross-state citizen movements, the policies of international organizations, creative market innovations, and religious organization are needed. But those larger constellations may not themselves move far in a positive direction unless they meet multiple constituencies primed to join them and geared to press them whenever they lapse into inertia. If a world resonance machine of revenge and counter-revenge stretches, twists, and constrains the classical image of sovereign units, regionally anchored creeds, uneven capitalist exchange, and international organizations, while drawing selective sustenance from all of them, a new counter-machine must do so too.

CHAPTER SIX

The Theorist and the Seer

If we live in a world of becoming, what difference does that make to the vocation of political theory? The conception of time in which my question is posed is not, of course, accepted by many scientists, philosophers, theorists, and citizens. Many adopt a punctual, linear conception of secular time most at home with itself in conjunction with an observational image of inquiry, an efficient concept of causality, a notion of probable progress, and a vision of the theorist as an autonomous agent who stands outside the world to be explained and judged. The latter idea of scientific autonomy assumes that the investigator has special standing as an "anthropic exception" above or outside the regularities governing nature, that does not need to be explained. This exception can be defended further via a Kantian distinction between the necessary shape of human understanding of the world and the unfathomable character of human freedom, or through some other compatibilist doctrine. Defenders of a linear, progressive conception of time also say that to be an agent of moral responsibility is to presuppose the possibility of moral progress in history. And since the kernel of a moral point of view is installed deeply in us, we must act "as if" time is progressive. It is our duty to do so, as Kant would say, even if empirical history often points in other directions.[1]

The question that guides this chapter will not command attention from those who find moral and linear conceptions of time utterly compelling. What about those in the hermeneutic tradition who often fold a soft notion of divine purpose into time? Some may find the thesis pursued here pertinent and may be sympathetic up to a point, for there is a partial connection between the image of time embraced here and that in which hermeneutics is often embedded. The point now, however, is to articulate a world of becoming sufficiently to clarify the parameters within which my exploration of the role of the theorist is set.

By time as becoming, I mean a bumpy, twisting flow reducible to neither linear causality nor providential design. With respect to a world of becoming, the universe itself is marked by an uncertain degree of openness. The bumpiness of time in an open universe is accentuated by the fact that several force-fields or tiers of chrono-time subsist — time measured by a clock. There is geological time, evolutionary time, neuronal time, civilizational time, the time of a specific state regime, the time of a human life, the time of a type of economic organization, and so on almost endlessly. As Alfred North Whitehead puts it in an admirable passage, "We shall find that there are in nature competing serial time-systems derived from different families of durations."[2] A temporal force-field previously setting the background or source of sustenance for another field may erupt or gradually become altered, introducing new pressures into a previously stabilized zone. The difference between the dictates of an old set of gods and a new set, heretofore co-existing uneasily together in the same time and place, might suddenly collide dramatically in the face of a new event to which they apply incompatible imperatives. A flock of geese, following one trajectory, might collide with a plane set on another, creating havoc for both the birds and humans. The intersections between an international trade in exotic animals and plants, owners disposing of unwanted pets in fertile areas, a tightly coiled hurricane in southern Florida, the particular climatic conditions in Florida, and the release of baby Burmese pythons in the Everglades by the hurricane, can eventually spark the northern march of thousands of pythons, potentially stretching north to Virginia and west to Texas. The cosmic forces of gravity and sun, in conjunction with a lifelong diet of red meat and bad air, might imperceptibly pull on the organs of patriarchs, until they eventually present a tired and wrinkled appearance to the young; one day a few go too far in punishing young critics, creating a local resistance that spreads like wildfire throughout the regime. Here, as in some of the other cases, an intersection between fields of different types triggers self-inflating tendencies in one or more of them, adding another force to the emergent condition.

And things can get more complicated. A new social movement in support of physician-assisted suicide, challenging the sense that a complete list of human rights has already been collected or "implied" in accepted principles, might itself face a surprising upsurge of religious feeling against voluntarily ending human life under any circumstances. And both of those constituencies might encounter new developments in medical technology set on a third tier of chrono-time, throwing them for another loop. The juxtaposition of the social movement, the religious response, and the medical technology may set a new resonance machine into motion. The participants in that spiral, in turn, may encounter a surge in global warming, itself the product of imbrications between climate change and the intensification of capitalism.

It is pertinent to see that in a world of becoming this or that force-field can go through a long period of relative equilibrium, or even gradual progression as defined by standards extrapolated from that equilibrium. Much of social thought and political theory takes such periods as the base from which to define time and progress themselves, making the practitioners all the more disoriented when a surprising turn occurs, that is, when a period of intense disequilibrium issues in a new plateau that scrambles the old sense of progress and regress in this or that way. There may be long chrono-periods of relative stabilization in several zones that matter to human participants, but during a time of accelerated disequilibrium the ethico-politics of judgment through extrapolation from the recent past to the medium or distant future becomes rattled or breaks down. It is now time to modify old extrapolations of possibility and desirability. During such periods Kantian and neo-Kantian ideas of the universal are retrospectively shown to have been filled with more material from a historically specific mode of common sense than their carriers had imagined. The Augustinian-Kantian sense that human beings are unique agents in the world, while the rest of the world must be comprehended through non-agentic patterns of causality, may turn out to be one of them. To the extent this idea takes hold, established notions of the human science and morality become ripe candidates for reconstitution.

What about affect in a world of becoming? Affective pressures travel from a variety of human and nonhuman sources — sunlight, electrical shocks, insulting statements, magnetic fields, a raging sea, inspirational actions, and so on — into the human sensorium. The latter affective states then become organized into feelings and higher emotions. Affect, in its most elementary human mode, is an electrical-chemical charge that jolts or nudges you toward positive or negative action before it reaches the threshold of feeling or awareness. Its action invoking pressure arrives before it takes the shape of culturally infused feelings, emotions, or moods. The affective charge, consisting of vibrations running through different parts of the nervous system, provides the initial, fast, subliminal response to something arriving from the outside. A painting of glistening sunflowers by Van Gogh, sunlight bathing the body, an unexpected caress, a screeching sound, a pungent smell, a dancing body in motion, a bolt of lightning — all these affect the sensorium before being organized by it into conscious perceptions, feelings, and reactions. The organization, indeed, results from a set of resonances between the new vibrations and sensorial habits already there, unless the affect overwhelms those habits. Affectively imbued action is underway even before a perception crystallizes. As when a driver is jolted into making a sharp turn even before a visual image is formed or a conscious feeling of danger arises. The thud in the stomach in this case follows the reflex action rather than preceding it because the formation of visual *information* moves faster than that of a visual *image*. That is why the apparent oxymoron of "blindsight" is possible for those who have lost the ability to form an image but retained the ability to receive visual information. Or take a youngster who lifts her finger from a hot stove even before feeling pain. These are instances of the half-second delay between an affective trigger to action and the conscious feeling that arrives later.

To say this is not to say that the force of affect prior to feeling is only genetically determined, while culturally organized feeling refines or represses these genetic determinants in this way or that. It means, rather, that affect itself receives a degree of cultural encoding and organization, as when cultural skills of baby chimps are encoded below conscious awareness, making a difference to their conduct; or the visceral memory of notes in a musical composition is retained so that a pianist plays the piece faster and more rhythmically than conscious control would allow; or, on another register, when the young Oedipus felt a strange premonition sweep over him at odds with his official conception of himself and his world, a premonition lodged in that fecund zone of indiscernibility between affective charge and interpreted feeling — too vague to be understood, too intense to be ignored.

Affect consists of relatively mobile energies with powers that flow into conscious, cultural feeling and emotion; yet these affective energies also exceed the formations they help to foment. Affect has an element of wildness in it. The human being thus absorbs pressures from the world that both help to compose its subjectivity and exceed it. There is no transcendental subject, but rather an emergent, layered subject. Emotion with no affect would be dead, merely a pile of words as empty containers; emotion and mood filled with affect often brim over with energy-potentials that exceed ready-made articulations. The outside, affect, and the politics of becoming are thus interinvolved. Seers make more of such a network of inter-involvements than most of us do.

To gather these preliminary points together, the idea of time as becoming involves at least three assumptions: first, the existence of multiple zones of becoming, each of which has at least some degree of openness; second, periodic encounters, not always predictable, between processes set on one tier of chrono-time and those on others, creating mergers, collisions, or potential for new vectors of development; third, an uncertain degree of pluri-potentiality inhabiting several such temporal tiers, so that a new encounter between two or more could trigger a new capacity of *self-organization* in one, propelling it in directions that exceed the external pressure, its previous mode of organization, and a simple combination of them. One example of self-organization is the creative moment at the inception of biological evolution when DNA, springing loose from its cellular host, swam to another cell, inciting a *creative response* that resulted in the first nucleated cell, the kind of cell from which the quirky path of biological evolution then proceeded.[3]

A Blind Seer

My objective, again, is less to defend such an image of affect and time now, and more to ask how political thinking might proceed if and when it is accepted.[4] What skills do those who embrace such an image need to cultivate? Why are they important? What relation, if any, is there between the vocation of political theory so defined and the activities of the seer, lodged in legend, several religious traditions, tragic dramas, and modern films? Do the two stand in productive tension or can they be harmonized into one? What is a seer, anyway? If the answers to these questions affect the activities of thinkers, theorists, and philosophers they may also add another consideration in favor of the notion of time in which the reflections are set, increasing its eligibility for possible acceptance. So the agenda is to think about the seer and to allow the insights gleaned to be carried over into the task of theory in a world of becoming.

Tiresias played a prominent role in two of the Oedipal tragedies of Sophocles. Through earlier encounters with snakes mating, according to one version of the Greek legend, he had first lost his male sex and become a female and then he reverted back to the male sex. When Hera and Zeus — themselves both sister/brother and man/wife — quarreled over which gender took the most pleasure in sex, they consulted Tiresias. He asserted that the woman receives nine parts of pleasure to the man's one. Hera, enraged, struck him blind for revealing the secret of her sex. Zeus took pity on Tiresias and endowed him with the powers of prophecy. According to some versions, Tiresias now mixed the powers of man and woman together, folding the sensitivity of a woman into the prowess of a man. S/he became a blind seer, renowned in legend, feared by rulers, and yet consulted by them at critical junctures.[5]

Consider a moment in *Antigone*. The situation has reached a critical moment. Antigone, herself the product of unintentional incest between Oedipus and Jocasta, has tried to bury her brother/uncle who had launched an attack on his own city over which he claimed to be the rightful ruler as the son/brother of Oedipus. She does so, she says, to obey an edict from the gods as immemorial as time that you must not allow a relative to die unburied. Creon has ordered her executed for disobeying his edict to leave enemies who attack the city unburied, supporting his edict by reference to the demands of city integrity and commands by another, newer set of gods. Haemon, betrothed to Antigone and son of Creon, has tried to coax his father to reverse course, showing us by his counsel that some humans in Greek tragedy can simultaneously sense an emerging crisis compounded by external and internal events and counsel creative negotiation to reshape or soften its terms. After being accused by his father of being too womanly, in stark contrast to Antigone whom Creon finds to be too manly, Haemon departs in a fury to meet his betrothed.

At this point, a young boy leads the blind Tiresias into the town square. Creon welcomes Tiresias as s/he enters the square. Called upon to speak, Tiresias says, "Then beware, you're standing once again upon the razor's edge." The pace of events has accelerated, as they do at pivotal moments in most Sophoclean plays, and an appropriate response to the new danger will now require flexibility on the part of the ruler and a willingness to act with due speed. The vicissitudes of pace and timing are critical to a seer. Put another way, a seer sees how crucial shifts in the pace of events and the timing of responses are to the world, while heroes and rulers invested with the hubris of consummate agency often fail to appreciate how they can become pawns of time, particularly when they lose sight of its shifting speeds and awesome power.

Creon's prompt obedience to the seer's warning—his rapid reversal of course—might avoid a tragic outcome otherwise in the offing, a possibility to be noted by those who interpret Greek tragedy entirely through the lens of hubris and an implacable fate set before the action starts. A delay, however, will be as disastrous as a refusal, a fact that calls us to heed the delicate relation between timing and fate. How does Tiresias see this? Here is what he says:

I'll read the signs and make them plain.
I was sitting by my ancient chair of augury, the haunt of every kind of
   bird,
When suddenly a noise not heard before assaults my ears:
A panic screeching and a pandemonium deafening jargon:
beaks and bloody talons tearing . . . , all shocked me as a portent . . .
See it — how the city sickens, Creon,
these the symptoms, yours the fanatic will that caused them . . .
Think, son, think!
Give death his due, and do not kick a corpse . . .
Believe me, I advise you well.
It should be easy to accept advice
so sweetly tuned to your good use.[6]

"When suddenly a noise not heard before assaulted my ears." The blind, an-
drogynous old codger encounters a new situation unimagined in advance; he
responds by reading omens from birds. He dwells in signs at a critical moment to issue a warning to a sovereign overly impressed by his own powers
and insight. The ruler promptly ridicules both the seer he had so recently
complimented as wise and the world of signs the seer invokes. He refuses the
advice. Here is Tiresias's reply as he feels a surge of rage rise up in him:

All right then! Take it if you can.
A corpse for a corpse the price, and flesh for flesh,
one of your own begotten.
The sun shall not run his course for many days
before you pay.
You plunged a child of light into the dark;
entombed the living with the dead; the dead
Dismissed unmourned, denied a grave — a corpse
Unhallowed and defeated of his destiny below.
Where neither you nor gods must meddle,
you have thrust your thumbs.
Do not be surprised that heaven — yes and hell —
have set the Furies loose to lie in wait for you,
Ready with the punishments you engineered for others.[7]

The vengefulness that infuses this prophecy reflects the seer's rage at Creon's
refusal to listen and adapt quickly at a critical fork in time. There was,
according to the seer, a crack through which resolute commitment to re-

negotiate the impasse between Creon and Antigone could save the ruler and the city, if only Creon acted in a wise, timely way. After that moment, things will be locked in place so that each turn taken tightens the noose. The tragic result is engineered in part by the brother's decision to make war against a city previously ruled by his father/brother, in part by the interplay between Creon and Antigone as each obeys an antagonistic principle ordained by a different set of gods, in part by a stubborn disposition installed in both, in part by a conflict already simmering in the city between an old set of Titan gods and a newer set of Olympian gods, in part by the wavering back and forth of the chorus, in part, perhaps, by Antigone's magnification of loyalty to her deceased brother/uncle because they are products of incest as well as siblings, in part by the persisting sense in the city that incest is a pollutant that must be purged, and in part by the (contingent?) *timing* of several of these actions and events. Haemon arrives too late to try to persuade Antigone; the seer arrives rather late himself; and Creon repents only after he and the others have set a fateful course of action into motion. The tragic denouement produces a definitive result from accumulating actions and statements marked by an acceleration of pace and filled with enough double meanings and apparent uncertainties to make an adamant postmodernist blush. The result shows how the themes of contingency and preordained fate can slide toward each other: the first setting a variety of opposed events and priorities into conflict amidst double meanings that exceed the grasp of the participants; the second emerging from the way those intentional meanings and purposive actions converge on a result preordained in advance. My sense is that Sophocles plays out this debate between a tragic denouement attributed to preordained fate and a concatenation of contingent events, hubris, and timing that only eventually congeal as fate, though I cannot prove this. Perhaps it is better to say that I receive *Antigone* as a dramatization of this debate.

Though the onto-theological context differs significantly, the scenario may find an eerie echo in that fateful moment when George W. Bush decided to invade Iraq and a large minority in the U.S. and many elsewhere warned him to reverse course before it was too late; or to the collision between early warnings by scientists about the dangers of global warming and the angry response by millions whose identities are tied to investment, work, and consumption habits at odds with those warnings. A world marked by multiple gods who do not place human welfare high on their list bears an uncanny affinity to a world of becoming composed of multiple, open force-fields of numerous types. The openness of any particular system in a world of becoming does not mean that an escape clause is *always* available: a city can die, a species can be overwhelmed, a civilization can go under. Openness and multiplicity in a universe without overarching providence promote vulnerability and creative possibility alike. This is why several philosophers of becoming also advance a modern variant of the tragic vision, a vision that remains open to the possibility of the worst happening through an unfortunate confluence of hubris, timing, and events.

But these murky connections across the significant distance between two eras, it will be said, are still poorly chosen. Tiresias read omens from birds as the gods spoke through them. Moderns do not have access to divinely ordained signs during periods of turbulence, unless prayer plays that role. We have empirical data and predictive power at our disposal. Climate scientists, for instance, have good reason to believe that the results of inaction will have serious effects, even though they can only predict them with degrees of probability and within a broad range of variation.

Yes and no. The seer does read omens, and that is a real difference. But the seer does so in a way that has *affinities* with how sensitive thinkers strive to read natural and cultural signs during fateful moments in modern life, when a new disequilibrium is emerging and established modes of knowledge and moral judgment may be insufficient. The risk of climate warming, remember, was posed publicly at least as early as the 1970s. When it was first announced, knowledge about it was uncertain, but early, protective action amidst that uncertainty might have warded off the worst at far less strain to the world. Today, we may see the danger more sharply, except for those whose image of divine providence makes it sinful to accept such interactions between human action and the course of nature. The question of whether protective action will be effective has *now* become more uncertain. Even in Greek tragedy, for god's sake, a moment arrives when some insightful humans see the handwriting on the wall. A few, like Haemon in *Antigone* and Jocasta in *Oedipus Rex,* sense danger over the horizon; they make recommendations that show the ability of some actors in Greek tragedy to respond creatively and flexibly to unexpected situations. Jocasta even advances the idea that chance is more important than predetermined fate, before she is driven to commit suicide. And Tiresias displays uncanny responsiveness to a surprising turn in time, whether that awareness is anchored in the omens s/he reads or expresses a cultivated sensitivity to diverse events, human powers, and foibles.[8]

Flashbacks and Premonitions

Should we, then, consider cultivating the powers of the seer in a late-modern world without gods set on diverse tiers of chrono-time? Is there a contemporary need to translate the powers of the Greek seer into our world? No one could predict the precise outcome of the Iraq invasion, but even without access to the latest "intelligence," many thoughtful people brought experience and sensitivity to bear on the situation before the invasion, reading signs, gauging potentialities in a volatile situation, sensing how immense the suffering could be, and how difficult it could become to change course once an invasion was launched. Well before the most recent economic crash several thinkers counseled caution with respect to placing too much trust in an unregulated market, even though they could not predict with certainty just when or how the danger would find expression. They had a sense of the human predicament and the dangers of overreaching, and also understood how inaction is not a real possibility at pivotal moments. They poured a degree of modesty into those models of the masterful political agent, the consummate market, and warriors of unlimited military prowess. The lesson is that you must act forward in a world replete with uncertainty, sensitive to possible ways in which old habits may be out of touch with new developments.

Let's turn to a seer in Hollywood's world of restless ambition, circulating through film plots, time obsessed directors, stunning leading ladies, and cool male actors. Consider the flashbacks in some Hollywood films, which illuminate the abyss of time and the skills of those who dwell thoughtfully in forking moments. According to Gilles Deleuze, the most compelling flashbacks do not return to a moment when a current event, character structure, or condition became unavoidable. They review forking moments, not apparent to most participants at the time. Some figures sense that they sit on the razor's edge during such moments, realizing that something fateful hangs in the balance, assessing potential turns from that moment even before the turns are complete, and seeking to nudge things in this direction rather than that. For Deleuze, in the most compelling flashbacks, "what is reported is always a skidding, a detour, a fork. But although the fork may in principle be discovered only after the event, through flashback, there is one character who has been able to foresee it, or grasp it at the time."[9]

The forking moment can shine retrospectively, *after* it has assumed the aura of precondition of the present. This is what makes a scene work as a flashback; this is why it would have been background noise — unless the music was turned up — at the time of its occurrence. At the time the moment was in play, it contained several potentialities — or half-formed trajectories of development. They are half-formed because what they actually become depends upon both their protean character and the timing and content of things that happen around them. This array of uncertain potentialities thus escapes the attention of most who participate in the moment, where a moment means a period of accelerated disequilibrium during which some elements become destabilized.

Sometimes, as Deleuze says, one figure has a premonition that others miss. I prefer Deleuze's phrase "grasp it at the time" to "foresee" to capture the sensitivity of this figure. It suggests a seer dwelling within a nest of partly formed potentialities jostling against and upon each other during a forking moment, with no potentiality settled enough to be foreseen with certainty.

Such an array is in play at a fateful moment in *All About Eve*. In the first conversation between Margo (Bette Davis), a beloved middle-aged star, and Eve (Anne Baxter), a lovely young fan who adores her so much she has followed every step of Margo's career, Eve speaks in a soft voice, with a muted note of sultriness mixed into smooth expressions of devotion. Margo's husband and everyone else at hand are impressed with Eve's sincerity, hard luck story, and care for Margo, including Margo. The men catch a whiff of sensuality in this sweet, obedient demeanor, in something like the way listeners of organ music are affected by vibrations below the level of audibility even without being able to identify the source of these effects. The tone affects listeners without being audible, and they are sometimes swept away like those listening to Eve.

The hairdresser stands out as the exception. "Birdie" (Thelma Ritter) at first hears Eve's voice from the adjoining room, receiving its resonances, intonations, and rhythms as so many signs. For one moment she becomes a blind seer. She strides abruptly into the room, staring coldly at the woman who seems to care so much for Margo even before having met her. Birdie's suspicion is aroused because she is old, has cultivated attentiveness to protean moments, has seen ambitious young things sweep middle-aged stars aside before, is sensitive to the possibility of being displaced herself, and, notably, she tuned into Eve's voice before she saw the expressions and gestures that helped to guide the other listeners' interpretation. An *absence* of one type of "evidence" in conjunction with a note in that voice turns the trick for Birdie — an interesting name in its own right. (The suspicions of the audience have been aroused already by the cynical columnist, introducing the cast and context in voice-over from a retrospective stance.)

The hairdresser is a seer, though not a Greek prophet. The way things actually turn out could deviate from her suspicion, even if she is really on to something. What if she herself carries too many disappointments into the room? Or what if a new event intervenes, such as a debilitating illness to the star, triggering a new current of thought-imbued affect in Eve that would otherwise have gone untapped? No single vector is certain in a forking moment. There is, however, a certain fecundity that some dwell within and others walk blithely past.

Birdie, the name given to a diminutive, flighty figure, does not have sufficient stature to act authoritatively upon her suspicions or to convince others to do so. Most modern seers are in a similar position with respect to key political moments and their standing. A seer by definition lives at the edge of power and events, not at the authoritative center: uncertainty and marginalization come with the territory. But this does not mean that such skills are useless or dispensable, unless there are in fact firmly tested, reliable, and replicable ways to proceed in forking, skidding moments. And there are not.

The hairdresser possesses some attributes of a modern seer. These include exquisite sensitivity to critical conjunctures *as* they unfold, dwelling in subtle signs in such forking situations, allowing layered experiences of the past — some of which may not have captured your attention at the time — to resonate as you encounter a protean moment not entirely reducible to those experiences, and a readiness to bracket one register of experience on occasion to focus on others that call for sensitive attention. To experiment with bracketing a single register of experience in favor of others, try watching Dick Cheney on television with the sound turned off.

The Nutty Professor and the Cheerleader

We need to explore further this disposition toward exquisite sensitivity to the world. It is relatively uncommon; it can be cultivated to some degree; it cannot be in play all the time if you also seek to act efficaciously; it is essential to creative thinking in a world of becoming; it can be extended to larger domains than that to which the hairdresser applies it; it limits those who cultivate this disposition unless balanced by other powers in tension with it; and it is not apt to be cultivated by those who accede too much to conventional wisdom or power, or seek always to be at the center of action.

Gilles Deleuze cultivated the powers of a seer, though this aspect of his mode of participation in a world of becoming has not been commented upon enough.[10] He thought that Jerry Lewis films could teach us something about what is involved in refined sensitivity to movements of the world. "Jerry Lewis's character," he says, "more involuted than infantile, is such that everything resonates in his head and soul . . . his smallest sketched or inhibited gestures, and the inarticulate sounds he comes out with, in turn resonate, because they set off a movement of world which goes as far as catastrophe . . . a metamorphosis of forms and mutation of sounds." Moreover, "the character places himself (involuntarily) on an energy band which carries him along and which is precisely movement of world, a new way of dancing."[11]

What do these formulations mean? The Lewis films noted by Deleuze include *It's Only Money* and *The Disorderly Orderly*. I find the traits Deleuze notes even more prominently on display, however, in *The Nutty Professor*, a 1963 film in which Lewis was both star and director. Teaching at a liberal arts college at which football players preside over the fraternity circuit and cheerleaders form the feminine brigade, assistant professor Kelp is an adult nerd devoted to teaching and his chemistry lab. He is exquisitely sensitive, however, to diverse pressures, moods, and passions that circulate through him, pressures relayed from disparate parts of himself, other people and animals, and nonliving nature. Had he stood on the outskirts of Thebes with Tiresias, who shares a few traits with him, Kelp might also have noted the frantic energies of the Sophoclean birds. He would surely note small animals that scurry around just before a storm breaks, or salt-water crocodiles who leave the Australian ocean for the marshes two or three days before a cyclone hits.

Kelp seems to feel something from every flow and force in the vicinity, even from his laboratory magpie, with whom he engages in conversation as if it were a parrot or one of the birds consulted by Tiresias. Kelp accentuates qualities that already find a coarser expression in us when we read a loyal dog as it wags its tail in a certain way or suddenly becomes poised in concentration when nothing in particular seems to be happening, or when Brazilian composers allow a cacaphony of sounds and rhythms from the rainforest to find expression in their music.

When the nutty professor walks and talks, his herky-jerky movements, blurted words, stutters and strange sounds, facial ticks, sudden shifts in expression—all these express a swarm of relatively unformed perceptions, feelings, actions, and judgments on the way. A chaotic mess of flows and counterflows, only a subset of which *could* pass through the schema of the organized subject to become well formed perceptions, judgments, and actions.

These incipient, thought-imbued tendencies are filled with pluri-potentiality before they become diverted, squelched, or crafted into this or that finished product. The eventual expression or blockage of an affect-imbued tendency is touched by other movements and responses in that half-second delay between inception and consolidation. That is why the entertaining little professor often hesitates a second too long before absorbing conventional invitations, suggestions, and cues: they all feel a bit new to him. Politicians, CEOs, economists, and media talking heads are more highly organized subjects than this goofy guy. They are well equipped to negotiate the everyday world: report the facts; be realistic; follow universal principles; order preferences rationally; give definitive interpretations; reduce findings to the context of their occurrence; stay the course; conform to reason; extrapolate from past generality to the probable future. Each of these types, indeed, constitutes a double of the nutty professor. They represent, though perhaps in too great abundance, *needed* traits, skills, and priorities with which he is under-supplied.

The powers of the nutty professor limit him from another direction: the unruly mass of incipiencies pressing urgently upon him inhibit his efficacy in everyday life; they can even stop an incipient thought from being consolidated enough to pose a challenge to this or that cliché — that is, to disturb something in settled understandings of God, identity, morality, tolerance, causality, justice, finance, reason, or scientific method. The unruly swarm of incipiencies consists of half-formed tendencies, while the operational world of well formed judgments and resolute action unavoidably blocks, diverts, or absorbs some things on the way in order to attain coherence and stability. This is the paradox residing in the human experience of temporality as such. Everyone, including the most creative thinker, is thus doomed to be less than they could be. This may explain why many viewers of *The Nutty Professor* tacitly include themselves among the objects of friendly disparagement, as they laugh good naturedly at the hapless teacher. Such laughter may express a paradox of being in the world: the persistent discrepancy between the stereotypes appropriate to action-oriented perception and communication on the one side and the loss of bearings needed to think experimentally under new conditions on the other. Both modalities are part of being in the world; each interferes with the efficacy of the other. This, again, is the paradoxical condition of being in the world that Henri Bergson understood so well and that theorists need to negotiate sensitively in the contemporary world of becoming in which things often move faster than heretofore. The need is to negotiate a new balance between action-oriented perception and dwelling in fecund moments of temporal disequilibrium.

"Incipience" again is not that which is complete but repressed, or even exactly that which is "implicit." The implicit is not altered fundamentally by being rendered explicit. If we inhabited a world in which the explicit was surrounded only by the implicit, transcendental arguments, dialectical reasoning, and immanent critique would be the most powerful tools of the theorist, for the implicit is presupposed by the explicit.[12] But incipience exceeds a presupposition. It is an affect-imbued inception on the way replete with pluripotentiality, something like a stem cell on the verge of becoming a definite kind of tissue. It could become a blood, bone, or brain cell, depending both upon its capacities and the environment to which it migrates, though it is not implicitly any of them. And there are things it could not become, such as a spark plug in an old Chevy. That's why incipience finds its most characteristic expression through *dramatization* and the implicit through *analysis*, setting the stage for competing modes of theory anchored in different conceptions of time. Both modes are needed, according to a theorist of becoming, but the emphasis between them shifts from time to time. In a world of becoming the implicit assumes partial command during periods of relative stabilization in this or that zone, and the incipient during moments of relative destabilization. At the latter moments, dramatization, never entirely absent, becomes more prominent. Now you strive to fabulate a potentiality on the verge of activation, giving it more priority than the others with which it contends, because you sense that to draw this potentiality into being is to participate in becoming in a way that speaks positively to our new circumstances. Analysis and dramatization are always wedded, but the appropriate distribution of emphasis between them varies from time to time.

The nutty professor allows aberrant gestures, stutters, facial ticks and stray words to take one more step forward than most of us do, even though such incipiencies do find nano-expression in our flickers of the eye, a hand over the mouth, a pursing of the lips, a thud in the gut, a tightening of the shoulders, a curl of the lip that might slide into a smirk, smile, or more enigmatic expression.

It can be both mesmerizing and disturbing to respond with exquisite sensitivity to new proto-thoughts or possibilities of action as they bubble to the edge of actuality, to dwell within a forking moment as it unfolds in this way or that. Such is the way of the thinker. But it is difficult to wow your colleagues or to get dates if you wallow in such ambiguous states too often. So, professor Kelp the chemist, in consultation with the beloved magpie in his lab, eventually concocts a formula to crystallize Buddy Love from the swarm of incipiencies that stalk his life. All this was imagined in 1963, before

Figure 2. *The Nutty Professor*, Professor Kelp and Stella Purdy.

designer drugs were officially invented. Buddy is the aggressive, smooth talking, finger snapping crooner who acts like Dean Martin, the erstwhile partner of Jerry Lewis. He is well designed to negotiate the world of cliché. His sarcasm and musical performances wow the students, for sarcasm is a mode of humor that compares actuality to shared clichés that are not themselves up for reflection.

Stella Purdy, a cheerleader and chemistry student, herself strangely sensitive to aberrant movements of world, is drawn to Buddy even more than to the football star who is her boyfriend. She also senses how insufferable he could become. Who wants to make love to someone whose pluri-potentiality has congealed? Even more, however, she is attuned to fugitive circuits coursing between her at critical junctures when Buddy entertains the student body and his formula begins to lose its punch. This happens twice: as Buddy entertains the roaring crowd, a squeaky voice suddenly breaks in, followed by awkward gestures; and the strange, slight protrusion of those buck teeth. At these two moments Professor Kelp becomes highly vulnerable to public surveillance and humiliation. Stella, though, falls into a trance each time, sinking into a crystal of time in which qualities of the public Buddy and the previously suppressed nutty professor resonate confusingly back and forth. During the second occasion a new possibility seems to synthesize itself in her imagination: she visualizes how to mix one or two tendencies of the crooner into the awkward sensitivity of the teacher. Dean Martin—who closed his career as a sidekick in John Wayne films, would hate this combination. So would Dick Cheney and the King of Kings in the book of Revelation. Stella revels in it.

Stella grasps the dilemma. As a nut, the professor responds to a mass of

Figure 3. *The Nutty Professor*, Buddy Love and Stella Purdy.

incipient movements. But he can barely negotiate the everyday world of cliché that — as Bergson teaches — we must engage to eat breakfast, drive a car, and get to class on time. Kelp's chemistry experiments often blow up. When smoothed into the confident, overbearing Buddy, however, he lives entirely in the world of cliché. Or should I say theory? Stella eventually negotiates this dilemma because she already balances each tendency against the other in her mode of being. She, after all, already brought the cheerleader and chemistry student into a precocious balance. She runs off to marry the nutty professor, while quietly stuffing two bottles of that serum into the back of her jeans. A bit of juice may be needed from time to time.

Exquisite sensitivity to unexpected events, balanced against the capacity to allow some incipiencies to well up into new concepts, judgments, or strategies of intervention, is the torsion that defines Stella.

The Torsion of Theory

As the preceding accumulation of examples suggests, a seer does not only express premonitions about an uncertain future at protean moments. Those same skills and sensitivities are also indispensable to the formation of new maxims, judgments, concepts, and strategies at untimely moments when a collection of old precepts, habits, and standards of judgment are insufficient to an emerging situation. Cultivation of some of the capacities of a seer is thus pertinent to several onto-philosophical traditions, except perhaps to the most closed variants of analytic philosophy, rational choice theory, and logical empiricism. The consolidation of such skills is particularly pertinent to theorists who care about the future and know they cannot read it definitively. *If* we inhabit a world of becoming composed of interacting, heterogeneous force-fields in which the old gods are inactive, over which no providential God presides, and which no concept of efficient causality or simple calculus of probability suffices to explain, then it is wise from time to time to dwell in the world as a seer, allowing new thoughts, judgments, and experiments to ferment. In a world of becoming, however — where communion with authoritative gods is unavailable — it is particularly important to *recoil* back upon such ideas and judgments after they emerge, testing, revising, and refining them in a variety of ways. Tiresias was more confident of his prophecies than we can be. Perhaps Jesus was too, depending on whether you receive him as the sensitive Son of Man or the unique son of an omniscient God.

A set of pertinent skills and dispositions to the enterprise of theory can be distilled from leading philosophers of time as becoming, particularly if you allow each to be adjusted in the light of considerations advanced by the others. I refer to Friedrich Nietzsche, William James, Alfred North White-head, Henri Bergson, and Gilles Deleuze, though, as we have seen, others such as Ilya Prigogine, Stuart Kauffman, Marcel Proust, Merleau-Ponty, and Catherine Keller could be added to the list. I will concentrate here, however, on the first group. Taken together, at least four commendations can be distilled from them:

1. To work upon the self and the culture to which you belong, amplifying the feeling of attachment to the most fundamental character of existence as such, as you *yourself* confess those terms in a theistic or non-theistic vein.

2. To cultivate the capacity to dwell sensitively in historically significant, forking moments.

3. To seek periodically to usher new concepts and experimental actions into the world that show promise of negotiating unexpected situations.

4. To recoil on those interventions periodically to improve the chance that they do not pose more dangers or losses than the maxims they seek to correct.

The first task, to amplify attachment to this world, is important to all five thinkers, but it finds perhaps its most fervent expression in the work of Nietzsche and Deleuze. To them, life in a world of becoming carries the obdurate risk of fomenting cultural formations infused with drives to existential revenge seeking available outlets. Both those who embrace and those who deny this image of time face this risk, however. So it is imperative to overcome resentment of the fundamental terms of existence as such, as you understand them, in order to marshal the energy and drive to address the specific dangers and injustices you perceive. Otherwise what starts as a fight in favor of something positive can all too easily be twisted into a crushing demand to punish others for faults you secretly resent about the most fundamental order of being itself (as you understand it). Bergson, James, and Whitehead concur on this point too, though it may find less dramatic expression in their work. Bergson and James embrace a limited God as they cultivate gratitude for being, while Nietzsche and Deleuze, at their best, exude gratitude for an abundant world of becoming without divinity. Whitehead, whose thought is still relatively new to me, seems to support the idea of an impersonal divinity that absorbs "external objects" and sets limits of the possible in a world of becoming. His stance is perhaps tied to a more beneficent view of the outer reaches of possibility than that advanced by Nietzsche, Deleuze, and me. We seek to amplify attachment to the most fundamental character of this world, amidst the tragic possibilities that inhabit a world neither providential in the last instance nor susceptible to consummate human mastery.

The thinkers listed above also concur on the importance and method appropriate to points 2 and 3, though perhaps again they differ in emphasis. There is a subordinate difference between Bergson and Nietzsche on point 2 that is difficult to state with precision. Bergson treats the virtual as that which is below human awareness while periodically surging up into it to make a difference. But his virtual is also infused with degrees of divine intelligence and agency. Nietzsche's "powers of the false" are not divinely infused, even though Nietzsche does acknowledge differential degrees of agency beyond the human estate. This subtle difference may mean that becoming goes through more complex passages for Nietzsche. At its most protean or unformed level the Nietzschean "false" is that which presses upon life, thought, and action but is not shaped like thought itself. At higher thresholds it moves close to Bergson's virtual without perhaps being identical to it. This difference, I think, issues in another difference between Bergson and Nietzsche. The latter plays up the tragic possibilities that prowl through a universe without a special predisposition to humanity, while the former evinces a more benign image of the universe from the vantage point of the human estate. This difference, in turn, finds expression in the larger breaks, discontinuities, and shocks Nietzsche locates periodically in human experience by comparison to Bergson's theme of alteration through continuity. I find myself drawn more to Nietzsche when it comes to these issues, though it is difficult to settle the differences between them definitively. Even with these differences in mind, however, there are significant affinities between the false and the virtual, particularly by comparison to the mechanistic and organic philosophies with which both thinkers break: according to both philosophies we participate in a world of becoming that distributes creativity to and across heterogeneous force-fields.

A difference in emphasis with respect to point 3 is discernible as well. Nietzsche and Deleuze, because each emphasizes multiple fields of becoming in a nonprovidential universe, are more committed to activism than Bergson and Whitehead, and in Deleuze's case to a militant activism of the left. The universe of becoming seems to me a bit smoother and harmonious in Bergson and Whitehead. For that reason neither plays up tragic possibility, nor do they emphasize the periodic need for resolute political action. These are, however, differences of degree rather than kind. I find myself drawn most to Deleuze on this front for reasons made clear in chapter 5.

There are also differences of emphasis among our five exemplars on point 4. Bergson and James, as we have noted, seek to commune periodically with a God who informs their insight and inspires them to action. To dwell in protean moments of incipience, for them, is to open a window to a mystical relation with transcendence. Bergson articulates this pursuit for both in saying, "When [James's] book *The Varieties of Religious Experience* appeared, many saw in it only a series of very vivid descriptions . . . The truth is that James leaned out upon the mystic soul as, on a spring day, we lean out to feel the caress of the breeze on our cheek . . . For him those truths it is most important for us to know, are truths which have been felt and experienced before being thought."[13] James and Bergson find it advisable to recoil back upon the insights that emerge from dwelling in protean moments. The *limited* God with whom they commune participates in the world of becoming, and is therefore neither entirely in charge nor completely certain what is coming over the horizon. Their God is close to the God Catherine Keller draws from Judeo-Christian scripture, which we reviewed in the last chapter. And Whitehead, perhaps more than the others, insists that the flights of imagination that are essential to wise human participation in a world of becoming must eventually be forged as concepts with experimental implications, so that they can be subjected to live experimentation and speculative consistency. He does not think that any such philosophical system will be proved, but will rather remain "speculative" and seek new ways to test itself comparatively against other competitors. Whitehead's notions of process, prehension, feeling, and eternal objects are speculations designed to bring the poetic expressions of Wordsworth and Shelley into communication with more recent scientific formulations. Whitehead contends, along with Prigogine, that the themes of philosophers such as Bergson and James can be translated into scientific concepts with experimental implications. He seeks to bring art and science into close communication. I find myself drawn to him on these points, sharing his aspiration to reform our conceptual armory to bring it into contact with recent developments in science and to incorporate into science, political thought, and everyday life alike more appreciation of a world of becoming. A philosophy of becoming thus contains speculative assumptions and concepts that may be revised in the light of future experience, experiments, and tests of coherence.

So existential gratitude, periodic suspension, creative political action, and reflective recoil are important to all five philosophers of becoming, though each inflects and informs the items on this list in a distinctive way. Moreover, each evinces respect for the idea that existential gratitude for the world as you conceive it is apt to find its most noble expression when you acknowledge the element of contestability in your onto-philosophy and pursue relations of agonistic respect with other perspectives. James is the most dramatic in articulating that part of the vision, but it is discernible in the others as well.

Even the idea of a world of becoming *could* become a critical object of review by them and us, particularly if a new candidate came along to challenge it. But, as things stand now the ideas of becoming, gratitude, dwelling, periodic experimental action, and recoil shape and qualify each other.

One senses that the seed of the idea of becoming itself was sown in each thinker as he found himself suspended uncannily in a crystal of time, feeling layers of the past press upon the vicissitudes of the moment as he also addressed the insufficiency of some established concept or other. Zarathustra vindicates such a sense in Book III of *Thus Spoke Zarathustra* in the vivid section entitled "The Vision and the Riddle." Zarathustra arrives at his image of time in a dreamlike state, and the shepherd, who eventually turns out to be him, soon acquires the courage to affirm that vision without existential resentment during a dream about a big black snake that crawls down his throat and attaches itself. The shepherd bites off the head of the snake to avoid swallowing the theme of original sin and the temper of *ressentiment* that so easily accompanies it. Such a temper can also, however, accompany acceptance of becoming, as Zarathustra finds when he encounters the ape who fills Zarathustra's substantive themes with a frothy temper of *ressentiment* expressed as categorical hatred for constituencies who confess other onto-theological perspectives. That is why Nietzsche finds it so important to cultivate attachment to the world of becoming, rather than to allow resentment of it to well up behind one's back. This is perhaps the most important lesson that modern seers, led by Nietzsche and Deleuze, teach the late-modern theorist, not just about the larger world but about the temperament appropriate to reflective engagements with it.

Is it also reasonable to project such experiences of creative dwelling into the thought of Ilya Prigogine, the Nobel-prize-winning scientist of physical systems that periodically pass through imperfect equilibrium toward radical disequilibrium and then sometimes to a novel organization of imperfect equilibrium? At a culminating moment in his life of research, he can finally say, "Our universe is far from equilibrium, nonlinear, and full of irreversible processes."[14] This succinct formulation seems to consolidate a life of addressing loose ends in established scientific theories. His reflections upon those loose ends were inspired by a close reading of Bergson, touching off explorations that resonated with discrepancies in received theories and Bergson's philosophy. Prigogine then devised creative experiments to test and refine the resulting concepts. If he did not include the sensitivity of a seer among his impressive repertoire of mathematical skill, conceptual innovation, and experimental rigor, the conception of a universe far from equilibrium, nonlinear, and resistant to reversibility might not have found such robust expression in his experimental work.

Duration and Causality

Let's turn from tragedy, comedy, romance, theo-politics, and the natural sciences to a contemporary example in the human sciences. Suppose your work has made you vaguely dissatisfied with established conceptions of efficient causality and fixed registers of probability. You find efficient causality to work in simple situations, but for others it separates too sharply elements that both interpenetrate to some degree *and* impinge upon one another. You also find that fixed distributions of probability apply fairly well to stabilized systems but not to the emergence of *new* formations following periods of accentuated disequilibrium. Suppose, too, that you also find vaguely inadequate the tendency of interpretationists to bracket the idea of causality itself because of these very deficiencies. How to proceed? You might study philosophies of time that contest the image in which established concepts of cause and interpretation are lodged. You might then explore allied fields such as neuroscience and biological evolution, where received ideas of causality have also become a problem.[15] At the same time you might return to a work such as Hesiod's *Theogony*, in which the ancient Greek poet explores relations between the gods and the human estate too complex to be captured by either a simple model of efficient causality or a simple model of probability in which the parameters of possibility are already known. Sex, love, sensuality, and deceit provide better metaphors from which to think about causality in his world than the idea of humanly designed mechanisms from which the Newtonian, mechanistic idea of efficient cause is drawn. Absorption, swallowing, intermingling, digestion, and strengthening are all modes through which defeat, transformation, and transfiguration occur. Look for instance at the moment when "Zeus took Hera [his sister] as his wife to bear him children . . . Likewise Semele, Cadmus' daughter, lay with him in love and became the mother of a son with a glorious destiny— Dionysus, the giver of joy. She was mortal when she bore her immortal son; now they are both immortal."[16] Dionysus is born into an Olympian system of gods through human-god intercourse; this androgenous figure combines an element of wildness in the world, extreme sensitivity to things, and a temper of joyousness toward the fundamental terms of existence as such, bringing these three qualities to bear as he enters into multiple compositions with gods and humans. If you were to translate these gods into force-fields of diverse types, as some of Hesiod's philosophical successors themselves soon began to do, you would be on the road to a concept of emergent causality and to the exploration of uncanny affinities (not identities) between this stream of early Greek myth and emerging strains of late-modern thought. You could also achieve a similar sense by comparing the Theophany in the *Book of Job* to new developments in complexity theory.[17]

After running such thought experiments you might thereafter dwell experimentally in fecund moments in which dissatisfaction with received images, the insights from other fields and discourses, and a new appreciation of time as becoming reverberate, almost mindlessly. At some point a specific idea may bubble forth from these sporadic bouts of vertigo, not an entirely new idea, but one with distinctive dimensions.

The idea of *emergent causality* may now grip you. Even if others have delineated a concept with family relations to it, you were not perhaps *gripped* by it until you brought your doubts about this or that established concept to points of creative interruption in experience. The experience and the doubts then jostle each other, encouraging a creative adjustment in your operational concepts.

It now becomes imperative to render the protean idea more clear without trying too hard to meet all the demands proponents of other methods insist in advance such a concept must meet. For you and they probably disagree about the character of time in a way that is relevant to the issue and difficult to bring to a common court of adjudication.

The idea of emergent causality does not apply well to micro or macroprocesses in contexts of relative stability. Efficient causality, or more richly, multicausal intersections work rather well under those circumstances.[18] Emergent causality is most pertinent when a previously stabilized force-field enters a period of heightened instability. Emergent causality is *causal* — rather than reducible to a mere web of definitional relations — in that a movement in one force-field helps to induce changes in others. But it is also *emergent* in that: first, some of the turbulence introduced into the second field is not always knowable in detail in itself before it arrives darkly through the effects that emerge; second, the new forces may become *infused* to some degree into the very organization of the emergent phenomenon so that the causal factor is not entirely separate from the latter field; third, some of these forces also continue to impinge from the outside on the emerging formation; fourth, the new infusions and impingements may trigger novel capacities of *self-organization* or *autopoiesis* within one of the two systems that had not been spurred into motion before; and fifth, a series of resonances may now roll back and forth across two partially separated and partially conjoined force-fields — sometimes generating a new stabilization and sometimes intensifying disequilibrium.[19] The emergent condition is affected by external forces that infect, invade, or infuse it and by activation within itself of previously untapped capacities of self-organization. The emergent grows out of spiraling movements — or resonances — back and forth between these elements. Sometimes an accumulation of internal stresses and fractures assumes priority, eventually reaching a tipping point at which an abrupt change occurs. Sometimes the initial trigger comes from outside, spurring a new response of self-organization inside that succeeds or fails. Often the two processes interact in an intimate way. If you now introduce looping entrant and re-entrant combinations across several relatively open temporal systems moving at different speeds with different degrees of agency, emergent causality becomes yet more complex.[20]

Such complexity is endemic to an econo-political world bound to natural and cultural systems of multiple sorts, with each system moving at a distinct speed, with differential degrees of openness and periods of gestation in each, with several both infiltrating into and impinging upon others, and with such intersections periodically triggering novel modes of self-organization in one or more of the systems. Sometimes, of course, a system expires, leaving simmering remains behind available for scavenging or colonization by others at another time.

Such a new, emergent formation throws a set of received assumptions about system autonomy into question. One can imagine that dinosaurs at a key moment, if they had talked together, would have drawn a bright future from past tendencies and regularities, noting the convergence of multiple factors but not noticing the asteroid shower poised to smash into their world. Sometimes a received principle of moral judgment is also thrown out of balance by a radical twist in time. Or, at least, its established interpretation is thrown into doubt until a new one is crafted to fit a transformed situation. For instance, the future invention by bioscientists of biorobots, who simulate some human capacities of mobility, feeling, and reproduction while displaying capacities of complex calculation faster than ours, could throw a series of notions about species superiority, God, moral obligation, biological evolution, and temporal progress into turmoil.[21] They might introduce issues into our thinking about what feeling and thinking involve, which agents participate in them, and how we can relate to a species that has powers of perception and comprehension exceeding some of ours. Perhaps our current tendency to invest the provincial assumptions of our species with the imprint of universality would undergo revision. Would such beings be gods?

The concept of emergent causality can thus be tested, if perhaps not proven definitively, by applying it to specific situations during periods of accentuated disequilibrium. One recent case is the formation of a distinctive evangelical-capitalist resonance machine in the United States in which constituencies in very different subject positions have amplified bellicose dispositions in each other. As each exacerbates complementary tendencies in the other, through the definition of shared projects and enemies, an aggressive theo-econo machine emerges larger and more intense than the sum of its separate parts.[22] Another is the global resonance machine of mutual antagonisms that has arisen in the aftermath of the Cold War. These two machines, of course, are connected. You could also compare both machines to a "rogue wave" that, once a certain point of expansion has been reached, grows itself by "self-amplification."[23] On another front, you might explore volatile inter-changes between a surge in global warming, the pressures it places on estab-lished modes of capitalist investment, deregulation, and consumption, and the political responses of constituencies whose identities are tied to estab-lished modes of faith, investment, deregulation, and consumption. These interacting force-fields may then enter into spirals of resonance with re-ligious and spiritual forces in other regions of the world, creating a global machine that exceeds the state, market, and religious forces upon which it depends and from which it was organized. "Resonance" is not merely a metaphor in such an account: it speaks to real rhythms of inter-infusion exceeding mechanical modes of causality. The composition of the universe itself involves multiple vibrations, rhythms, and resonances working at dis-tinct levels and speeds, periodically dampening or amplifying each other. Indeed, the quantum brain proceeds by reverberations within and between different segments of it and affective entries into it, sometimes creating the potential for new thoughts, concepts, or strategies to emerge.

With the introduction of the concept of emergent causality a tradition of assumptions about sharp differences between human agency, on the one hand, and a world of objects governed by efficient causality or simple proba-bility, on the other, requires reconfiguration. The line between agency and cause is historically linked to Cartesian and Kantian contrasts between hu-man beings invested with the powers of free will and nonhuman force-fields susceptible to explanation through nonagentic causes. But the powers of self-organization expressed to varying degrees in open systems of different types translate that first disjunction into a matter of degree. Kant starts to pave the way for these adjustments in his third Critique when he encounters the resistance of organisms to the mode of explanation he had projected, though the implications of that encounter are not allowed to compromise his theory of the unique human agent sufficiently. Pursuing this trail, it now becomes plausible, as in Stuart Kauffman's work, to reconstruct the agency/causality duality as a distributive conception of agency and causality in a world of becoming.[24] Bacteria, stem cells, pheromones, hurricanes, dung beetles, viruses, yeast, chimps, parrots, rogue waves, and lava flows now assume one or two characteristics previously reserved entirely for human agents, even if they do not emerge as agents of the most complex sort. Some pursue simple ends; some participate in a degree of creativity; some are invested with something close to purpose, meaning, and habit, and so on. In a world of becoming, as we began to see in chapter 1, sharp divisions between causality and agency are relocated to a distributive register, softening the human/nature divide that still carries so much weight in many secular and monotheistic quarters.

Emergent causation spawns real effects without being susceptible to full explanation in a Newtonian or classical sense, partly because what emerges was not adequately *conceptualized* before its production and partly because of the strange element of creativity operating inside these spiraling movements. The spirals are not quite reducible to chance either—if that idea is set in a simple contrast between things that are either subject to classical causality or rise above causality altogether. What is operating here is closer to spiral causality. Nor does emergent causality correspond to actions undertaken in a world endowed with a final purpose—though meanings and limited purposes do circulate through it. Emergent causality consists of resonances within and between force-fields in a way that is causal but beyond the power to isolate and separate all elements in determinate ways. An element of mystery or uncertainty is attached to emergent causality.

Yes, some interactions now taken to embody emergent causation may someday be reduced to a more fixed notion of causality, even though that new conception too may not be entirely reducible to efficient causality. But the wager or faith of those imbued with an image of time as becoming is that concepts such as rhythm, vibration, reverberation, resonance, amplification, autopoiesis, and emergence will remain pertinent to particular domains of nature during periods of heightened disequilibrium, to several domains of culture much of the time, and to numerous periods of volatile inter-involvement between them.

Common Sense and Thinking

Did it take seers—those who cultivated exquisite sensitivity to the accelerated pace in several zones of life—to visualize time as becoming, as they sunk into moments when sensitivity intensified and the action-oriented sense of chronology blurred? Did they revisit in a new key that exquisite experience of duration that has been with us, in one way or another, since the inception of human life? This seems probable. Are there partial affinities, across significant differences, between the visions of Hesiod and Sophocles, on the one hand, and those of Friedrich Nietzsche, Henri Bergson, William James, Alfred North Whitehead, and Gilles Deleuze, on the other? This too seems right. None is committed to a smooth, linear concept of time, though their positive visions differ significantly. All sensed how the course of human events accelerates at times and slows down at others. All found it essential to dwell in pregnant moments from time to time, allowing new thoughts to emerge or reading omens, as the case may be, sometimes emerging from that vertigo with a new insight, mode of empathy, proposal, demand, concept, or edict. They differed in the degree to which they invested those insights with transcendent authority, and that difference is important. But in other respects they are all more critical of the lawlike model of nature, logical empiricism in the human sciences, neo-Kantianism, noncausal cultural interpretation, and rational choice theory than of each other. And most seek to affirm the most fundamental character of the universe they inhabit, however they themselves project that universe to be.

A political theorist who appreciates a world of becoming gives a degree of presumptive weight to common sense during periods of relative stability, even while appreciating or sensing how the terms of common sense can suffocate otherwise admirable possibilities. Such visceral presumptions weigh upon us unconsciously and are essential to thinking. But they are paradoxical, both enabling thought to proceed and, often enough, inhibiting it from adjusting creatively to a new or emerging situation. Thinking is beset by this paradoxical coupling of its dependence upon and limitation by layers of habit. This double condition is constitutive of thinking, as is the constitutive tension between dwelling in time to amplify sensitivity to unfolding events and acting resolutely when and if it seems wise to do so.

Today, however, it is important for more people to hone some of the capacities of a seer and to exercise them periodically. When a period of turbulence arises in a zone that had been relatively quiescent, you revisit a habitual pattern of thought by slipping into a creative suspension of action-oriented perception, doing so to allow a new insight or tactic to bubble forth if it will, as if from nowhere. You may then intervene in politics on the basis of that insight, ready to recoil back on the insight in the light of its actual effects. You soon launch another round as you maintain a relation of torsion between following a train of thought, dwelling in duration, and exploring a revised course that has just emerged, until your time runs out. Even those trains of thought will be punctuated by little jumps and bumps, as they ride on rough tracks more akin to those between New York and Washington than the smooth ones on the Kyoto–Tokyo line. Such are the joys, risks, and travails of thinking and action in a world of becoming — composed of multiple force-fields, and marked by small and large moments of real creativity.

Postlude

Do you know what the world is to me?
A colossus of diverse energies, without beginning or end, with each flowing over, through, and around others, generating new currents and eddies.

> A play of waves, forces, and perceptions on different scales of complexity, endurance, and time, with some swelling as others subside, with perhaps long cycles of repetition, but none that simply repeats those preceding.

You and I are drops in this sea of flows, feelings, and surges, my friend. So, if you die before you wake, well, I pray your God your soul to take.

> And Yahweh, Hesiod, Jesus, Moses, Sankara, and Buddha? They send out ripples of passion that persist, sometimes flowing into each other, before melting into larger waves.

And that mosquito buzzing around, sensing you as heat, movement, and food? Are you a god to it? A demon?

> It, too, perceives, hopes, and acts, living long and intensely on its temporal scale and briefly on yours. It too makes a difference, as when it alters your DNA while feeding, or deposits a virus.

As does the yeast fermenting in the dough.

> And those bursts of laughter, bouts of sensual heat, workers' movements, consumption habits, hurricanes, geological formations, climate patterns, contending gods, electrical fields, spiritual upheavals, civilizational times, species changes, and planetary rotations—they, too, participate in this veritable monster of energies, making a difference before melting down, to be drawn again into new currents, and again.

And the monster itself? It never completes itself, always rolling out and rolling in, with no outside or end-times, like a Möbius strip or Möbius current, never simply repeating, eternally evolving, and dissipating.

A monster that feeds on its own excretions, that knows no joy, existential resentment, weariness, or horror, even as it houses all these, and more.

Many strive and connect to others in such a world, seeking to amplify existential gratitude for the world as they comprehend it.

Others resent either this world or the different account of it they embrace.

That is the world to me. And you, my friend and rival?

What is it to you?

Acknowledgments

My thinking on this project has greatly profited from numerous conversations and seminars. In the fall of 2008, Mark Blyth and I taught an exploratory seminar on "Complexity Theory and Politics." The readings and discussions in that class have filtered into this book, particularly the first chapter. A second seminar of mine, "Immanence and Transcendence in Politics," has similarly affected my thinking. Besides Mark, several graduate students in these classes and elsewhere have informed my thinking. I thank Adam Culver, Drew Walker, Noora Lori, Mabel Wong, Kellan Anfinson, Nate Gies, Stefanie Fishel, Dot Kwek, Derek Denman, Katherine Goktepe, and Tim Hanafin for their thoughts and contributions. Bhrigu Singh, a recently minted PhD in Anthropology at Johns Hopkins, has been a very important sounding board and contributor to this project. So has Jairus Grove, who is finishing his graduate work at Hopkins. Anatoli Ignatov not only served as a valuable interlocutor, but also gave the entire manuscript a final editorial reading and helped to organize the index.

We have a rich group of theory faculty at Hopkins inside and outside the political science department. Jane Bennett, Sam Chambers, and Jennifer Culbert in political science, and Paola Marrati, Hent de Vries, Naveeda Khan, Veena Das, Amanda Anderson, and Francis Ferguson in allied departments, have been very helpful to me in thinking through this project. Several faculty members at other universities have also been influential. Davide Panagia, Kam Shapiro, Thomas Dumm, Mort Schoolman, Bonnie Honig, Nathan Widder, James Williams, Kathy Ferguson, Kathleen Skerrett, Ben Anderson, David Campbell, David Howarth, Lars Tønder, and Catherine Keller are people whose insights readily spring to mind. I am sure there are others. Several of these chapters have been presented as papers at symposia and conferences. I note recent presentations at Durham University, England, the University of Essex, the Watson Center at Brown University, the New School for Social Research, the University of Missouri, Emory University, the University of Ottawa, and the CUNY Graduate Center as places in which the discussions that ensued have been particularly helpful and challenging.

I would like to thank the publishers of the following two essays for letting me republish significantly expanded versions of articles originally written for them. I note that chapter 3, "Belief, Spirituality, and Time," significantly revised and extended, is reprinted by permission of the publisher from *Varieties of Secularism in a Secular Age*, edited by Michael Warner, Jonathan VanAntwerpen, and Craig Calhoun (Cambridge, Mass.: Harvard University Press, Copyright 2010 by the President and Fellows of Harvard). Chapter 4, "The Human Predicament," is a revised and extended version of an essay published by that title in *Social Research: An International Quarterly* 76, no. 4 (Winter, 2009), 1121–40.

I am lucky to work with such thoughtful people at Duke University Press. Courtney Berger is full of insight and savvy, and Timothy Elfenbein has been very helpful too.

Jane Bennett, already noted above, commented extensively on each chapter in this book. I like to think of the final product as a companion to her recent book on the vibrancy of material assemblages. I dedicate this book to graduate students in theory with whom I have worked. They give vibrancy to the enterprise and keep thought alive.

Notes

Chapter 1. Complexity, Agency, and Time

1 Stuart Kauffman offers an excellent discussion of pre-adaptations unstateable in advance in *Reinventing the Sacred: A New View of Science, Reason, and Religion* (New York: Basic Books, 2008). That book is relevant to several points in this essay. For the discussion of pre-adaptations, see in particular 131–38.

2 Ilya Prigogine, *The End of Certainty: Time, Chaos and the New Laws of Nature* (New York: Free Press, 1996).

3 Brian Goodwin, *How the Leopard Changed Its Spots: The Evolution of Complexity* (New York: Scribner, 1994).

4 William E. Connolly, *Capitalism and Christianity, American Style* (Durham, N.C.: Duke University Press, 2008).

5 See Kauffman, *Reinventing the Sacred*, 48.

6 Prigogine, *The End of Certainty*, 158, 162, and 166.

7 I explore this dimension of Kantian theory in *Why I Am Not a Secularist* (Minneapolis: University of Minnesota Press, 1999). One of the formulations that moves Kant closer to Augustine occurs in *Religion Within the Limits of Reason Alone*, trans. Theodore Greene and Hoyt Hudson (New York: Harper Torchbooks, 1960), where Kant says,

> "Now if a propensity to this [evil] does lie in human nature, there is in man a natural propensity to evil; and since this very propensity must be in the end sought in a will which is free, and can therefore be imputed, it is morally evil. This evil is *radical* because it corrupts the ground of all maxims; it is, moreover, as natural propensity, *inextirpable* by human powers . . . yet at the same time it must be possible to overcome it, since it is found in man, a being whose actions are free" (32, emphasis in original).

It is at this point that Kant opens his ambiguous discussion of the will's need for grace, its hope for grace, and our inability to translate that hope into a confident assertion of philosophy.

8 Kauffman, *Reinventing the Sacred*, 72, 74.

9 Ibid., 78.

10 See Bonnie Bassler, "Discovering Bacteria's Amazing Communication System," *TED Talks*, April 2009, http://www.ted.com/ (accessed 18 May, 2010). I thank Stephanie Fishel, a graduate student at Johns Hopkins University, for calling my attention to this example and for discussing its implications in a seminar on Spinoza and Ecophilosophy in 2009.

11 Jane Bennett, *Vibrant Matter: A Political Ecology of Things* (Durham, D.C.: Duke University Press, 2010), 23–24. In other chapters Bennett explores such things as metallic vibrancy, food metabolism and stem cell pluri-potentiality, all in the service of a "vital materialism" that widens ecological experience while contesting the alternatives of mechanical materialism and deep ecology.

12 It could be objected that I have smuggled in the idea of "decision" without explaining it. I am, however, merely trying to characterize differences of capacity without dissecting or explaining each capacity entirely. I do not know to what extent the latter can be done. I do know that active defenders of the idea of agency as free will operate in a similar way, as for example, when Augustine arrives at the idea of free will by *eliminating* other possible options to it, rather than by showing how it actually operates. The debate between us is (so far) not whether either can further specify agency or will, but whether human agency arises from lower processes that enter into its current constitution or is given to humans from above as a unique capacity. For a discussion of Augustine's argument by elimination by which he isolates the will, see William E. Connolly, *The Augustinian Imperative: A Reflection on the Politics of Morality* (New York: Roman and Littlefield, 1993), ch. 4.

13 Giacomo Rizzolatti and Corrado Sinigaglia, *Mirrors in the Brain: How Our Minds Share Actions and Emotions,* trans. by Frances Anderson (New York: Oxford University Press, 2008).

14 Sophia Roosth, "Screaming Yeast: Sonocytology, Cytoplasmic Milieus, and Cellular Subjectivities," *Critical Inquiry* 35, no. 2 (Winter 2009), 339. I thank Davide Panagia for calling this essay to my attention.

15 Alfred North Whitehead, *Process and Reality: An Essay in Cosmology,* ed. by David Ray Griffin and Donald Sherburne (New York: Free Press, 1978 [1929]), 222, 125.

16 Whitehead, *Process and Reality*, 163.

17 Friedrich Nietzsche, *The Will to Power*, trans. by Walter Kauffman (New York: Random House, 1967), #636, 339–40. I am indebted to Anatoli Ignatov for bringing this note to my attention.

18 The research is summarized in a report from the National Science and Technology Center, Canberra, Australia, in 2006, http://strikeachord.questacon.edu.au/.

19 William James, *A Pluralistic Universe* (Lincoln: University of Nebraska Press, 1996, originally 1909), 34, 44.

20 Ibid., 252–53.

21 Ibid., 254.

22 Someone will say, "But this shows that time is progressive, since those concepts are better than the ones that preceded them." Not exactly. The introduction of

new concepts and experiments does throw some old ones into crisis. One set of advocates had extrapolated the future of science in one way. And now others do so in another way. But in doing so the new advocates may draw selectively upon concepts and philosophies that had been dumped under the old conception of progress. Heraclitus, Hesiod, Lucretius, Spinoza, James, Whitehead, and Bergson, all of whom had been shuffled to the sidelines by recent conceptions of scientific progress, now receive renewed attention. They become shining points rather than dead figures. *And we now project forward along a changed path*, with the new projection of progress turning away from the previous projection. So the sense of what is progressive changes with each significant shift in thinking. When the next crisis comes, the most recent extrapolation will shift again. That suggests to me the need for a "double-entry orientation" to the idea of progress. You extrapolate a new path during each new consolidation, drawing sustenance alike from past achievements and previous experiments that had been dropped under those aspects of the regime now called into question. And this new extrapolation, in turn, may itself be twisted and turned in a new direction at a later date, setting off a revised set of extrapolations of what constitutes progress. Such twists and turns fit with an image of time as becoming, particularly when you see how each break in a previous temporal projection may demand corollary modes of creative thought in the domains of ethical judgment, political priority, and the like. One key difference between Newton and Prigogine, for instance, is that the former thinks time is reversible in principle — meaning that any process in one direction could be carried out in the opposite direction too, while the latter contends that time is irreversible, meaning that any change now in a domain will find some expression in the future, even if it is not what we now term progressive. The collapse of the human species, if it occurred, might be irreversible, but few of us would say, if we were there after the fact, that it was progressive. To say that time is *irreversible* is thus not equivalent to saying that it corresponds to a single line of *progress* in which the end to be reached is already glimpsed in the general outline of the present, or that it is linear, or that the temporal horizon is in principle closed. The idea of a double-entry orientation to time is pursued in chapter 4 of my book *Pluralism* (Durham, N.C.: Duke University Press, 2005).

23 Charles Taylor, *A Secular Age* (Cambridge, Mass.: Harvard University Press, 2007). See particularly chapter 15, "The Immanent Frame." A more detailed engagement with several themes in Taylor's study can be found in chapter 3 of the present book.

Chapter 2. The Vicissitudes of Experience

1 You could speak, as Merleau-Ponty occasionally does, of transcendence without the Transcendent. But such a formulation may blur a contestation between alternative faiths/philosophies that needs to be kept alive. In the next chapter I dis-

tinguish between mundane and radical transcendence as two visions of the "outside."

2 Gilles Deleuze and Felix Guattari, *A Thousand Plateaus: Capitalism and Schizophrenia*, trans. Brian Massumi (Minneapolis: University of Minnesota Press, 1987), 266.

3 In the introduction to *Problems and Methods in the Study of Politics*, ed. Ian Shapiro, Rogers M. Smith, and Tarek E. Masoud (Cambridge: Cambridge University Press, 2004), the editors report me as saying that "the world is in a state of constant and unpredictable flux" (11). Does that mean that awareness of one side of my position has been blocked by the shock of meeting the other?

4 Ilya Prigogine, *Is Future Given?* (New Jersey: World Scientific Press, 2003), 65.

5 Maurice Merleau-Ponty, *Nature: Course Notes from the College de France*, trans. Robert Vallier (Evanston, Ill.: Northwestern University Press, 2003), 206.

6 The formulation in fact suggests the doctrine of parallelism introduced by Spinoza in the seventeenth century. For a fine study in neuroscience that draws upon both Spinoza's philosophy of parallelism and his idea that affect always accompanies perception, belief, and thinking, see Antonio Damasio, *Looking for Spinoza: Joy, Sorrow and the Feeling Brain* (New York: Harcourt, 2003).

7 See V.S. Ramachandran, *Phantoms in the Brain: Probing the Mysteries of the Human Mind* (New York: William Morrow, 1998). Some implications of this research for cultural theory are explored in my *Neuropolitics: Thinking, Culture, Speed* (Minneapolis: University of Minnesota Press, 2001), ch. 1.

8 Merleau-Ponty, *Nature*, 152.

9 See, besides the references to Damasio, Prigogine, and Ramachandran above, Brian Goodwin, *How the Leopard Changed Its Spots*. In *The Structure of Evolutionary Theory* (Cambridge, Mass: Harvard University Press, 2002), Stephen Jay Gould emphasizes how close his revision of Darwinian theory is to the notion of genealogy developed by Nietzsche.

10 Merleau-Ponty, *Nature*, 156.

11 The phrase, "the half-second delay" comes out of work in neuroscience pioneered by Benjamin Libet. Merleau-Ponty was certainly aware, however, of a time lag. An excellent discussion of the delay and its significance can be found in Brian Massumi, *Parables for the Virtual: Movement, Affect, Sensation* (Durham, N.C.: Duke University Press, 2002).

12 Merleau-Ponty, *Nature*, 100.

13 Merleau-Ponty, *Phenomenology of Perception*, trans. Colin Smith (London: Routledge, 1995), 52.

14 Ibid., 100.

15 This theme is increasingly accepted in neuroscience today. See Bruce Durie. "21 Senses: Doors of Perception." *New Scientist* 185, no. 2484 (29 January 2005), 28–33. The authors of this article agree, too, that the senses are inter-involved.

16 Laura U. Marks, *The Skin of the Film: Intercultural Cinema, Embodiment, and the*

Senses (Durham, N.C.: Duke University Press, 2000), ch. 3, "The Memory of Touch."

17 Merleau-Ponty, *Phenomenology of Perception*, 183. Such a pattern of inter-involvement will seem impossible only to those captured by the analytic-synthetic dichotomy, in which every connection is reducible either to a definitional or an empirical (causal) relation. Once you break that dichotomy, you can come to terms with the series of memory-infused inter-involvements through which perception is organized. You are also able to consider models of causality that transcend efficient causality.

18 Ibid., 209, 211.

19 Ibid., 228.

20 Ibid., 235.

21 Rizzolatti and Sinigaglia, *Mirrors in the Brain*, 125. Rizzolatti thinks that language would not have developed without this base of prelinguistic experience enabled by the cultural coding of mirror neurons. (I am aware that the word "linguistic" can be stretched to include such processes, but the value in not doing so is to help us understand how language evolved out of cultural experience rather than popping up all at once and to appreciate more closely the multilayered character of experience.) Rizzolatti also sprinkles his book with quotations from Merleau-Ponty, appreciating numerous points at which his observational experiments support the phenomenological work the former had already accomplished. One point at which his work suggests a modest revision to me, however, is that it points to the way that tactics of the self and media micropolitics help to code cultural experience by multimedia means that exceed the ready reach of intellectual self-consciousness. He draws us, then, into political territory mapped by Michel Foucault and Gilles Deleuze.

22 Ibid., 189.

23 Another pertinent text here is Nathan Widder, *Reflections on Time and Politics* (University Park: Pennsylvania State University Press, 2008). One high point in that text is his account of the three syntheses of time in the work of Gilles Deleuze.

24 Ricard Solé and Brian Goodwin, *Signs of Life: How Complexity Invades Biology* (New York: Basic Books, 2000), 142–43. This examination of oscillation between points of instability and stability speaks to Stuart Kauffman's theory of the "quantum brain" discussed later.

25 In fact, Henri Bergson is better than Merleau-Ponty at focusing attention on the role that the imperative to make perceptual judgments rapidly as you run through the numerous encounters of everyday life plays in creating the subtractions and simplifications of operational perception. It is beyond the scope of this book to explore the comparative advantages and weaknesses of each perspective. But if I were to do so, the above limitation in Merleau-Ponty would be balanced against his reflective appreciation of the numerous sensory "inter-involvements" that make perception possible. The starting point to engage Bergson on these issues is

his *Matter and Memory*, trans. N. M. Paul and W. S. Palmer (New York: Zone Books, 1988).

26 Merleau-Ponty, *Phenomenology of Perception*, my italics, 219.

27 Diana Coole, *Negativity and Politics: Dionysus and Dialectics from Kant to Poststructuralism* (London: Routledge, 2000), 132. This book prompted me to take another look at Merleau-Ponty in relation to Foucault and Deleuze. Some will protest her assertion, saying that priority must be given either to the subject *or* to the object. But they then have to come to terms with the multiple inter-involvements elucidated by Merleau-Ponty and his judgment that you can't unsort entirely—once these mixings and remixings have occurred—exactly what contribution is made by one "side" or "the other." "Even the painter, alert to his powers of perception, is not able to say (since the distinction has no meaning) what comes from him and what comes from things, what the new work adds to the old ones, or what it has taken from the others . . ." Merleau-Ponty, "Indirect Language and the Voices of Silence," in *Signs*, trans. Richard McCleary (Evanston, Ill.: Northwestern University Press, 1964), 58–59.

28 Merleau-Ponty, *The Visible and the Invisible*, trans. Alfonso Lingis (Evanston, Ill.: Northwestern University Press, 1968), my italics, 13. That text also deepens our experience of "the flesh" in ways that extend all the points made about the sensorium discussed above. But we cannot pursue that pregnant topic here.

29 Sean Dorrance Kelly, "Seeing Things in Merleau-Ponty," in Taylor Carman and Mark Hansen, eds., *The Cambridge Companion to Merleau-Ponty* (Cambridge: Cambridge University Press, 2005), 85 and 92.

30 Michel Foucault, *Discipline and Punish: The Birth of the Prison*, trans. Alan Sheridan (New York: Pantheon Books, 1977), 25.

31 For a review of the neuroscience literature on bodily and cultural elements in the formation of sight see Adam Zeman, *Consciousness: A User's Guide* (New Haven, Conn.: Yale University Press, 2002), ch. 5 and 6.

32 In April of 2005, the *Johns Hopkins Gazette* released the following bulletin: "Continuing its efforts to enhance the security of students, faculty and staff, the university has installed . . . a state of the art closed-circuit TV system . . . The system can be programmed to look for as many as 16 behavior patterns and to assign them a priority score for operator follow-up . . . The cameras are helping us to make the transition to a more fully integrated 'virtual policing' system."

33 Foucault, *Discipline and Punish*, 172.

34 Robert Heath, *The Hidden Power of Advertising: How Low Involvement Processing Influences the Way We Choose Brands* (Henley-on-Thames: Admap, 2005), 67. Heath is not speaking of subliminal inserts here, but about advertisements that distract attention from themselves and encourage the viewer to be distracted too as they insert connections between affect, words, and images.

35 Mark B. N. Hansen, *New Philosophy for New Media* (Cambridge, Mass.: MIT Press, 2004), 198.

36 Ibid.

37 In *Pluralism*, I focus on the most recent elements that help to drive what is there called multidimensional pluralism.

38 Taylor, *A Secular Age*. For one discussion of the conditions under which "belief" became more "optional," see 1–94.

39 The quotations are found in *Cinema 2: The Time Image*, trans. Hugh Tomlinson (Minneapolis: University of Minnesota Press, 1997 [1989]), 171, 172.

40 Ibid., 181.

Chapter 3. Belief, Spirituality, and Time

1 See, for example, the symposium on the mind-body relation organized by Antonio Damasio in *Daedalus* 135, no. 3 (Summer 2006). The essays by Antonio and Hanna Damasio and Gerald Edelman are particularly relevant, with the first discussing the implications of the discovery of "mirror neurons" for understanding how the sociality of experience precedes language and the second suggesting that consciousness is an afterglow rather than an antecedent to action. My essay in that symposium ("Experience and Experiment," 67–75) seeks to connect themes in Spinoza and contemporary neuroscience to an understanding of how tactics of the self and micropolitics work on the visceral register of cultural life.

2 Stephen Mitchell, ed., *The Gospel According to Jesus: A New Translation and Guide to His Essential Teachings for Believers and Unbelievers* (New York: Harper, 1991), 123–24.

3 William E. Connolly, "Catholicism and Philosophy: A Nontheistic Appreciation," in *Charles Taylor*, ed. Ruth Abbey (Cambridge: Cambridge University Press, 2004), 166–86.

4 See Taylor, *A Secular Age*, ch. 15, "The Immanent Frame," especially 544–50.

5 Jane Bennett, in *The Enchantment of Modern Life: Attachments, Crossings, and Ethics* (Princeton, N.J.: Princeton University Press, 2001), explores modes of enchantment that are reducible neither to a theological tradition nor to the disenchantment themes of Weber and Blumenberg.

6 See Kauffman, *Reinventing the Sacred*.

7 William James, *A Pluralistic Universe*.

8 At the American Political Science Association meeting in 2006, a commentator on a paper of mine said that for me, "all that is solid melts into air." He missed the theme, reviewed again in this chapter, that while force-fields vary in their pace and rate of metamorphoses, most go through periods of both relative stabilization and active disequilibrium. All the thinkers I call philosophers of becoming in this book hold such a view.

9 Angela Carter, *The Infernal Desire Machines of Doctor Hoffman* (London: Penguin, 1972).

10 In a thought provoking essay, Bonnie Honig explores differential rates of becom-

ing in aspects of the human estate, as well as the need to accept the acceleration of pace in some zones while seeking to slow down others. Her discussion of the slow food movement is particularly pregnant. I concur with her reading. See Bonnie Honig, "The Time of Rights: Emergent Thoughts in an Emergency Setting," in David Campbell and Morton Schoolman, eds., *The New Pluralism: William Connolly and the Contemporary Global Condition* (Durham, N.C.: Duke University Press, 2008), 85–120.

11 For discussions of the relation between the level of sunspot activity and weather, climate, and electrical activity on the earth see "Sunspot Mysteries," posted 30 November 2002 on The Electric Universe website, http://www.holoscience.com/; and for a more dramatic version, "Sunspot cycle rising," posted 8 May 2009 on the Armageddon Online website, http://www.armageddononline.org/. There are, apparently, discernible cycles between active and inactive periods of sunspot activity, of approximately eleven years. But so far, at least, significant variations in the cycles with respect to both timing and intensity escape successful prediction.

12 Taylor's discussions of immanent materialism can be found in pages 360–68, 398–401, 541–50, and 595–98 of *A Secular Age*.

13 The themes I am advancing in relation to Taylor's concept of transcendence share a lot with those of Patrick Lee Miller in his responses to Taylor. See "Heraclitean Spirituality: Divine Conflict," posted 22 December 2008 on The Immanent Frame blog, http://www.ssrc.org/blogs/immanent_frame/. I also appreciate the conversations we had after reading each others' contributions to the blog.

14 In *Post-Secular Faith: Toward a Religion of Service* (Pulau Pinang: Penerbit Universiti Sains Malaysia, 2008), Fred Dallmayr enters into comparative conversations with William James, Charles Taylor, and me on the role of spirituality and belief in a pluralist world. He is particularly alert to the ubiquity of faith in each perspective and to differences in spirituality that can accompany the same formal creed.

15 I pursue such an experiment in an essay entitled "Shock Therapy, Dramatization, and Practical Wisdom," in George Levine, eds., *The Joys of Secularism* (Princeton, N.J.: Princeton University Press, forthcoming), originally delivered as a paper at the University of Essex in 2008.

16 Charles Taylor, *Sources of the Self: The Making of the Modern Identity* (Cambridge, Mass.: Harvard University Press, 1989), 74, 96.

17 St. Augustine, *Concerning the City of God against the Pagans*, trans. Henry Bettenson (Harmondsworth: Penguin, 1985), book 11, ch. 13, 446.

18 Benjamin Libet, Anthony Freeman, and Keith Sutherland, eds., *The Volitional Brain: Towards a Neuroscience of Free Will* (New York: Imprint Academic, 1999).

19 For an excellent study of the role of ethos in politics, see Stephen White, *The Ethos of a Late Modern Citizen* (Cambridge, Mass.: Harvard University Press, 2009). White places Taylor and me into conversation with him as the text proceeds, and he plays up the importance of our engagement with mortality as a possible common resource to draw upon in sustaining a pluralist ethos.

20 I explore these issues in Connolly, *Capitalism and Christianity, American Style*. The point now is to make the case more explicitly as to why symptomatic readings are needed today.

21 I worked upon that earlier self-orientation in *Why I Am Not A Secularist*.

Interlude

1 Heraclitus in *The Art and Thought of Heraclitus: The Fragments with Translation and Commentary*, ed. Charles Kahn (Cambridge: Cambridge University Press, 1979), 53.

2 Friedrich Nietzsche, *The Pre-Platonic Philosophers*, trans. Greg Whitlock (Chicago: University of Illinois Press, 2006), 60–61.

3 Heraclitus in *The Art and Thought of Heraclitus*, 33.

4 Nietzsche, *The Pre-Platonic Philosophers*, 61.

5 Alfred North Whitehead, *Process and Reality*, 222.

6 William E. Connolly, *A World of Becoming*, 94.

7 Marcel Proust, *Time Regained*, vol. VI of *In Search of Lost Time*, trans. Andreas Mayer and Terence Kilmartin (New York: Modern Library, 1983), 419–20.

8 Alfred North Whitehead, *The Concept of Nature* (Cambridge: Cambridge University Press, 1920), 55.

9 Gilles Deleuze, *Proust and Signs*, trans. Richard Howard (Minneapolis: University of Minnesota Press, 2000), 122.

10 Kauffman, *Reinventing the Sacred*, 209.

11 Whitehead, *The Concept of Nature*, 223.

12 Heraclitus in *The Art and Thought of Heraclitus*, 61.

13 Friedrich Nietzsche, *The Will to Power*, # 636, 339.

14 Henri Bergson, *Creative Evolution*, trans. Arthur Mitchell (New York: Dover, 1998), 106.

15 Heraclitus in *The Art and Thought of Heraclitus*, 65.

16 Kauffman, *Reinventing the Sacred*, 116.

17 Heraclitus in *The Art and Thought of Heraclitus*, 85.

18 Ilya Prigogine, *Is Future Given?*, 64.

19 William James, *A Pluralistic Universe*, 328.

20 Heraclitus in *The Art and Thought of Heraclitus*, 33.

Chapter 4. The Human Predicament

1 Connolly, *Capitalism and Christianity, American Style*.

2 John J. Thatamanil, *The Immanent Divine: God, Creation, and the Human Predicament* (Minneapolis: Fortress, 2006), 10.

3 Ibid., 19.

4 Ibid., 21.

5   Paul Tillich, *Christianity and the Encounter of World Religions* (New York: Columbia University Press, 1963), 83.

6   Sankara, quoted in Thatamanil, *The Immanent Divine*, 40. I have been reading Sankara in Eliot Deutsch and J. A. B. van Buitenen, eds., *A Source Book of Advaita Vedanta* (Honolulu: University of Hawaii Press, 1971). The themes and Sankara quotations used here, however, come from Thatamanil, reflecting my current lack of confidence in presenting an independent reading. Tillich, in the book quoted above, creates an "encounter" between Christianity and Buddhism, without extending it to Hinduism.

7   These themes find expression in several of Bergson's books. But perhaps the book closest to the concerns we are exploring is Bergson, *The Two Sources of Morality and Religion*, trans. R. Ashley Audra and Cloudesley Brereton (New York: Henry Holt, 1934).

8   Thatamanil, *The Immanent Divine*, 186.

9   Ibid., 190.

10 Catherine Keller, *The Face of the Deep: A Theology of Becoming* (New York: Routledge, 2003), xv. I was first alerted to Keller's work when Kathleen Skerrett sent me an essay in which she compared Keller on time to a chapter on that issue in a recent book of mine. I look forward to seeing Skerrett's essay in its final form, and I want to acknowledge a debt between what I say about Keller and Skerrett's account of her.

11 Ibid., 198.

12 Ibid.

13 Ibid., 227.

14 This relation comes out most clearly in Keller, *On the Mystery: Discerning Divinity in Process* (Minneapolis: Fortress, 2008). There Keller explores connections between her reading of scripture and Whitehead's process theology, in which God functions as a lure. She already, as it were, forges some of the connections across difference we seek to promote in this book.

15 One superb example of this is Kauffman, *Reinventing the Sacred*.

16 See Keller, *God and Power: Counter-Apocalyptic Journeys* (Minneapolis: Fortress, 2005).

17 For an excellent version of the latter account, see Nuno Nabias, *Nietzsche and the Metaphysic of the Tragic* (London: Continuum, 2007). Nuno makes a fine case that Nietzsche outgrew the early version of eternal return. But since Nabias does not ask what conception of time replaces it, he fails to consider the possibility that the maturation involved growing into time as becoming.

18 Friedrich Nietzsche, *The Will to Power*. Just to give a couple of examples from *The Will to Power*, in note #1064, 547, he says that "at any precise moment of a force, the absolute conditionality of a new distribution of all its forces is given: it cannot stand still. 'Change' belongs to the essence, therefore also temporality." By contrast, note #1067 has elements that point both toward eternal becoming and

toward return as long cycles. The Postlude to the present book can be read in part as my attempt to rewrite note #1067, so that the statement "what 'the world' is to me" is retained while the ambiguity about eternal return is turned toward a world of becoming.

19 For an earlier account, see William E. Connolly, *Neuropolitics: Thinking, Culture, Speed*, ch. 6. I now think of that account as a prelude to this one: it focuses on the politics of acceleration more than the relation between becoming and the human predicament; it does not bring the powers of the false into sharp focus; and above all, it does not place different affirmative accounts of the human predicament into conversation.

20 Friedrich Nietzsche, *Thus Spoke Zarathustra*, trans. Walter Kaufmann (New York: Penguin, 1978), 157–58.

21 Ibid., 166, 198.

22 See Søren Kierkegaard, *Philosophical Fragments* (Princeton, N.J.: Princeton University Press, 1936). You must be "born anew" to appreciate the profundity of the Kierkegaardian moment. Nietzsche's Danish friend Georg Brandes recommended that he read Kierkegaard, and he promised to do so. But the promise was made late and no writing on the topic emerged. I hope to make an extended comparison sometime. The only point to be made now perhaps is that the invaluable contrast Kierkegaard makes between the Socratic mode and the receipt of the miracle he himself commends speaks to but inadequately captures the difference between Kierkegaard and Nietzsche. Socrates pursues education to a higher mode without grace, but he differs from Nietzsche as to what the higher mode is.

23 See Hannah Arendt, *The Life of the Mind* (New York: Harcourt, 1978), ch. 14, entitled "Nietzsche's Repudiation of the Will." There are other places where she does not offer such a reading.

24 A detailed discussion of significant changes between the world of Zarathustra and the world of today that impinge on the decisions of both Zarathustra and Nietzsche can be found in William E. Connolly, *Identity/Difference: Democratic Negotiations of Political Paradox* (Minneapolis: University of Minnesota Press, 2nd edition, 2002), ch 6.

25 Nietzsche, *Thus Spoke Zarathustra*, 276.

26 Ibid., 277.

27 These thoughts about desire are informed by an unpublished paper by Bhrigupati Singh, a recent graduate student in Anthropology at Johns Hopkins University, entitled "Preliminary Work for a Future Morality: Spiritual and Political Exercises in Gandhi, Thoreau, and Nietzsche." I also note his dissertation, "Gods and Grain: Lives of Desire in Rural Central India," completed in the fall of 2009. Singh's explorations of connections between shifting valences of local life, the attributes of traveling gods, and the contemporary global condition are highly pertinent to the issues posed above.

28 I engage this dimension in the next chapter. I am also aware that the words

"positive," "productive," and so on will disturb some who believe you cannot make ethical judgments unless you adopt a morality of universal principle set in a progressive image of time. Having addressed this issue earlier I will now merely say that during breaks and shifts in the trajectory of time in which we are located, these traditional modes become insufficient. At such junctures, the right *ethical response* is to join care for this world to creative reflection upon a distinctive situation.

29 For a study that carries Adorno's theorization of the gap between the concept and the thing close to the formulations about the powers of the false in this chapter, see Morton Schoolman, *Reason and Horror: Critical Theory, Democracy and Aesthetic Individuality* (New York: Taylor and Francis, 2007).

30 Marcel Proust, *Time Regained*, 247–48.

31 Friedrich Nietzsche, *The Will to Power*, # 676, 357.

Chapter 5. Flows, Decisions, and Resonance Machines

1 Georg Wilhelm Friedrich Hegel, *Elements of the Philosophy of Right*, trans. H. B. Nisbet (Cambridge: Cambridge University Press, 1991), #241, #244 and addition to #244, 265–67.

2 I do not dig deeply here into the debate between those who think that *Geist* in Hegel's account of civil society and the state can be reduced to natural processes of historical realization without a trace of divinity, and those who think that *Geist* is initially an incomplete divine direction that progressively materializes (and realizes) itself through the tears of history. On the latter reading, *Geist* is touched and moved by worldly history, but it also brings something from the outside to it. If *Geist* were simply an emergent property, with no transcendent dimension, Hegel's official optimism about the future of the interstate system could be derailed at multiple points. There would be no supra-historical pressure within history — no divinized outside — to promote balance between new historical needs that arise and their provision. Things would be very chancy. On the other hand, there is considerable evidence that the heavy rendering of *Geist* apparent in *The Philosophy of Right* is compromised in later lectures, even if those lectures are not then carried back to his reading of capitalism, the state, and the world order (see note 4). Charles Taylor in *Hegel* (Cambridge: Cambridge University Press, 1975) provides a thoughtful account of the complex role of *Geist* in Hegel before the later lectures on aesthetics. He contends that *Geist* is an incomplete divinity which can only realize itself through historical actualization, but that, correspondingly, Hegelian progress also depends upon the searching telos of *Geist*. Patchen Markell, in *Bound by Recognition* (Princeton, N.J.: Princeton University Press, 2003), criticizes the logic of recognition in Hegel and replaces it with one of acknowledgment. To the extent a teleological conception of time is replaced by time as becoming, acknowledgment provides a promising reconfiguration of a dialectical

logic of recognition. And what about those who say you can never escape the dialectic, even when you try hard to do so? I would reconfigure such a claim: it is very difficult to avoid the dialectic when you are looking back at what has happened, even though you can qualify it. When you are lodged in the complexity of the present, however, acting forward into a future populated with uncertain degrees of uncertainty, the persuasive power of a philosophy of becoming looms larger. And we do live forward into the future, even as we drag the effects of the past along in doing so. In thinking about these issues it is important not to allow the irreversibility of time — its inability to repeat itself perfectly — to become equated with progressive time. All of the figures we have explored in this text, including Whitehead, Deleuze, and Prigogine, accept the thesis of irreversibility.

3 Hegel, *The Philosophy of Right*, # 339, 371.

4 See Hegel's *Aesthetics: Lectures on Fine Arts*, trans. T. M. Knox (Oxford: Oxford University Press, 1998). I am indebted to Terry Pinkard, in a lecture at Johns Hopkins University in the spring of 2009 entitled "The Dialectic of Freedom," for posing this side of Hegel so dramatically. As Pinkard acknowledges, these openings in Hegel sing the most if you do not turn to his engagement with religion in the same text. It is also important to remember that Hegel wrote well before Darwin; he thought that the world itself had not been in existence very long. Given such a short time horizon, species evolution made no sense to him, and he has a highly static view of nature as such. This is a fateful assumption, one with profound effects on his system and one already contested during his lifetime. Alfred North Whitehead, one might say, is Hegel after both the advent of Darwin and the critique of Newtonianism. Whitehead's elongated notion of evolution, his sense that degrees of agency, feeling, perception, and creativity extend far beyond the human estate, and his conviction that the co-evolution of the universe expresses a high degree of creative becoming could almost be taken for the work of a late-modern Hegelian, a post-Darwinian Hegel who prepares the way for complexity theory in the natural and social sciences. See Whitehead's *Process and Reality*. I thus would seek to have this chapter read in conjunction with chapter 1 of this book on "Complexity, Agency, and Time."

5 Immanuel Wallerstein, *World Systems Analysis: An Introduction* (Durham, N.C.: Duke University Press, 2004), 23.

6 This theme is in fact more developed in Giovanni Arrighi, *The Long Twentieth Century* (New York: Verso, 1994), which is rich with evocative detail. Both Wallerstein and Arrighi are devotees of world systems theory, and each is indebted to the other. I think the theme about a hegemonic state is implicit in what Wallerstein actually writes. Arrighi was my colleague at Johns Hopkins before his untimely death in 2009. We all miss him dearly.

7 These themes are presented more extensively in chapter 5 of Connolly, *Pluralism*. There I also discuss the global dimension of contemporary sovereignty.

8 These themes are elaborated in Foucault, *Security, Territory, Population: Lectures at the College de France 1977–1978*, ed. Michel Senellart and trans. Graham Burchell (New York: Macmillan, 2007).

9 Gilles Deleuze, *Negotiations*, trans. Martin Joughin (New York: Columbia University Press, 1995), Part V, with the two chapters entitled "Control and Becoming" and "Postscript on Control Societies," 167–82. I would like to thank Jairus Grove, a graduate student at Johns Hopkins University, for his comments on this entire essay, but particularly those on this section. He has helped me to see more clearly the difference between Deleuze and Foucault on this register, amidst the connection between them.

10 Giles Deleuze and Felix Guattari, *A Thousand Plateaus: Capitalism and Schizophrenia*, 512. For a thoughtful account of key aspects of their philosophy, including the relation between an abstract machine and chaotic elements that revolve within and around it, see Jeffrey A. Bell, *Philosophy at the Edge of Chaos: Gilles Deleuze and the Philosophy of Difference* (Toronto: University of Toronto Press, 2006). Bell also has a fine account of Hegel's philosophy of *Geist*, seeing how close Deleuze and Guattari are to it along one dimension and how far away along another.

11 For a discussion of Alan Greenspan and climate change, see William E. Connolly, "Climate Change, Spirituality, and Neoliberalism," posted 1 March 2010 on the Contemporary Condition blog, http://contemporarycondition.blogspot.com.

12 For an excellent account of the origin, systemic character, and uneven effects of this world financial market, see Edward LiPuma and Benjamin Lee, *Financial Derivatives and the Globalization of Risk* (Durham, N.C.: Duke University Press, 2004). They saw its potential for crisis rather early, while its neoliberal supporters, led by Alan Greenspan, treated it as a force for market stabilization. For a creative account of the role of money and credit in global capitalism *per se*, see Philip Goodchild, *Theology of Money* (Durham, N.C.: Duke University Press, 2009). That book, too, was written before the 2008 collapse, while identifying in advance several factors that created it.

13 Samuel P. Huntington, *The Clash of Civilizations and the Remaking of World Order* (New York: Simon and Schuster, 1996).

14 See Talal Asad, *On Suicide Bombing* (New York: Columbia University Press, 2007), 89. Asad and I also concur, I think, that the most bellicose factions working on each side of this divide first amplify existential and historic resentments already simmering and then seek to translate them into this machine. An additional point I would add is that no religious or existential creed in history to date has found such a surefire way to overcome human resentment against mortality and time that it provides sufficient spiritual resources by itself to transcend the danger. We must all work on this tendency, within and across the creeds that separate us. Such is a key element in the human predicament.

15 I explore a positive cosmopolitan machine consisting of heterogeneous constituencies in Connolly, *Neuropolitics*. The negative machine explored here is a counterpoint to that one.

16 That negative resonance machine is analyzed in Connolly, *Capitalism and Christianity, American Style*.

17 Naomi Klein, *The Shock Doctrine: The Rise of Disaster Capitalism* (New York: Metropolitan, 2007). As she shows, Milton Friedman first tested the shock doctrine in Chile during the Pinochet regime, using shocking events to get a recalcitrant public to accept neoliberal policies they would otherwise resist. She quotes Milton Friedman, who says, "Only a crisis produces real change . . . That I believe is our basic function: to develop alternatives to existing policies, to keep them alive . . . until the politically impossible becomes politically inevitable" (Klein, 140). So much for neoliberalism as pure economic doctrine. Klein sometimes acts as if the Right produces the crises to which it then responds. This is true on occasion, intentionally in Iraq, unintentionally in the 2008 economic meltdown. But often it is primed to respond with preset policies to outside events that surprise it too. Neoliberals seem to think that the shocks would dissipate if their doctrine were in place. I think that in a world of becoming, shocks will come periodically from surprising places.

Chapter 6. The Theorist and the Seer

1 See Immanuel Kant, "On the Proverb: 'That May Be True in Theory, But is of No Practical Use,'" in *Perpetual Peace and Other Essays*, trans. Ted Humphrey (New York: Hackett, 1983). While discussing our duty to assume moral progress even when we are in no position to prove by other means that it is true, Kant says,

> I will thus permit myself to assume that since the human race's natural end is to make steady cultural progress, its moral end is to be conceived as progressing toward the better. And this progress may be occasionally *interrupted* but it will never be *broken off*. It is not necessary for me to prove this assumption . . . For I rest my case on my innate duty . . . : the duty so to affect posterity that it will become continually better (something that must be assumed to be possible). (86)

He goes on to say that even if historical evidence belied this faith it would still remain our duty, given the conception of morality he takes to be "apodictic," to act "as if" it were operative in history.

2 Alfred North Whitehead, *The Concept of Nature*, 55.

3 See Lynn Margulis and Dorion Sagan, *What Is Life?* (Berkeley: University of California Press, 1995). Margulis introduced the term "symbiogenesis" into biology after her experiments with released streams of DNA that swim to other cells

after being released from their initial host, an idea that now seems widely accepted.

4 I have offered an account, indebted to some thinkers listed above, in *Pluralism*, chapters 3, 4, and Postlude.

5 Bonnie Honig first called my attention to the dual gender of Tiresias. A fine account can be found in Walter Burkert, *Greek Religion* (Cambridge, Mass.: Harvard University Press, 2006).

6 "Antigone," *The Oedipus Plays of Sophocles*, trans. Paul Roche (New York: Penguin, 1991), 5th Episode, 236–37.

7 "Antigone," *The Oedipus Plays*, 239.

8 Jacqueline de Romilly, in *Time in Greek Tragedy* (Ithaca, N.Y.: Cornell University Press, 1966), focuses on those sudden turns in time in Greek tragedy. She also suggests that Sophocles was himself closer to the thinking of minor figures such as Haemon, Ismene, and Jocasta than to heroes such as Oedipus (in the first play, at least), Creon, and Antigone, whose hubris, in concert with other events, teaches us by bringing tragic possibility to the fore. The heroes teach us through their hubris about our problematic relation to the universe; the other figures teach us more, perhaps, about how to negotiate such a world wisely. Unfortunately, it seems to take both types together to teach us wisdom, but we can at least hope that well crafted dramas enable more of us not to have to learn the hardest lessons through repetition.

9 Gilles Deleuze, *Cinema 2*, 51. I will, indeed, explore further an example that Deleuze cites.

10 Is this because the constituency who reads *A Thousand Plateaus* often diverges from that which reads the cinema books? Perhaps. At any rate, each text needs to be read in relation to the other. For a reading that is attuned to the first book, see Manuel De Landa, *A Thousand Years of Nonlinear History* (New York: Zone Books, 1997). For one sensitive to the task and promise of dwelling, see D. N. Rodowick, *Gilles Deleuze's Time Machine* (Durham, N.C.: Duke University Press, 1997).

11 Deleuze, *Cinema 2*, 65, 66.

12 For an excellent study that starts by comparing Deleuze to Kant with respect to the idea of a transcendental field in each and then clarifies the virtual-actual relation in Deleuze by reference to comparable themes in several other philosophers, see James Williams, *The Transversal Thought of Gilles Deleuze: Encounters and Influences* (Manchester: Clinamen, 2005). The discussion in that book of the similarities and differences between Deleuze and Whitehead is also excellent.

13 Bergson, *The Creative Mind: Introduction to Metaphysics* (New York: Citadel, 1992), 212–13. An engaging paper by Thomas Dumm, "William E. Connolly and the Politics of Embodiment," presented at a conference at the University of Swansea on my work in the spring of 2007, encouraged me to think again about

the similarities and differences between mystical experience and dwelling in duration in a world of immanence.

14   Ilya Prigogine, *Is Future Given?*, 65.

15   I summarize such debts to recent work in neuroscience in Connolly, "Experience and Experiment," *Daedalus* (Summer 2006), 67–75. Essays by Antonio and Hanna Damasio and Gerald Edelman from the symposium that gave rise to the issue of *Daedalus* also speak to the issue of causality in neuroscience. The discussion of the work of Giacomo Rizzolatti in chapter 2 of the present book is also pertinent to this question.

16   Hesiod, *Theogony*, trans. with intro. Norman O. Brown (Englewood Cliffs, N.J.: Prentice Hall, 1953), 79. Brown's introduction is superb. It brings out the moments of volatility and sharp twists of time in the *Theogony*. For an essay that places Hesiod and Kant into extended conversation, see my "Shock Therapy, Dramatization, and Practical Wisdom." The idea there is to use Hesiod to show how the "apodictic" starting points from which Kant constructs his arguments are already culturally infused, and then to explore what happens if you seek to dramatize those protean moments in ways different from Kant. Such an effort, I suggest, supports the idea of an ethic of cultivation over a morality of universal laws and also helps us to appreciate why theorists should seek to become like seers at protean moments.

17   I launched such an experiment in chapter 1 of *The Augustinian Imperative: A Reflection on the Politics of Morality*.

18   For a superb account of several interacting modes of causality, see Nancy Cartwright, *Hunting Causes and Using Them: Approaches in Philosophy and Economics* (Cambridge: Cambridge University Press, 2007). The mixed modes of causality she traces, often interacting in the same system, lay the groundwork for the notion of emergent causality considered here. The latter is most applicable when a more radical disequilibrium has occurred in one or more systems.

19   The Deleuzian idea of change through spiral repetition is relevant here. As Jane Bennett, in *The Enchantment of Modern Life: Attachments, Crossings, and Ethics*, summarizes, the "point about spiral repetition is that sometimes that which repeats itself also transforms itself. Because each iteration occurs in a . . . unique context, each turn of the spiral enters into a new and distinctive assemblage" (40). For other works that speak to emergent causation in social and cultural theory, see Brian Massumi, *Parables for the Virtual*, and Manuel De Landa, *One Thousand Years of Nonlinear History*. De Landa explores auto-catalytic loops that help to generate new forms out of old molds in the formation of granite, the consolidation of ecosystems, and the composition of national languages.

20   I present a preliminary version of this notion in chapter 3 of *Capitalism and Christianity, American Style*, without, however, exploring the way in which the idea of a world of becoming itself may emerge out of oscillations between new

encounters, dwelling, and analyzing. The paleontologist Stephen Gould emphasizes the need to rethink cause in evolutionary theory: In Darwin, "the organism supplies raw material in the form of 'random' variation, but does not 'push back' to direct the flow of its own alteration from the inside . . . By contrast the common themes . . . in this book all follow from serious engagement with complexity, interaction, multiple levels of causation, multidirectional flows of influence and pluralist approaches to explanation in general" (Gould, *The Structure of Evolutionary Theory*, 31). To keep these intersections between diverse thinkers in play it should be noted that Gould discusses how Nietzsche's genealogical mode of analysis prefigured the approach to biological evolution he adopts, though he did not realize this until a graduate student showed him late in the day. See 1214–18.

21 I borrow this example from Jairus Grove, a graduate student in Political Science at Johns Hopkins University, who is working on this question. His essay is entitled "William Connolly's Critical Responsiveness: Beyond the Limits of the Human Species," in Alan Finlayson, ed., *Democracy and Pluralism: The Political Thought of William E. Connolly* (London: Routledge, 2009).

22 For an account, see Connolly, "The Evangelical-Capitalist Resonance Machine," *Political Theory* 33, no. 6 (December 2005) and *Capitalism and Christianity, American Style*.

23 See "Freak Waves, Rogue Waves, Extreme Waves and Ocean Wave Climate," by Kristian B. Dysthe, et al., from the mathematics departments in Bergen and Oslo, Norway, http://folk.uio.no/karstent/waves/index_en.html (accessed February 2010); and "Rogue Waves," the Environmental Literacy Council, www.enviro literacy.org/article.php/257 (accessed July 2007).

24 See Stuart A. Kauffman, *Reinventing the Sacred*, especially ch. 6.

Bibliography

Arendt, Hannah. *The Life of the Mind*, 2 vols., ed. Mary McCarthy (New York: Harcourt, 1978).

Arrighi, Giovanni. *The Long Twentieth Century: Money, Power, and the Origins of Our Times* (New York: Verso, 1994).

Asad, Talal. *On Suicide Bombing* (New York: Columbia University Press, 2007).

Bell, Jeffrey A. *Philosophy at the Edge of Chaos: Gilles Deleuze and the Philosophy of Difference* (Toronto: University of Toronto Press, 2006).

Bennett, Jane. *The Enchantment of Modern Life: Attachments, Crossings, and Ethics* (Princeton, N.J.: Princeton University Press, 2001).

———. *Vibrant Matter: A Political Ecology of Things* (Durham, N.C.: Duke University Press, 2010).

Bergson, Henri. *Creative Evolution*, trans. Arthur Mitchell (New York: Dover, 1998).

———. *The Creative Mind: An Introduction to Metaphysics*, trans. Mabelle Andison (New York: Citadel, 1992).

———. *Matter and Memory*, trans. N. M. Paul and W. S. Palmer (New York: Zone Books, 1988).

———. *The Two Sources of Morality and Religion*, trans. R. Ashley Audra and Cloudesley Brereton (New York: Henry Holt, 1934).

Burkert, Walter. *Greek Religion* (Cambridge, Mass.: Harvard University Press, 2006).

Carter, Angela. *The Infernal Desire Machines of Doctor Hoffman* (London: Penguin, 1972).

Cartwright, Nancy. *Hunting Causes and Using Them: Approaches in Philosophy and Economics* (Cambridge: Cambridge University Press, 2007).

Connolly, William E. *The Augustinian Imperative: A Reflection on the Politics of Morality* (New York: Rowman and Littlefield, 1993).

———. *Capitalism and Christianity, American Style* (Durham, N.C.: Duke University Press, 2008).

———. "Catholicism and Philosophy: A Nontheistic Appreciation." *Charles Taylor*, ed. Ruth Abbey (Cambridge: Cambridge University Press, 2004).

———. "The Evangelical-Capitalist Resonance Machine," *Political Theory* 33, no. 6 (December 2005), 869–86.

——. "Experience and Experiment." *Daedalus* 135, no. 3 (Summer 2006), 67–75.

——. *Identity/Difference: Democratic Negotiations of Political Paradox,* 2nd edn. (Minneapolis: University of Minnesota Press, 2002).

——. *Neuropolitics: Thinking, Culture, Speed* (Minneapolis: University of Minnesota Press, 2002).

——. *Pluralism* (Durham, N.C.: Duke University Press, 2005).

——. "Shock Therapy, Dramatization and Practical Wisdom." *The Joys of Secularism,* ed. George Levine (Princeton, N.J.: Princeton University Press, forthcoming).

——. *Why I Am Not A Secularist* (Minneapolis: University of Minnesota Press, 1999).

Coole, Diana. *Negativity and Politics: Dionysus and Dialectics from Kant to Poststructuralism* (London: Routledge, 2000).

Dallmayr, Fred. *Post-Secular Faith: Toward a Religion of Service* (Pulau Pinang: Penerbit Universiti Sains Malaysia, 2008).

Damasio, Antonio. *Looking for Spinoza: Joy, Sorrow and the Feeling Brain* (New York: Harcourt, 2003).

De Landa, Manuel. *A Thousand Years of Nonlinear History* (New York: Zone Books, 1997).

Deleuze, Gilles. *Cinema 2: The Time-Image,* trans. Hugh Tomlinson and Robert Galeta (Minneapolis: University of Minnesota Press, 1989).

——. *Negotiations,* trans. Martin Joughin (New York: Columbia University Press, 1995).

——. *Proust and Signs,* trans. Richard Howard (Minneapolis: University of Minnesota Press, 2000).

Deleuze, Gilles, and Felix Guattari. *A Thousand Plateaus: Capitalism and Schizophrenia,* trans. Brian Massumi (Minneapolis: University of Minnesota Press, 1987).

Deutsch, Eliot, and J. A. B. van Buitenen, eds. *A Source Book of Advaita Vedanta* (Honolulu: University of Hawaii Press, 1971).

Durie, Bruce. "21 Senses: Doors of Perception." *New Scientist* 185, no. 2484 (29 January 2005), 33–36.

Foucault, Michel. *Discipline and Punish: The Birth of the Prison,* trans. Alan Sheridan (New York: Pantheon, 1977).

——. *Security, Territory, Population: Lectures at the College de France 1977–1978,* trans. Graham Burchell, ed. Michel Senellart (New York: Macmillan, 2007).

Goodchild, Phillip. *Theology of Money* (Durham, N.C.: Duke University Press, 2009).

Goodwin, Brian. *How the Leopard Changed Its Spots: The Evolution of Complexity* (New York: Scribner, 1994).

Gould, Stephen Jay. *The Structure of Evolutionary Theory* (Cambridge, Mass.: Harvard University Press, 2002).

Grove, Jairus. "William Connolly's Critical Responsiveness: Beyond the Limits of the

Human Species." *Democracy and Pluralism: The Political Thought of William Connolly*, ed. Alan Finlayson, 183–202 (London: Routledge, 2009).

Hansen, Mark B. N. *New Philosophy for New Media* (Cambridge, Mass.: MIT Press, 2004).

Heath, Robert. *The Hidden Power of Advertising: How Low Involvement Processing Influences the Way We Choose Brands* (Oxford: Admap, 2001).

Hegel, G.W.F. *Aesthetics: Lectures on Fine Arts*, trans. T. M. Knox (Oxford: Oxford University Press, 1998).

———. *Elements of the Philosophy of Right*, trans. H. B. Nisbet, ed. Allen W. Wood (Cambridge: Cambridge University Press, 1991).

Hesiod. *Theogony*, trans. Norman O. Brown (Englewood Cliffs, N.J.: Prentice Hall, 1953).

Honig, Bonnie. "The Time of Rights: Emergent Thoughts in an Emergency Setting." *The New Pluralism: William Connolly and the Contemporary Global Condition*, ed. David Campbell and Morton Schoolman (Durham, N.C.: Duke University Press, 2008).

Huntington, Samuel P. *The Clash of Civilizations and the Remaking of World Order* (New York: Simon and Schuster, 1996).

James, William. *A Pluralistic Universe* (Lincoln: University of Nebraska Press, 1996).

Kahn, Charles. *The Art and Thought of Heraclitus: An Edition of the Fragments with Translation and Commentary* (Cambridge: Cambridge University Press, 1979).

Kant, Immanuel. *Perpetual Peace and Other Essays*, trans. Ted Humphrey (Indianapolis: Hackett Publishing, 1983).

———. *Religion Within the Limits of Reason Alone*, trans. Theodore M. Greene (New York: Harper and Row, 1960).

Kauffman, Stuart. *Reinventing the Sacred: A New View of Science, Reason and Religion* (New York: Basic Books, 2008).

Keller, Catherine. *The Face of the Deep: A Theology of Becoming* (New York: Routledge, 2003).

———. *God and Power: Counter-Apocalyptic Journeys* (Minneapolis: Fortress, 2005).

———. *On the Mystery: Discerning Divinity in Process* (Minneapolis: Fortress, 2008).

Kelly, Sean Dorrance. "Seeing Things in Merleau-Ponty." *The Cambridge Companion to Merleau-Ponty*, ed. Taylor Carman and Mark Hansen, 74–110 (Cambridge: Cambridge University Press, 2005).

Kierkegaard, Søren. *Philosophical Fragments* (Princeton, N.J.: Princeton University Press, 1936).

Klein, Naomi. *The Shock Doctrine: The Rise of Disaster Capitalism* (New York: Metropolitan, 2007).

Libet, Benjamin, Anthony Freeman, and Keith Sutherland, eds. *The Volitional Brain: Towards a Neuroscience of Free Will* (New York: Imprint Academic, 1999).

LiPuma, Edward, and Benjamin Lee. *Financial Derivatives and the Globalization of Risk* (Durham, N.C.: Duke University Press, 2004).

Margulis, Lynn, and Dorion Sagan. *What is Life?* (Berkeley: University of California Press, 1995).

Markell, Patchen. *Bound by Recognition* (Princeton, N.J.: Princeton University Press, 2003).

Marks, Laura U. *The Skin of the Film: Intercultural Cinema, Embodiment, and the Senses* (Durham, N.C.: Duke University Press, 2000).

Massumi, Brian. *Parables for the Virtual: Movement, Affect, Sensation* (Durham, N.C.: Duke University Press, 2002).

Merleau-Ponty, Maurice. *Nature: Course Notes from the College de France*, trans. Robert Vallier (Evanston, Ill.: Northwestern University Press, 2003).

———. *Phenomenology of Perception*, trans. Colin Smith (London: Routledge, 1995).

———. *Signs*, trans. Richard McCleary (Evanston, Ill.: Northwestern University Press, 1964).

———. *The Visible and the Invisible*, trans. Alfonso Lingis (Evanston, Ill.: Northwestern University Press, 1968).

Mitchell, Stephen. *The Gospel According to Jesus: A New Translation and Guide to His Essential Teachings for Believers and Unbelievers* (New York: Harper, 1991).

Nabias, Nuno. *Nietzsche and the Metaphysic of the Tragic*, trans. Martin Earl (London: Continuum, 2007).

Nietzsche, Friedrich. *The Pre-Platonic Philosophers*, trans. Greg Whitlock (Chicago: University of Illinois Press, 2006).

———. *Thus Spoke Zarathustra*, trans. Walter Kaufmann (New York: Penguin, 1978).

———. *The Will to Power*, trans. Walter Kaufmann and R.J. Hollingdale (New York: Random House, 1967).

Prigogine, Ilya. *The End of Certainty: Time, Chaos, and the New Laws of Nature* (New York: Free Press, 1997).

———. *Is Future Given?* (River Edge, N.J.: World Scientific Press, 2003).

Proust, Marcel. *Time Regained*, vol. VI of *In Search of Lost Time*, trans. Andreas Mayer and Terence Kilmartin (New York: Modern Library, 1983).

Ramachandran, V.S., and Sandra Blakeslee. *Phantoms in the Brain: Probing the Mysteries of the Human Mind* (New York: William Morrow, 1998).

Rizzolatti, Giacomo, and Corrado Sinigaglia. *Mirrors in the Brain — How Our Minds Share Actions and Emotions*, trans. Frances Anderson (Oxford: Oxford University Press, 2008).

Rodowick, D. N. *Gilles Deleuze's Time Machine* (Durham, N.C.: Duke University Press, 1997).

Romilly, Jacqueline de. *Time in Greek Tragedy* (Ithaca, N.Y.: Cornell University Press, 1966).

Roosth, Sophia. "Screaming Yeast: Sonocytology, Cytoplasmic Milieus, and Cellular Subjectivities," *Critical Inquiry* 35, no. 2 (Winter 2009), 332–50.

Saint Augustine. *Concerning the City of God against the Pagans*, trans. Henry Bettenson (Harmondsworth: Penguin, 1985).

Schoolman, Morton. *Reason and Horror: Critical Theory, Democracy and Aesthetic Individuality* (New York: Taylor and Francis, 2007).

Shapiro, Ian, Rogers M. Smith, and Tarek E. Masoud, eds. *Problems and Methods in the Study of Politics* (Cambridge: Cambridge University Press, 2004).

Singh, Bhrigupati. "Gods and Grains: Lives of Desire in Rural India." Ph.D. dissertation. Johns Hopkins University, 2009.

Solé, Ricard V., and Brian Goodwin, *Signs of Life: How Complexity Invades Biology* (New York: Basic Books, 2000).

Sophocles. *The Oedipus Plays of Sophocles: Oedipus the King, Oedipus at Colonus, Antigone*, trans. Paul Roche (New York: Plume, 1996).

Taylor, Charles. *A Secular Age* (Cambridge, Mass.: Harvard University Press, 2007).

———. *Hegel* (Cambridge: Cambridge University Press, 1975).

———. *Sources of the Self: The Making of the Modern Identity* (Cambridge, Mass.: Harvard University Press, 1989).

Thatamanil, John J. *The Immanent Divine: God, Creation, and the Human Predicament* (Minneapolis: Fortress, 2006).

Tillich, Paul. *Christianity and the Encounter of World Religions* (New York: Columbia University Press, 1963).

Wallerstein, Immanuel. *World Systems Analysis: An Introduction* (Durham, N.C.: Duke University Press, 2004).

White, Stephen. *The Ethos of a Late Modern Citizen* (Cambridge, Mass.: Harvard University Press, 2009).

Whitehead, Alfred North. *The Concept of Nature* (Cambridge: Cambridge University Press, 1920).

———. *Process and Reality: An Essay in Cosmology*, ed. David Ray Griffin and Donald W. Sherburne (New York: Free Press, 1978).

Widder, Nathan. *Reflections on Time and Politics* (University Park: Penn State University Press, 2008).

Williams, James. *The Transversal Thought of Gilles Deleuze: Encounters and Influences* (Manchester: Clinamen, 2005).

Zeman, Adam. *Consciousness: A User's Guide* (New Haven, Conn.: Yale University Press, 2002).

Index

Abstract machine, 194n10; civil society as, 124; defined, 135–36; of global antagonism, 128, 138–42; the outside and, 136. *See also* Force-field

Adorno, Theodor, 192n29

Affect, 152; abstract machine and, 136; belief and, 10, 59, 85, 184n6; defined, 150–51; discipline and, 54–55, 57, 186n34; feeling and, 150–51, 160; intersensory experience and, 46–47, 49, 57; modulation of, 134; the outside and, 150–51; politics of becoming and, 15, 152; thought-imbued tendencies and, 97, 159, 160–62, 173; visualization of activity and, 68

Agency: abstract machine and, 136–38, 142; bacteria and, 24–25, 28, 31, 173; demarcation between cause and, 111, 173–74; desire and, 26–27, 101–4; distributed agency, 12, 22–23, 29–30, 37–38, 83, 85, 167, 173–74; differential degrees of, 5, 7, 15, 17, 21, 24–27, 31–32, 35, 39–40, 42, 70–71, 80–82, 115, 118, 136, 166, 171, 193n4; Hegel and, 26, 125, 141; human agency, 7, 25, 64–65, 101–2, 107, 115, 120, 153; scientific autonomy and, 148. *See also* Creativity; Proto-agency

Agonistic respect, 77, 79, 85, 115, 123, 168

Al Qaeda, 41, 53, 140, 144

All About Eve, 158–59

Anthropic exception, 21–22, 25, 29, 148. *See also* Human estate

Anthropomorphism, 23

Anticipation, 3–4, 33, 36, 69; anticipatory structure of perception, 46, 48–51, 56–57

Antigone (Sophocles), 153–56, 196n8

Arendt, Hannah, 86; on Nietzsche, 104, 113

Arrighi, Giovanni, 193n6

Asad, Talal, 41, 139, 194n14

Assemblages, 14; as abstract machine, 135–36; of desire, 14, 115–16, 120, 123; inter-agency, 22, 27–28; pluralist, 13; political, 42, 75, 91–92; resonant, 146; role performance and, 143–44, 146; spiral repetition and, 197n19; vitality of "actants" in, 25

Attractors, 49, 55–58

Augustine: Connolly on, 182n10; existential sensibility and, 86–87; on human predicament, 98, 105, 107; on human will, 22, 25, 81–82, 98, 107, 111, 150, 181n7, 182n12

Autopoiesis, 71, 78, 171, 174. *See also* Self-organization

Avatar, 128

Barton Fink, 1–2, 4–5, 9

Bassler, Bonnie: "quorum sensing" of bacteria, 24

Bateson, Gregory: double bind, 128

Becoming: affirmation of, 6, 98, 113–15, 127; atheological register of, 109–16; atheological vs. theological regis-

Becoming (*cont.*)
 ter of, 119–20; defined, 9, 149; differential rates of, 187n10; eternity of,
 105–6, 190n18; "innocence" of, 118–
 19; litter and, 72; periods of stability
 and, 21, 30, 37, 44, 46, 73, 111, 127,
 149–50, 158, 161–62, 169, 171–72,
 175, 187n8; philosophy of, 23, 36, 44,
 70, 72, 109, 127, 192n2; politics of, 3,
 151; question of, 106; theological register of, 104–9; Whitehead on, 94,
 193n4. *See also* Equilibrium; Force-
 field; Open system; Time
Belief: affect and, 10, 59, 85, 184n6; affirmation and, 79–83; autonomy of,
 129; faith and, 39, 112; multiple
 strands of, 108; "optional," 59–60,
 187n38; proto-belief, 85; role performance and, 14, 145–47; spirituality
 and, 13, 85–91, 130, 188n14. *See also*
 Belief in this world
Belief in this world: Deleuze on, 12, 59,
 61–67, 109; Merleau-Ponty and, 12,
 65; Taylor on, 59–62, 66, 109
Belonging: belief in this world and, 12, 52,
 54, 57–58, 61, 63–65, 80, 121, 165–66,
 169; powers of the false and, 64–65, 67,
 116, 119; to time, 5, 8, 10, 102, 108
Bennett, Jane, 187n5, 197n19; on actants, 25
Bergson, Henri, 88, 165, 182n22,
 190n7; dwelling in duration and, 7,
 68–69, 71, 75, 102; on human predicament, 13, 102, 104–6, 115; imma-
 nence/transcendence and, 71, 75,
 166–67; Merleau-Ponty and, 185n25;
 Prigogine and, 168–69; Sankara and,
 102; Thatamanil and, 105–6; two registers of time, 2, 77, 102, 106, 115,
 161, 164, 174; virtual and, 166–67
Bifurcation, 130; point of, 19, 63, 116
Bin Laden, Osama, 53, 142, 144
Brain, the, 27, 65, 111, 162; body/brain
 processes, 17, 36, 45, 48–49, 52, 73,

76–77, 82; quantum brain, 94–95,
 118, 173
Buddhism, 60, 73, 104, 190n6
Bush, George W., 53, 90, 142, 155

Capital flows, 84, 124, 128, 130, 132
Capitalism: altered "conditions of belief" and, 59; climate change and, 7,
 19–20, 36–37, 73, 99, 120, 133, 136–
 37, 141, 150, 173, 194n11; complexity
 theory and, 130; discipline and, 54;
 ecological balance and, 42; expansion
 of, 122, 126–35, 140–41; as interstate
 system, 127–33, 142; money and,
 194n12; as an open system, 36–37,
 129; the outside and, 129–30; state
 capitalism, 14, 27, 125–26, 143,
 192n2. *See also* Evangelical-capitalist
 resonance machine; Market
Carter, Angela, 72
Cartwright, Nancy, 197n18
Causality, 7, 15, 80, 161; complexity theory and, 109; efficient, 6, 45, 71, 75, 78,
 81–82, 111, 118, 148–49, 165, 169–71,
 173–74, 185n17; efficient vs. emergent,
 44, 58, 170–71, 173–74, 197nn18–19;
 emergent, 19, 130, 170–74, 197nn18–
 19; God and, 100; Hume and James on,
 34–36; mechanical, 24, 45; multiple
 modes of, 197n18, 197n20; neuroscience and, 197n15; non-agentic patterns of, 150; probabilistic, 19, 71, 165,
 169–70, 173; resonance and, 77; Whitehead on, 34–36, 94
Channeling apparatuses, 134–35
Cheney, Dick, 159, 163
Christianity, 41, 60, 62, 68, 70, 100, 131,
 133, 142, 190n6; pluralism and, 78–
 79, 101
Civil society, 135, 138; equilibrium and,
 124; "rabble" and, 124–28; state and,
 124–29, 132, 143, 146, 192n2
Clash of Civilizations, The (Huntington), 139, 142

Climate, 188n11; climate change, 7, 19–20, 73, 99, 120, 133, 136–37, 139, 150, 156, 173, 194n11; climate crises, 141; as a force-field, 5, 36–37; patterns of, 37, 73, 176. *See also* Capitalism: climate change and Global warming

Coen Brothers, 1–2, 4–5, 9

Color of perception, 47–51, 55

Complexity, 57, 122, 176; agentic, 17, 23–27, 30–31, 37, 42, 171–72; of experience, 83; of perception, 12, 46–52, 55–56; of sovereignty, 132; theory of, 7, 12, 17, 20, 23, 35–36, 40, 42, 58, 107, 109, 120, 130, 170, 193n4. *See also* Pre-adaptation; Self-organization

Connectionism, 12, 35–37, 42

Consciousness: agency and, 24–26; as an afterglow, 187n1; media micropolitics and, 185n21; the powers of the false and, 64, 118; quantum coherence and, 94–95

Consumption, 27, 31, 87–88, 176; infrastructure of, 99, 134; investment and, 61, 89, 91, 104, 116, 120, 133, 140, 143–44, 155, 173; underconsumption, 124–26

Contestability: of conceptions of human agency, 22; of faith/creeds, 37–42, 66, 87, 91, 112, 120; images of time and, 8, 16; onto-philosophy and, 168

Coole, Diana, 50

Cosmos, 2, 8, 66, 112, 119

Creativity: agency and, 8, 27, 38, 74, 83, 85, 94, 167, 173–74, 193n4; becoming and, 63–64, 71, 78, 84, 107–9, 113–14; estrangement and, 101; force-fields and, 5, 38, 94, 105–6, 165, 167, 175; God and, 8, 21, 38, 105, 107–9; thought and, 116–19, 161. *See also* Agency

Creed, 12, 58, 76, 79, 100–101, 111; contestability of, 40, 66, 87, 112; ethos and, 108; existential resentment and, 114, 139–40, 145, 147, 194n14; immanence/transcendence and, 39–42, 60, 71, 77; minoritization of world and, 60, 66, 68, 84–89, 128; spirituality and, 13, 19, 77, 83–92, 188n14; uncertainty and, 140

Crocodile, 160; the feeling of, 28, 31

Cynicism: desire for authority and, 54–55

Dallmayr, Fred, 41, 188n14; monotheism and, 81

Damasio, Antonio, 45, 184n6, 187n1, 197n15

Damasio, Hanna, 187n1, 197n1

Das, Veena, 41

Da Vinci Code, The, 68

De Landa, Manuel, 196n10, 197n19

Deleuze, Gilles, 84, 185n23; abstract machine, 135, 194n10; "asymmetry of nature," 46; "belief in this world," 59, 61–67, 109; capitalist axiomatic, 36–37; on causality, 77; cinema and, 157–60; *Cinema II*, 63, 116; Hegel and, 194n10; immanent naturalism and, 71, 74; Kant and, 196n12; Merleau-Ponty and, 12, 43, 46, 65, 186n27; micropolitics and, 116, 133–34, 185n21, 194n9; powers of the false and, 63–64, 116, 118–19; radical immanence and, 37–38, 44; systems of "control," 133–34; time as becoming and, 7, 165–67, 169, 174, 192n2; Whitehead and, 196n12

Democritus, 71

Descartes, Rene, 29

Desire, 73, 108, 191n27; Augustine on will and, 81; belief, spirituality and, 91; dwelling and, 104; experience of lack and, 103, 115; first-order desire, 26; microtactics of the self and, 26, 114–16, 119, 121; perception, action and, 101–5; revenge and, 56, 58, 87, 90; role performance and, 14, 64, 91,

Desire (*cont.*)
144–47; second-order desire, 26–27.
See also Assemblages
De Vries, Hent, 41
Discipline: expressive sovereignty and,
133–35; perception and, 12, 50, 52–
55
Disorderly Orderly, The, 160
DNA, 77–78, 152, 195n3
Double-entry orientation, 182n22
Dumm, Thomas, 196n13
Duration, 40, 74: causality and, 169–74;
chrono-time vs., 71; complexity of,
58, 80; dwelling in, 5, 7, 15, 36, 38,
51, 68–72, 75–79, 84, 102, 104, 115,
165, 174–75, 196n10, 196n13; time
as, 2, 10, 72, 77; Whitehead on, 29,
94, 149. *See also* Seer
Dwelling. *See* Duration; Seer

Epicurus, 71, 84; swerve, 77
Equilibrium, 30; disequilibrium and,
18–20, 44, 46, 71–73, 76–77, 96, 111,
136, 149–50, 156, 158, 161–62, 169,
171–72, 174, 187n8, 197n18; reflective, 10
Eternal Sunshine of the Spotless Mind,
65
Ethics, 5, 8, 92, 110, 191n28; cultivation
and, 10, 16–17, 26, 31, 40–41, 79–86,
102, 104, 113–16, 119–20, 123, 156–
59, 164–66, 169, 174, 191n28,
197n16; desire and, 103, 115–16, 119,
121; family and, 132; immanent realism and, 44, 79; warrior ethic, 144–45
Ethos: bellicosity and, 135; collective,
74; creed and, 108; of engagement,
84–85; of existential resentment, 88;
of gratitude, 41; pluralist, 188n19; of
politics, 5, 119; of reciprocal involvement, 16
Evangelical-capitalist resonance machine, 19, 99, 143; governmentality
and, 134; resonance machine of

global antagonism and, 172–73; spirituality and, 87–91
Experiment, 93, 164; Augustine and,
81; dwelling and, 7, 75–77, 165, 168,
170; experience and, 7, 9–10, 35, 35–
37, 39, 45, 67, 159, 167–70; media
and, 56–57, 63; micro-economic,
145; nonhuman modes of expression
and, 28, 31–32; neuroscience and, 48–
50; symbiogenesis and, 195n3; time
and, 7, 108, 110, 112, 119–20

Faith, 21, 71, 100, 104; "apodictic" morality and, 195n1; belief in this world
and, 59–62, 65–66; contending faiths,
11, 13, 40–42, 66, 84–91, 112, 122,
140, 173, 183n1; defined, 39–40; desubstantialization of divinity and,
106; evangelical-capitalist resonance
machine and, 134, 137; evolution of,
73; immanence/transcendence and,
37–38, 65, 76, 80; Kierkegaard on,
112; life after death and, 18; Nietzsche on, 112; omnipotent God and,
82, 107, 109; providence and, 56, 120;
revenge and, 140, 145; spirituality
and, 74, 188n14
False: defined, 64, 116–17; powers of, 4,
14, 63, 67, 116–19, 166, 191n19,
192n29; virtual and, 166–67
Feeling, 4, 117, 149, 165, 168, 172, 176;
affect and, 46, 57, 150–51, 160; differential degrees of, 23, 25, 28–29, 31,
38–39, 42, 193n4; of the divine, 107–
8; resentment and, 55, 87
Film, 1, 15, 56, 97, 145, 152, 163; contemporary condition and, 127–28;
Deleuze and, 77, 157, 159–60; flashbacks and, 63, 157–58; interruptions
of experience and, 62–65; intersensory experience and, 47; irrational
cuts and, 63; time and, 7, 9, 58, 68–
69, 109, 120, 157–64; tactics of the
self and, 116

Fluctuations, 20. *See also* Resonance; Vibrations

Force-field: agency and, 15, 23, 31, 38, 70, 80–82; capitalism and, 37, 137; creativity and, 5, 38, 94, 105–6, 165, 167, 175; cultural life and, 17; defined, 5; electrical, 20, 176; emergence and, 44, 71–78, 149–50, 171, 173–74; emergent causality and, 171, 174; Greek gods as, 155, 170; layered dimension of thought and, 94; litter and, 36; the outside and, 7, 30, 39, 71, 74, 129–30, 133, 136, 142, 147, 171; resonance machine and, 14, 135–36, 173; tiers of temporality and, 9, 44, 71–72, 149–50. *See also* Abstract machine; Open system; Tiers of temporality

Foucault, Michel: discipline and, 52–55, 57; governmentality, 133–34, 194n9; immanent naturalism and, 71, 74; Merleau-Ponty and, 12, 43, 52, 54, 57, 186n27; micropolitics and, 116, 133, 185n21

Friedman, Milton, 37; "shock doctrine" and, 195n17

Gandhi, Mahatma: warrior ethic and, 144, 191n27

Geist, 126–27, 130–32, 141–42, 192n2, 194n10

Gimzewski, Jim: the feeling of yeast, 28–29

Global warming, 41, 88–89, 120, 133, 137, 145, 150, 155–56, 173. *See also* Climate

Globalization: of capital, 7, 14, 133, 140; of contingency, 42

God, 56, 137, 161, 172, 176; agency and, 21–23, 27, 30, 70, 107, 137; becoming and, 11, 106–10, 113, 120, 165–67; belief in this world and, 59, 65–66; contending gods, 4, 149, 165, 176; creativity and, 8, 20–21, 38, 105, 107–

9; grace and, 4, 22, 39, 65, 81, 98, 107–8, 112; immanence/transcendence and, 10, 43–44, 70, 74–75, 80–81, 85–86, 99–100; limited, 74–75, 85–86, 108, 166–67; as a lure, 190n14; Nietzschean gods, 110; Olympian gods, 98, 152–57, 170; original sin and, 25, 82, 107, 119; traveling gods, 191n27; Whitehead on, 38–40, 94, 166, 190n14

Goodwin, Brian, 18, 45–46, 77

Gould, Stephen Jay, 45, 197n20

Guattari, Felix: abstract machine, 135; radical immanence and, 44

Half-second delay, 46, 50, 58, 82, 151, 161, 184n11

Hansen, Mark, 56: perceptual confusion and, 57, 63

Haptic image, 34

Hardin, Garrett: tragedy of the commons, 99

Heath, Robert, 54, 186n34

Hegel (Taylor), 192

Hegel, G. W. F.: agency and, 26, 125, 141; on civil society and its "rabble," 14, 124–28, 138; expressive dimension of collective life, 130, 132, 134, 139–41, 143; nature and, 127, 193n4; radical immanence and, 127; Taylor on, 192n2; Wallerstein and, 130; Whitehead and, 193n4; world-historical state, 126–27, 129, 141. See also *Geist*; State

Hesiod, 174, 176, 182n22; Kant and, 76, 197n16

Heraclitus, 11, 13, 182n22

Hesitation, 3, 55; desire and, 104; fecundity of, 68

Hinduism, 60, 104, 190n6

Holism, 6, 12; connectionism vs., 35–37, 42; defined, 32; James on, 32–34

Honig, Bonnie, 187n10, 196n5

Human estate, 83, 187n10; abstract machines and, 136; degrees of agency beyond, 5, 15, 22–24, 26–27, 29, 31–32, 35, 38–40, 70–72, 166, 193n4; god(s) and, 106–8, 111, 170; mastery over world and, 6–7, 10, 31–32, 70, 72, 79–80, 98, 108, 112, 118, 120, 141–42, 166; nature and, 45, 108; nonhuman processes and, 21, 79, 136, 150; the powers of the false and, 117. *See also* Anthropic exception; Humanism

Human predicament, the, 6, 141, 157, 194n14; affirmation of, 98, 100–101, 113–15, 121, 123, 191n19; Augustine and, 98, 105, 107; Bergson and, 102; Deleuze and, 61–62; desire and, 121; guilt and, 43; human condition vs., 97–98; Keller and, 106–9; minoritization of world and, 122; Nietzsche and, 109–16; Sankara and, 101–3; Sophocles and, 98, 105; Taylor and, 61, 85; Thatamanil and, 105; Tillich and, 100–101; versions of, 13–14, 98–100, 104–5, 115, 120, 122

Humanism, 115; as exclusive, 28, 31–32, 60, 69, 71, 79–80, 88

Hume, David, 29; causality and, 34–36

Huntington, Samuel, 139, 142

Immanence, 21, 196n13; defined, 43–44; Deleuze on, 44; divine form and, 99–100, 122; naturalism and, 60, 70–71, 74, 78, 81–83; naturalism vs. realism, 74; the outside and, 39, 65, 74–75, 183n1; radical form and, 13, 37–39, 42, 44, 74–76, 80, 127; realism and, 39, 44, 71, 74–76; Taylor on, 13, 38–39, 41; transcendence and, 12–13, 21, 37–45, 60, 65, 70–71, 74–77, 80–81, 86; versions of, 12, 37–38, 40–42

Implicit, the: the explicit and, 162; implicit belonging, 67; implicit learning, 54; incipience and, 162

Incipience, 3, 76, 82, 167; the false as,

64, 116–19, 166; the implicit and, 162; thought and, 78, 160–61, 164–65

Individualism, 6, 12; compensatory, 114; connectionism vs., 35–37, 42; defined, 32; James on, 32–34

Iraq war, 88, 140, 142, 155, 157, 195n17

Islam, 41, 59–60, 101, 139, 142, 144

It's Only Money, 160

I ♥ Huckabees, 65

James, William, 7, 88, 106, 174, 182n22; as "connectionist," 35–36; contestability of faith and, 41, 168; Dallmayr and, 188n14; immanence/transcendence and, 71, 75, 165–67; "litter," 35–36, 72; as radical empiricist, 33–34

Jesus Christ, 68–69, 72, 74, 78, 84, 86–87, 165, 176

Judaism, 60

Kafka, Franz, 62

Kant, Immanuel, 30, 76, 109; "apodictic" morality and, 76, 148, 195n1, 197n16; Deleuze and, 196n12; existential sensibility and, 86–87; on human will, 22, 81–82, 111, 150, 173, 181n7; on induction, 122; laws of nature and, 29

Kauffman, Stuart, 12, 165; complexity of agency and, 23–24, 26, 28–31, 173; creativity and, 20–21; immanence and, 37

Keller, Catherine, 13, 122; belief in this world and, 109; monotheism and, 81; Nietzsche and, 106, 109, 119–20, 122; time as becoming and, 106–9, 115, 119–20, 165; transcendence and, 41, 167; on Whitehead, 190n14

Kelly, Sean Dorrance, 51

Keynes, John Maynard, 37

Kierkegaard, Søren, 13, 62; on belief and faith, 112; Nietzsche and, 112, 191n22

Klein, Naomi: "shock doctrine," 146, 195n17

Language, 30, 84, 197n19; complexity of perception, 46–49; fecundity of, 34; human capacity of, 31; inter-involvement with affect, 26, 36, 48, 185n21, 187n1; intersubjective web of, 32; life, labor and, 52; teleological, 24; transcendence of, 44
Lava flow, 72, 135–36, 173
Lazzarini, Robert, 57
Lewis, Jerry, 15, 159–60
Libet, Benjamin, 82, 184n11
Litter: James and, 35–36, 72
Lucid dreaming, 31, 76
Lucretius, 84, 86, 182n22; immanent naturalism and, 71, 74
Lures: positive and negative, 15–16

Magritte, Rene, 50, 62
Margulis, Lynn, 45, 77, 195n3
Market, 14, 134; as abstract machine, 136–37; as derivative machine, 137–39, 143, 194n12; employment market, 31; the outside and, 136–37, 139, 142; as purportedly self-regulating system, 36–37, 56, 88–89, 132, 136–37, 142, 146; resonance machine of global antagonism and, 140–41; state regulation and, 89, 124, 127, 137, 143–44, 146, 157, 173; transactions, 18; volatility of, 56, 113, 137, 142, 144, 157. See also Open systems; State: market and
Marks, Laura, 47
Marxism, 37
Massumi, Brian, 184n11, 197n19
Materialism: mechanistic, 43–44; mechanistic vs. immanent, 74, 81; mechanistic vs. vital, 182n11. See also Immanence: naturalism and
Media, 41, 60, 66, 84, 89, 120, 122, 126; micropolitics of perception and, 12,

17–18, 54–56, 58–59, 61, 63, 87, 134, 145, 185n21; resonance machines and, 138–45
Merleau-Ponty, Maurice, 88; belonging to the world and, 12, 54, 57–58, 61, 65; Bergson and, 185n25; color and, 47; Deleuze and, 12, 43, 46, 65, 186n27; depth and, 50–51; double movement and, 43; Foucault and, 12, 43, 52, 54, 57; half-second delay and, 184n11; "imbalance," 46, 49; immanence and, 43–44; Kelly on, 51; nature and, 43–46, 65; neuroscience and, 45, 48–49, 54, 185n21; time as becoming and, 7, 165; transcendence without the Transcendent, 183n1
Micropolitics, 5; counter-resonance machine and, 146–47; of discipline, 52–55, 133–35; macropolitics vs., 91; multi-media, 17–18, 145, 185n21; of perception, 55–58; tactics of the self and, 75, 115–16, 187n1
Miller, Patrick Lee, 188n13
Minoritization of world, 7, 42, 61, 66–67, 84, 87, 89, 120, 122–23, 128, 133, 138–42; defined, 59–60
Mirror neurons, 26, 48, 187n1

Nature, 40, 79, 93–94, 113–15, 149, 160; culture vs., 8, 10, 18, 20–22, 43–46, 105, 108, 115, 156, 174; Hegel on, 127, 193n4; law-like model of, 23, 29, 111, 148, 175; Merleau-Ponty and, 43–46, 65; neoliberal conception of, 137; the subject and, 30, 43. See also Human estate
Neoliberalism, 146; desire and, 103; neoliberal economic theory, 37, 136–37, 140; pervasiveness of, 122; "shock doctrine" and, 146, 195n17
Newton, Isaac, 29, 182n22
Nietzsche, Friedrich, 84; contestability of philosophy / faith and, 41; Deleuze on, 62; dwelling and, 104; eternal re-

Nietzsche, Friedrich (*cont.*)
turn, 110–11, 168, 190nn17–18; genealogy and, 184n9, 197n20; "gift giving virtue," 115; on human
predicament, 14, 104, 106, 109–16,
119–20; immanence and, 37–38; Kauffman, Whitehead and, 30–31; Keller and, 106, 109, 119–20, 122;
Kierkegaard and, 112, 191n 22; on
meaning of faith, 112; modes of "interpretation" and, 34–35; powers of
the false and, 4, 63, 116, 118–19, 166–
67; radical "subjectivism," 30, 95; *ressentiment*, 14, 61, 87–88; spiritualization of enmity, 112; Taylor on, 70, 77,
92; and time as becoming, 7, 11, 13,
118–19, 165–69, 174; warrior ethic
and, 144, 191n27
Noise, 36, 96, 154, 157
Nutty Professor, The, 15, 160–64

Open systems: complexity of, 12, 17, 27,
30, 83, 173; intersections between, 7,
9, 19–20, 37–39, 43, 136–37, 146–47,
171–73; vulnerability and, 155–56.
See also Force-field; Tiers of temporality
Outside, the: abstract machine and, 136;
affect and, 150–51; capitalism and,
129–30; of experience, 112; force-
fields and, 7, 30, 71, 74, 136, 147, 171;
Geist and, 192n2; immanence/tran-
scendence and, 39, 65, 74–75, 183n1;
market and, 136–37, 139, 142; Nature
and, 45; sovereignty and, 129–30,
133, 139, 142

Perception: action-oriented, 2, 4–5, 33–
35, 38, 51–52, 69, 77, 102, 106, 161,
174–75, 185n25; of depth, 51–52; desire and, 102, 104; Humean concept
of, 35–36; Merleau-Ponty on, 12, 43–
51; 57–58; micropolitics of, 55–58;
multisensory organization and, 46–

49, 52, 185n17; normative construction of, 49–51; points of instability
and, 49; Proust on, 94; species
provincialism and, 172; unconscious
organization of, 17, 58, 66, 150–51,
160, 184n6; Whitehead on, 29, 193n4.
See also Anticipation; Color of perception; Discipline
Phenomenology: Deleuze, Foucault
and, 12, 43; experience and, 46–51,
57–58; nature and, 43–46
Philosophy of Right, The (Hegel), 14,
124, 127, 192n2
Pinkard, Terry, 193n4
Pluralism, 16; as deep and multidimensional, 78, 90, 92, 187n37; deep vs.
multidimensional, 83–84
Pluralistic Universe, A (James), 32
Pre-adaptations, 19–20; defined, 18
Precursors: to human agency, 23–24,
32; to human will, 82
Prigogine, Ilya, 12, 165; Bergson and,
168–69; disequilibrium and, 45–46;
immanence and, 37, 71, 74, 78; irreversibility of time and, 20–21, 44, 96,
169, 182n22, 192n2; "Poincare resonances" and, 18; Whitehead and, 25,
168
Process, 51, 55, 136, 137, 192n2; agency
and, 22–25, 29–30, 182n12; bio-
cultural processes, 36–37, 80; body-
brain processes, 17, 36, 45, 48–49, 52,
73, 76–77, 82; bumpiness of time
and, 9, 65, 149; causality and, 19, 44,
171; creative processes, 5, 63, 71–72,
119, 152; disciplinary processes, 55,
133–34; disequilibrium and, 19; irreversibility of time and, 20–21, 44, 96,
169, 182n22; market processes, 130,
139; nonhuman processes, 15, 21, 23,
79, process philosophy, 39–40, 168,
190n14; self-organization and, 15, 74;
temporal interfolding and, 33–34,
69–70; will to power and, 95

Proto-agency, 23–26, 28, 115, 173. *See also* Agency

Proust, Marcel, 2, 7, 62, 68–69, 71, 165; Deleuze on, 94; powers of the false, 4, 116–18

"Rabble," 14, 124–25, 127–28

Ramachandran, V. S., 45

Resentment: affirmation and, 6, 60–61, 64, 79, 81–82, 87, 91, 98, 114, 120–21, 123, 168–69; contestability of creed and, 8, 13, 16, 66, 73, 85–89; dogmatic cynicism and, 54–55; estrangement and, 100–101; global resonance machine of revenge, 133, 138–41, 145, 147, 194n14; market-state regime and, 125–26; mortality and, 108, 138, 140, 194n14; as *ressentiment*, 55, 61, 66, 114, 168–69; time as becoming and, 106, 112, 119–21, 165–66, 176

Resnais, Alain, 62, 64

Resonance, 58; abstract machine and, 135; below the level of attention, 29, 31; between constituencies, 19, 89; between force-fields, 171, 173–74; between incipience and actualities, 116–17; "Poincare," 18; self-organization and, 74; between tiers of time, 69, 71, 115, 159; between vibrations and sensorial habits, 151

Resonance machine, 150; as counter, 91, 142–47; of global antagonism, 14, 121, 138–42, 144, 147, 172–73; 194n14; negative, 195n16; political, 41–42; positive, 195n15; systems of "control" and, 134; world resonance machine, 14, 135–42. *See also* Abstract machine; Evangelical-capitalist resonance machine

Ressentiment, 14, 55, 61, 63, 66, 81, 88, 90, 114, 122, 168–69

Rizzolatti, Giacomo, 26, 48, 185n21, 197n15

Sankara, 176; on human predicament, 13–14, 99–105, 115; ignorance and, 14, 101, 103, 120, 122

Secular Age, A (Taylor), 13, 38, 183n23

Secularism: expressive dimension of life and, 140–41; "predicament" and, 97–98; time and, 8, 10–11, 68–70; versions of, 13, 15–16, 58, 75, 88–90, 108–9, 174

Seer, 86, 151, 153–56, 164; dwelling in forking moments, 77, 154, 157–62, 165, 167–70, 174–75; theorist and, 152, 164–65, 197n16. *See also* Duration; Tiresias

Self-organization, 15, 18, 20, 44, 74, 77–78, 109, 135, 146–47, 152, 171–73. *See also* Autopoiesis

Shapiro, Ian, 184n3

Singh, Bhrigupati, 41, 191n27

Social position: insufficiency of, 85, 88, 121; political stance and, 58, 85–90; spirituality and, 85–90, 121

Sophie's dream: creative moment in Jesus and, 69

Sophocles, 152, 155, 174, 196n8; agency and, 26; on human predicament, 98, 105

Sources of the Self (Taylor), 78

Sovereignty, 14: as ambiguous practice, 131; channeling apparatuses and, 134–35; Connolly on, 193n6; divine, 131; expressive, 140–41, 143; expressive vs. decisional, 132–35, 139; governmentality and, 133–34; internal and external, 133; multiple modes of, 128, 138; the outside and, 129–30, 133, 139, 142; positional, 131

Species provincialism, 23, 31–32, 172

Spinoza, Baruch, 71, 75, 77, 84, 86, 182n22; neuroscience and, 184n6, 187n1

Spin the bottle, 3–4

Spirituality, 8, 10, 121; belief and, 13, 85–91, 130, 188n14; bellicose, 134; creed and, 13, 19, 77, 83–92, 188n14;

Spirituality (*cont.*)
    existential uncertainty and, 109; faith
    and, 74, 188n14; resentment and, 60–
    61; transcendence and, 39
Star Wars, 127
State, 9, 21, 40–41, 63, 73, 84; Christian
    state, 78–79; civil society and, 124–
    29, 132, 143, 146, 192n2; expressive
    state, 132–33; hegemony and, 129–
    31, 134, 137–38, 141, 193n6; market
    and, 124–30, 132, 139, 145–46, 173;
    national-security state, 52–53; sov-
    ereignty and, 14, 126, 128–29, 131–
    33, 140–42, 147; world-historical
    state, 126–27, 129, 141
Subject, the: affect and, 151, 160–61;
    color of perception and, 47–48;
    evangelical-capitalist resonance ma-
    chine and, 19, 172; Foucault on, 52–
    53; Hegel on, 14, 124–25; Merleau-
    Ponty on, 43; object vs., 28–31, 49,
    72, 186n27; resonance machine and,
    41; transcendental, 31, 76, 79–80;
    transcendental vs. emergent, 151; uni-
    versal moral, 31; world and, 34–35
Sunspot activity, 9, 73, 188n11
Symbiogenesis, 77–78, 152, 195n3

Tactics of the self, 26, 57, 75, 79, 83,
    115–16, 165, 185n21, 187n1. *See also*
    Ethics; Micropolitics
Taylor, Charles: "conditions of belief,"
    59–62, 66, 109; contestability of faith
    and, 41, 84–85, 91–92; Dallmayr and,
    188n14; disenchantment and, 70–72;
    exclusive humanism and, 60, 69, 71,
    80; immanence/transcendence and,
    13, 38–39, 41, 70, 74–75, 77–81, 83,
    86, 188nn12–13; incipience and, 78;
    Miller and, 188n13; monotheism and,
    81; on Nietzsche, 70, 77, 92; plural-
    ism and, 83, 188n14, 188n19; secular-
    ism and, 68–71, 89
Thatamanil, John J., 101, 104, 120, 122,

190n6; desire and, 103; divine imma-
    nence and, 99–100; eternity as ac-
    tivity, 105–6
Theism: belief in this world and, 59–60,
    62; nontheism and, 60, 62, 84–86, 98,
    103, 116, 165
Theogony (Hesiod), 170
Thoreau, Henry David, 191n27; imma-
    nent naturalism and, 71, 74; warrior
    ethic and, 144
Thus Spoke Zarathustra (Nietzsche),
    110, 168
Tiers of temporality, 2, 7–9, 19–20, 32,
    71–73, 77, 149–50, 152, 157. *See also*
    Force-field; Open system
Tillich, Paul, 13, 99, 103–5, 115, 122,
    190n6; estrangement, 14, 100–101,
    120; supranaturalism, 107
Time: as becoming, 7, 9–12, 15–16, 20–
    21, 37–39, 58, 70–71, 75, 80–81,
    105–6, 109–11, 114–15, 119–20,
    148–49, 151, 165, 170, 174, 182n22,
    190n17, 192n2; as chrono-time, 19,
    44, 71–73, 76–77, 149, 152, 157; as
    civilizational, 71, 149, 176; crystal of
    time, 69, 163, 168; as evolutionary,
    149, 176; as geological, 71, 149; as in-
    finite circle, 71, 110; as irreversible,
    20–21, 23, 44, 96, 169, 182n22,
    192n2; linear vs. durational, 77, 174–
    75; mechanical vs. organic, 6; the
    "moment," 4, 110–12, 115, 158, 168;
    as neuronal, 71, 149; as progressive,
    8, 148, 182n22, 191n28, 192n2; as
    punctual, 5, 38, 148; punctual vs. be-
    coming, 110, 115; secular image of
    time, 68–69, 148; theory and, 162;
    time forks, 14, 18, 154, 157–59, 162,
    165; the tragic and, 153–56, 196n8;
    two registers of temporal experience,
    2, 4–6, 15, 38, 42, 99–104, 106, 120,
    161; vicissitudes of, 66, 98, 104–6,
    108, 153. *See also* Duration; Force-
    field; Tiers of temporality

Time Code, 65
Tiresias, 15, 152–56, 160, 165, 196n5
Tradition: minor, 79
Tragic: Oedipal plays of Sophocles and, 152–55; time and, 153–56, 196n8; tragic possibility, 6–7, 16, 65, 79, 166–67, 196n8; tragic vision, 110, 156
Transcendence, 167, 188n13; belief in this world and, 59–61, 64–65; dogmatism and, 15; immanence and, 12–13, 21, 37–45, 60, 65, 70–71, 74–77, 80–81, 86; as intensification, 39; mundane form and, 76–78; the outside and, 39, 65, 74–75, 183n1; radical form and, 10, 16, 41, 70, 79–80, 83, 183n1; radical vs. mundane, 74–75, 183n1; senses of, 74–75; theology of, 17, 70; versions of, 12, 40–42, 60, 64, 175

Uncertainty, 3, 55, 58–60, 155, 159; abstract machine and, 136; becoming and, 20, 107–9, 152, 157–58, 192n2; capitalism and, 130, 137, 142–43; climate change and, 156; creed and, 140; emergent causality and, 174; human predicament and, 103, 112–14; pre-adaptations and, 18–19; the will and, 83
Uneven exchange, 133, 137–39, 141, 147; Wallerstein on, 129–31

Varieties of Religious Experience, The (James), 167
Vertigo, 50, 57, 170, 175
Vibrations, 108; affective charge and, 150; composition of the universe and, 173–74; litter and, 36; sub-audible, 28–29, 31, 118, 150–51, 158; Zarathustra and, 115
Visceral register: belief and, 85; of bio-cultural life, 17–18, 32, 151, 175; tactics of the self and, 57, 87, 187n1;

Visibility, 7, 140, 145; feeling visible to nonhuman world and, 50–51, 53; invisibility and, 50

Waking Life, 65
Wallerstein, Immanuel, 128–31, 193n6
Weber, Max: disenchantment and, 70, 187n5
Welles, Orson, 62, 64
White, Stephen, 188n19
Whitehead, Alfred North, 7, 12, 165, 174, 182n22; contestability of faith and, 41; Deleuze and, 196n12; fallacy of misplaced concreteness, 35, 37; feeling and, 28–29; Hegel and, 193n4; immanence/transcendence and, 38–40, 71, 94, 166; "innocence" of becoming and, 118–19; irreversibility of time and, 192n2; James and, 34–36; Kauffman, Nietzsche and, 30–31; Keller on, 190n14; multiple durations and, 29, 94, 149; "speculative" philosophy, 167–68; vitality of non-organic elements and, 25
Widder, Nathan, 185n23
Will: as divided against itself, 22, 81–82, 98, 111; as emergent, 82; human agency and, 107, 173, 182n12; philosophy of immanence and, 13; as two-sided, 82–83
Will to Power, The (Nietzsche), 35, 110, 190n18
Wittgenstein, Ludwig, 34

Yeast, 173, 176: the feeling of, 28, 31

Zarathustra, 113: Connolly on, 191n24; dwelling and, 77, 115; existential resentment and, 112, 168; Kierkegaard and, 112; multiple images of time and, 110–11, 168; Zarathustra's ape, 114, 168–69

William E. Connolly is Krieger-Eisenhower
Professor of Political Science at The Johns Hopkins
University. He is the author of many books,
including *Capitalism and Christianity, American Style*
(2008), *Pluralism* (2005), *Why I Am Not a Secularist*
(1999), and *Identity/Difference: Democratic
Negotiations of Political Paradox* (1991).

Library of Congress Cataloging-in-Publication Data
Connolly, William E.
A world of becoming / William E. Connolly.
p. cm.
Includes bibliographical references and index.
ISBN 978-0-8223-4863-4 (cloth : alk. paper)
ISBN 978-0-8223-4879-5 (pbk. : alk. paper)
1. Democracy — Philosophy. 2. Political science —
Philosophy. 3. Cultural pluralism — Political aspects.
I. Title.
JC423.C693 2010
320.01 — dc22
2010028793